"As 'roots' and 'wings' show up in famous quote
Christian thought and the long tradition of int ̠ authors demonstrate a
deep understanding of Christian mental health care. At the same time, they challenge us to grow wings, to be innovative and bold as we confront the needs of our world alongside beautiful possibilities for the church. The stories are poignant, the writing is effective, the reflection questions are wise and challenging, and the authors are leaders in the field. This is a fantastic book. Be inspired to imagine the possibilities *Beyond the Clinical Hour.*"

Mark R. McMinn, author of *Sin and Grace in Christian Counseling* and professor emeritus at George Fox University

"*Beyond the Clinical Hour* by Sells, Trout, and Sells is a comprehensive and very helpful guide to how Christian mental health professionals can partner with churches to deal with the mental health crisis before us. It includes integration of Christian approaches to mental health and a biblical theology for the foundation of Christian care. It also emphasizes and covers in detail the topics of supervision, consultation, church development and evaluation, and the ethics and economics of care. Highly recommended!"

Siang-Yang Tan, senior professor of clinical psychology at Fuller Theological Seminary and author of *Counseling and Psychotherapy: A Christian Perspective*

"This is one of the most unique, timely, and long-overdue resources for those committed to meeting the pressing needs of the men and women in today's world. The authors give us a fresh and much-needed biblically based, socially informed, clinically sound, and comprehensive model of providing meaningful Christian care. In some ways it provides an invaluable paradigm shift for understanding the essential role of the counselor and the church working together. This encouraging, empowering, and vision-casting resource is a book that you'll be reading more than once and wanting to share with your friends."

Gary J. Oliver, executive director of the Center for Healthy Relationships and professor emeritus of psychology and practical theology at John Brown University

"An insightful look into the mental health crisis, this book offers innovative solutions that emphasize the collaboration of pastors and counselors. Rather than abiding by the current default of church and mental health systems working at odds with one another, the authors present a vision for teamwork and unity of purpose. Their ideas are truly integration in action, ushering in a new era of creativity for pastors and Christian mental health professionals. Rife with examples of strategic partnership, *Beyond the Clinical Hour* is a must-read for pastors, counselors, and churchgoers who want to think outside the box to address the mental health challenges we face."

Kristen Kansiewicz, assistant professor at Evangel University and a licensed professional counselor

"How can a church respond to the mental health crisis? This practical book could help solve the crisis in your community! The authors guide church leaders using their unique insights into the process of mental health care within a congregation. The concepts are both theologically thick and psychologically informed. This book is innovative, clear, and full of pathways to new ideas for congregational mental health care."

Jennifer Ripley, Hughes Endowed Chair of Christian Thought in Mental Health Practice at Regent University and coauthor of *Couple Therapy*

"*Beyond the Clinical Hour* provides an important and timely call to action for pastors and mental health professionals to partner together to address the global mental health crisis. With wisdom, theological depth, and psychological sophistication, the authors lay out strategies for expanding the mission of the church to include spiritually sensitive and competent care for those suffering from mental health concerns. I look forward to introducing my students to this inspiring vision for living out our Christian integrative commitments."

Terri S. Watson, professor of psychology at Wheaton College and author of *Developing Clinicians of Character*

"*Beyond the Clinical Hour* eloquently navigates the intersection of faith and mental health, urging believers to extend compassion as a divine imperative. With profound insights, this book reveals the transformative power of a church united in understanding and support, fostering a community of care that echoes the teachings of the Bible. It is a beacon of hope, guiding believers to embrace the complexities of mental health with love, compassion, and spiritual resilience. *Beyond the Clinical Hour* delivers a timely and powerful message inviting the church to build bridges of understanding and healing in our communities."

Samuel Rodriguez, president of the National Hispanic Christian Leadership Conference

Beyond the Clinical Hour

How Counselors Can Partner with the Church to Address the Mental Health Crisis

James N. Sells, Amy Trout & Heather C. Sells

Foreword by Ed Stetzer

ivp
Academic
An imprint of InterVarsity Press
Downers Grove, Illinois

InterVarsity Press
P.O. Box 1400 | Downers Grove, IL 60515-1426
ivpress.com | email@ivpress.com

InterVarsity Press® is the publishing division of InterVarsity Christian Fellowship/USA®. For more information, visit intervarsity.org.

All Scripture quotations, unless otherwise indicated, are taken from The Holy Bible, New International Version®, NIV®. Copyright © 1973, 1978, 1984, 2011 by Biblica, Inc.™ Used by permission of Zondervan. All rights reserved worldwide. www.zondervan.com. The "NIV" and "New International Version" are trademarks registered in the United States Patent and Trademark Office by Biblica, Inc.™

While any stories in this book are true, some names and identifying information may have been changed to protect the privacy of individuals.

The publisher cannot verify the accuracy or functionality of website URLs used in this book beyond the date of publication.

Cover design: David Fassett
Interior design: Daniel van Loon

ISBN 978-1-5140-0104-2 (print) | ISBN 978-1-5140-0105-9 (digital)

Printed in the United States of America ∞

Library of Congress Cataloging-in-Publication Data
Names: Sells, James Nathan, 1958- author. | Trout, Amy, author. | Sells,
   Heather, 1965- author.
Title: Beyond the clinical hour : how counselors can partner with the
   church to address the mental health crisis / James Sells, Amy Trout, and
   Heather Sells.
Description: Downers Grove, IL : IVP Academic, [2024] | Includes
   bibliographical references and index.
Identifiers: LCCN 2023041939 (print) | LCCN 2023041940 (ebook) | ISBN
   9781514001042 (print) | ISBN 9781514001059 (digital)
Subjects: LCSH: Church work with the mentally ill. | Mental
   illness–Religious aspects–Christianity. | Counseling–Religious
   aspects–Christianity. | BISAC: RELIGION / Christian Ministry /
   Counseling & Recovery | PSYCHOLOGY / Clinical Psychology
Classification: LCC BV4461 .S45 2024 (print) | LCC BV4461 (ebook) | DDC
   259/.42–dc23/eng/20231114
LC record available at https://lccn.loc.gov/2023041939
LC ebook record available at https://lccn.loc.gov/2023041940

31 30 29 28 27 26 25 24 | 13 12 11 10 9 8 7 6 5 4 3 2 1

To our parents who first taught us to love God and others:
HAROLD AND VIRGINIA | NEAL AND JOANNA

And to our children and their spouses who
model lovingkindness and grace:
LAURA AND JOSH | NATHAN AND EMMA | PETER AND MOLLIE

And countless others in the church who inspire
and encourage us in the journey.

JS/HS

———————

The Church has been my anchor, a wellspring of strength and faith.

I dedicate this work to those laboring in his name, especially
DENNIS, LINDA, AND CORY
my partners in care and compassion.

To my children,
JULIANA, RACHAEL, AND CHRISTIAN,
You inspire me to live his light.

May this book glorify him
through shared love and commitment
as we walk together.

AT

Contents

Foreword

ED STETZER

I'VE WRITTEN ABOUT and advocated for mental health for a long time. When I was a young church planter, I wanted to help my people. But I quickly realized that I was not equipped to help them as fully as they needed. In the years since that first ministry experience, I have been glad to see movement away from stigmatizing mental health to recognizing its importance. Mental health matters, because we all have battles emotionally and mentally.

Nevertheless, polling suggests many Christians still believe that mental health issues can be solved by prayer and Bible study alone. God can do and sometimes does do miracles in our bodies and in our minds. That said, we should apply the same standard to mental health as we do to physical health. We know that medication is neither an enemy to be rejected nor a savior to be worshiped. Medication is not mutually exclusive with Scripture and divine aid. I've seen people healed miraculously. I have also seen people healed through the guidance of health care workers. In the same way, we need to see counseling and therapy as complementary friends of spiritual resources rather than their enemies.

The pandemic escalated mental health issues and awareness. We saw a much higher level of stress, especially among younger generations. Many schools now allow teens to take a mental health day without penalty if they need it. According to the National Institutes of Health, social distancing added to these mental health challenges, and health care workers reported an increase in mental health issues of 60 percent.[1] Some have called the rise in mental health cases a tsunami

---

[1] Natarajan Kathirvel, "Post COVID-19 Pandemic Mental Health Challenges," National Library of Medicine, September 22, 2020, www.ncbi.nlm.nih.gov/pmc/articles/PMC7507979.

of mental illness since 2020. A wide range of people have experienced a wide range of mental health challenges, from mild anxiety all the way to PTSD from the challenges of COVID-19. In March 2022, WHO reported a 25 percent increase globally in anxiety and depression.[2] The groups most likely to suffer were young people and women.

The church must create safe environments, and the church must create them now. The church must provide spaces where people can discuss and deal with mental health challenges. The church is made up of broken people who have been redeemed and experienced a measure of healing. God has reassembled their broken pieces, and then he calls these broken people to partner with him on his redeeming, healing mission for other broken people. Indeed, a church without broken people is a broken church.

We have never needed accessible and helpful mental health counseling services more urgently than we do at this moment. Again, I have advocated for mental health awareness and care in churches for many years. I rejoice that we are seeing a shift slowly from removing the stigma of mental health toward seeing it as a part of life and growth. The book *Beyond the Clinical Hour* offers hope at exactly this critical point. There is a wide gap between people seeking help with mental health needs and providers who can help meet those needs. Sells, Trout, and Sells are helping narrow the gap, offering a pathway to accelerate connection, relief, and relationships for people and families.

Their work in this book will remind you about the staggering mental health needs in America. Under the current model, we would need hundreds of thousands of trained workers at a cost into billions of dollars. They show this model to be both unrealistic and even unnecessary. They call instead for an intentional, collaborative opportunity: one where therapists, counselors, and church leaders

---

[2]World Health Organization, "COVID-19 Pandemic Triggers 25% Increase in Prevalence of Anxiety and Depression Worldwide," March 2, 2022, www.who.int/news/item/02-03-2022-covid-19 -pandemic-triggers-25-increase-in-prevalence-of-anxiety-and-depression-worldwide.

come together to serve the millions of people walking in brokenness and in need of mental health expertise. Division and polarization may currently seem as common as a cold, but this book calls together a network of people who care about the whole person. This vision leverages church facilities and youth groups, local psychologists and counselors. It sees a way that these resources can all collaborate together to offer hope. Workshops, seminars, and more can bring these resources together with capable lay leaders in churches. And all together they can stand for people who are too often overlooked. Their vision, like that of a local church, is to gather people in a community to do more together than they could do apart.

This book might inspire you with the possibilities of what God could do. Imagine with me, as I imagine with these authors. Imagine a rising number of churches who are rooted in the gospel and guided by God's Word. Imagine these churches as they partner with believing mental health professionals to develop a holistic approach to bring good news and practical help to many people. This book will help you imagine this better future, and not just imagine it but help accomplish it. Read this book and learn how to become a part of changing things for the better.

Preface

EVERY BOOK IS A TALE OF TWO STORIES. The first is the one it narrates, the essence captured within its pages. In this book, that story is the burgeoning mental health crisis and the pivotal role that the church, particularly those who train Christian counselors, can play in responding to this urgent challenge.

The second, more elusive story is the one behind the book itself. It's the unspoken journey of inspiration, dedication, and collaboration that drives authors to invest endless hours in research, contemplation, and creation.

The seed of this book was planted in a keynote speech I (Jim) delivered at the Christian Association for Psychological Studies in 2018. There I outlined the alarming rise in mental health needs and the parallel decline in our ability to address them. I suggested that the church, and those within CAPS, held a key to bridging this gap. Jon Boyd, an editor at InterVarsity Press, saw the potential and approached me, envisioning this idea as a book.

In the following year, spirited discussions brought the idea to life. Dr. Amy Trout, a pioneer in church-psychology collaboration, became a core contributor. Along with Dr. Thomas Suk we presented our ideas at the next CAPS Conference and found them to be well received. A book was being formed. But when academics tell a story it sounds, obviously, academic. We also envisioned a storyteller who could glean examples from the culture of emerging trends and examples. Heather Sells has three decades of print and broadcast journalism experience. Together we sculpted our thoughts into a cohesive and compelling narrative.

Then COVID arrived, reshaping everything. The already rampant mental health crisis flared, fanned by the pandemic's sweeping chaos.

The urgency to complete this book was never more apparent. We owe tremendous gratitude to many, including those at Regent University, such as Jennifer Ripley, Bill Hathaway, Kelly Drye, Logan Battaglini, Tasha Mortimer-Mitchell, Steve Stuhlreyer, Deja Miles-Bogger, Sam Thompson, and Caitlin Overfelt.

The beginning of my (Amy) journey started in the midst of my studies. I found something that resonated with me: the chance to collaborate with the church in ways unexplored. Mark McMinn, more than a mentor, ignited a vision that led to creative work at the Center for Church-Psychology Collaboration at Wheaton College.

Those early days were filled with discovery, and since then, doors have continued to open. This work has enriched not only the community but my life in ways I never anticipated. I feel driven to continue this path, inspiring others along the way. It's about more than assistance; it's about personal fulfillment in doing profound good.

The journey has been winding, filled with faith, care, and collaboration. Together, we've woven a tapestry of good work, creating something that goes beyond a mere career. It's a calling, and through these pages, we invite you to explore it with us. The stories within this book reflect not only the voices of those seeking solutions but also the hearts and minds of those willing to reach out and make a difference. It's an invitation to a journey, and we hope you'll join us as we embark on this meaningful path.

My (Heather) participation in this book came at the invitation of Jim to add my gifts in storytelling as we sought to lean into the good work already being done at the intersection of church ministry and mental health intervention. I've been inspired and encouraged by those who are creatively imagining and implementing a new world where church leaders and mental health professionals collaborate to meet the needs of the wounded in their midst.

A Sign Tells a Story

A SIMPLE SIGN CAN TELL A VERY BIG STORY. The marquee in front of a small church on a state highway in Anderson County, South Carolina, communicated just three words: "FAMILY COUNSEL AVAILABLE."

It is common to see a marquee in front of churches of all kinds. These signs share the most essential information in just a few words, things such as "Jesus Saves!," "Prayer Meeting: 6:00 Wednesday," or "Softball game Friday at 7:15." Signs are supposed to communicate the purpose, priorities, or proclivities of the church: "God loves you . . . Have a nice day!" But on that country road, at that church, the message shared was that families could get help there and that the type of help offered was something called "counsel." Three words meant to connect with parents and spouses who suffered, letting them know that hope could be found here in this country church. Family. Counsel. Available.

That small sign in front of that small church located in that small rural area is a very big deal. The sign suggests that change is happening in how and where mental health is delivered. As professors walking close to both the mental health profession and the church, we see a momentum shift that has the potential to affect churches and people everywhere. This church and thousands of others are responding to the needs within their communities and congregations. *People hurt. We can help.*

We have written this book with a vision toward human care and what the mental health profession can become given the pervasive need and current trends in our world. Our primary audience is the

Christian counselor, the mental health student, and the professors who train them. We also want to reach pastors and church lay leaders who seek to partner with those in the mental health field toward effective and affordable care.

Think Big

A paradigm shift occurs when the ways we have understood certain ideas, contexts, or experiences no longer explain the current realities we're seeing.

There are many events, ideas, and creations that have sparked major shifts in human culture. Martin Luther King Jr.'s "I Have a Dream" speech changed how society viewed racial restoration. Likewise, the Ten Commandments transformed Israel's understanding of God. The gospel was the ultimate paradigm shift; Jesus declaring "A new commandment I give you" (Jn 13:34) changed everything. Paradigm shifts are not just words, however. They can be inventions like the cell phone or new ways to meet needs—like getting counseling at your church. We believe the mental health care paradigm must change to meet overwhelming demand, and we invite Christian counselors, educators and pastors to collaborate in that process. We will explain the demand, cast a vision for new collaboration between counselors and churches, and provide specific recommendations.

Part one makes the case that despite advancements in science and practice, we have not been successful in adequately reducing mental health needs. In fact, mental health demands continue to increase despite our effective medical and psychological interventions. This section offers an alternative path, utilizing the church, and describes how the path might be implemented.

Part two offers a new perspective on the relationship between the church and the clinic, emphasizing the importance of integration. We describe the historic tension between faith and mental health practice and suggest innovative solutions using the term "faith articulation."

Part three provides recommendations for training future Christian mental health professionals in four essential areas: biblical scholarship and theology, supervision, consultation, and organizational development and evaluation. This section underscores the need for these skills to effectively bring mental health care into the church.

The purpose of this book can be succinctly encapsulated: as the existing mental health framework falls short of addressing humanity's profound needs, it's imperative for the church to join forces with Christian mental health experts to tackle the escalating crisis. This collaboration necessitates a transformative approach in the delivery of care, the training and understanding of Christian mental health professionals, and the church's recognition of its divine mandate in ministry. Culminating its insights, the book exhorts readers to forge ahead with audacity, sagacity, innovation, and empathy to usher in a redefined paradigm of mental health care, amalgamating the strengths of both the church and the profession. The symbiosis between these institutions is paramount to counter the mounting challenges in our communities. The call to action is immediate, and this book stands as a beacon for visionaries eager to envision and actuate a more holistic path forward.

"I Want You to Come to This Bible Study"

Travis was falling through the cracks, and he knew it. For years, he had used what he describes as the positive traits of his schizoaffective disorder, along with a substance abuse addiction, to build a lucrative career in commercial real estate. Working 100- to 120-hour weeks was not unusual. "In a confused state, I could do anything," he recalls. "I made a lot of money, and all I cared about was making money because I needed more money to fuel my addictions."

It all caught up to him in the San Diego hotel room where his brother and sister found him. "I was in bad shape, and they got me to rehab. That stopped the downward spiral, but when I got back from rehab I still wasn't really well." Travis's body had been detoxified from his physical dependence on the alcohol that had fueled him in part but his mind wasn't well, and his life was chaotic.

For the next month, Travis didn't leave the house—or his bed. Then his pastor Joe called and asked if a friend, Kyle, could reach out. Kyle called and asked to meet. When Travis reluctantly agreed and the two got together, Kyle shared that he had lost a profitable family business because of his addictions and challenged Travis. "I want you to come to this Bible study; it's full of guys like you," he said.

Travis refused but Kyle persisted. The night he finally attended, the study simply featured a Bible study video with a teaching on Philippians. Still, it got Travis thinking, and he watched the video repeatedly later at home.

"I started going to AA because you know what—step 2 is admitting that there's a God who is able to help me with my addiction and I was able to do step 2 because I started to believe again."

"I started going to the Sunday school class that my pastor taught, and everything started making sense to me. Slowly I started to actively pursue recovery," he recalled.

Today, Travis credits his pastor, Kyle, and his church with helping him get out of his pit—and staying out. "I spent so many years trying to prove to myself that there was no God for the sole purpose of removing the guilt and shame associated with the things that I was doing," he said. "So, I really needed to unlock that lie and exchange it for the truth, and once I did that it unlocked recovery for me."

For Travis, a big key to staying healthy is his involvement running his church's coffee bar and overseeing its kitchen for special events. He finds that remaining connected with the volunteers keeps him emotionally healthy. "Some days, that's the action that makes me take action toward my own recovery. So, the church has been integral. They were there for me when I had nothing and needed everything and now they give me a place to help other people, which is a huge part of my recovery today."

As mental health professionals, we believe that our unique training is essential in working with the complicated nuances of mental disease and relational disorder. And we believe that we must prepare the church, collaborate with it, consult, and be a resource as its frontline role of mental health ministry expands to address the need. To accomplish this, those who train Christian mental health professionals must expand beyond the current emphasis on clinical diagnosis and treatment. Educators must also prepare mental health students to be supervisors of lay counselors, consultants to pastors, and triage clinicians who can refer when necessary and attend to the direct and immediate need as individuals, couples, and families come to their door.

The ideas in this book may seem radical, as that is how paradigm shifts are supposed to feel. Not an unrealistic radicalism that would have no possibility of influencing change but an idea that serves as a response to a real and recognized need. Most in the mental health field know that the system is broken, meaning the needs continue to increase at very scary rates of growth, despite our efforts to educate, inform, and intervene. Our means of informing the public and our medicines are better, and there are more educated and licensed mental health professionals than ever before. Still, with all that we are doing to address the crisis, the problem grows worse.

In this book we highlight a small sample of the professionals who are already working with churches to address human suffering. They are among the hundreds of church/mental health partnerships emerging in communities around the country. These stories serve as models for others who feel called in the name of God and as ambassadors and stewards of his kingdom to act.

In the bigger picture, the overwhelmed mental health system needs a new model of care. Churches can play a crucial role in addressing this need without overburdening the national economy. However, to offer comprehensive mental health ministry, churches must change their understanding of Christian integration, embracing both religious and scientific knowledge.

This book emerges as a daring clarion call, championing a transformative shift in the way care is conceived and delivered. By shedding light on pressing challenges, dissecting their underlying causes, and mapping out viable solutions, it paves the way for groundbreaking change. The church, with its vast reach and spiritual foundation, stands poised to revolutionize the mental health landscape of communities far and wide. The hour beckons for action; let us rise to the occasion and set about this monumental task.

PART 1

Where We Are: Describing the Mental Health Crisis

You must never confuse faith that you will prevail in the end—which
you can never afford to lose—with the discipline to confront the
most brutal facts of your current reality, whatever they might be.

AT THE CLOSE OF THE VIETNAM WAR, Admiral James Stockdale held the respect of millions of Americans, thousands of Navy personnel, and hundreds of POWs who looked to him for leadership to survive the harshness of the Hanoi Hilton. Stockdale's paradoxical survival strategy was put forth in the bestselling book *Good to Great* by Jim Collins.[1] The first pillar of the paradox is the unwavering commitment to confront the current reality in its objective, unvarnished state—undeterred by the whirlwind of discouragement, shame, anger, or frustration that may ensue. Without an accurate assessment of the challenge at hand, envisaging transformative change

---

[1]Jim Collins, *Good to Great: Why Some Companies Make the Leap and Others Don't* (New York: HarperCollins, 2001).

becomes but a mirage. Adhering to the Stockdale strategy, chapters one and two of this book serve as our rigorous endeavor to paint a stark picture of the prevailing mental health crisis, spanning both the United States and the global spectrum.

While pinpointing the problem might appear straightforward, crafting collaborative solutions for diverse communities, each teeming with distinct needs and varied human and economic resources, is decidedly more intricate. In the face of such complexity, adversity is par for the course, underscoring the pertinence of Stockdale's axiom: an unclouded grasp of challenges is paramount for triumphant innovation.

The second tenet of Stockdale's paradox beckons an unwavering faith that, come what may, victory will be ours in the end. Even as the shadows of the mental health crisis loom large, we are buoyed by hope. The apostle Paul's words ring true, especially after his solemn acknowledgment of our human frailties and limitations: "And hope does not put us to shame, because God's love has been poured out into our hearts through the Holy Spirit, who has been given to us" (Rom 5:5). Embracing this spirit, part two delves into the harmonization of faith with modern strategies, ensuring the church's pivotal role in healing is well-understood and revered.

The two chapters of part one are our compass, guiding us toward tangible solutions. In chapter one we set the context, describing current mental health and ministry and offer a vision for what it might be. Then in chapter two we unfurl comprehensive data to lay bare the magnitude of the issues, navigate the labyrinth of economic and ethical quandaries that exacerbate the predicament, and fan the flames of optimism. Stockdale's paradox remains our North Star—encouraging us to maintain an astute cognizance of our condition, while anchoring our belief in the church's capacity to further God's mission, engendering change in our cultural tapestry.

Synthesis of Care

THE CONFLUENCE OF CULTURE, CHURCH, AND COUNSELING

We herd sheep, we drive cattle, we lead people.
Lead me, follow me, or get out of my way.

GEORGE S. PATTON

PEOPLE HURT AND the church can help. Nothing new here. The church has offered "benevolent programs"—care and share funds, food pantries, and housing assistance—for centuries. Anyone can see that churches do "nice" things for people. But the idea that the church can play a major role in the delivery of mental health in the United States and worldwide is not something many have considered. We believe governments, the mental health profession, insurance providers, and graduate programs should collaborate with religious institutions to address the need at levels impossible to attain through separate efforts.

The church should play a prominent role in providing mental health care for several reasons. First, the need is growing at an alarming pace. Second, the cost to treat those in need will bankrupt the health care system. Third, even if everyone had the funds to pay for the service, the number of clinicians required to treat those in need is beyond the scope of our educational system. These are the conditions facing us in the twenty-first century. In the current system of mental health care, funded by government support, private medical insurance, and self-payment, there is no mathematical regression equation in which the problem is adequately addressed with the funds and the human resources available. None.

This chapter will examine factors in the current cultural context that could prevent systemic change regardless of the need. The main problem we'll consider here is leadership. Addressing the mental health care demand will require collaboration of a plurality of groups, each very powerful in overlapping spheres. In an age where entities neither trust nor collaborate, they must learn to work together for the greater good.

Searching for Christian Community

Jess met Jesus in high school, sitting on a mountainside perch at a Christian camp in Colorado. "I just felt Jesus there," she explains emphatically. A friend told her she'd been praying for Jess for a long time.

Soon after she battled a life-threatening disease that led to surgery. For months, she found herself very lethargic but attributed it to the recovery process.

In her freshman year of college, the struggle to meet normal life demands began in earnest. She started missing classes and lying in bed for hours. A roommate suggested she might have depression and soon after she received her diagnosis: depression with mixed features. Jess didn't even know what the diagnosis meant, but she remembers ripping up her medical paperwork and rejecting what she had just been told.

Despite her diagnosis, Jess devoted herself to her studies and joined the worship team of her on-campus ministry organization, rehearsing and leading music weekly. Still, she quickly found her depression getting in the way and, equally as difficult, a Christian community that misunderstood her.

"I was very Pentecostal in college. They thought I was just very in tune with the Holy Spirit. There'd be strings of nights when I didn't sleep at all because I was having a manic episode," she said. During those sleepless nights, she would often turn to her music and song writing. In turn, her community praised her for her talents.

When she would confess her deep despair over her mental health struggles, she found Christian leaders minimizing it. "Adults kind of wrote it off, especially the older they were." They said, "You're fine. You just need more exercise or whatever." And she found her own friends keeping their distance, not understanding what she was experiencing.

Some of those friends later apologized to Jess for not understanding, a move she warmly received. For several years she joined a women's Bible study group and found herself supported and accountable to others. But still, she noticed she kept downplaying her personal battles and asking instead for prayer for her mom's cancer. To her, a mental health prayer request felt scandalous.

Today, Jess has put dreams she once had of owning a business on hold, possibly permanently. In her thirties now, she lives with her sister and is searching for work that will give her financial independence. She is also searching for a Christian community that can understand her. She feels support from her friends but is not free to express how deeply she struggles.

Defining the Problem

To meet the mental health demand within the United States using our current model of care, we would need to train hundreds of thousands more clinicians to serve *millions* more who suffer from the full spectrum of mental health disorders at a cost of *billions* of dollars per year.

To use a metaphor, let's say that the number of cars on the already congested roads and freeways was increasing in number at a rate of 20 percent per year. In just a few years we would double the number of cars on the road. One solution might be to build more roads. But no matter how fast roads are built, the number of cars keeps increasing. Imagine a major freeway being thirty lanes wide yet still congested.

There is no more money to design and build more roads. At some point local leaders begin to see that the traffic doesn't seem to be solved with more roads. This illustration suggests two different kinds of problems: the traffic and the political will to imagine and implement a different system.

When it comes to the church, Ed Stetzer identified the problem as a training and guidance deficiency: "Pastors need more guidance and preparation for dealing with the mental health crisis. . . . Pastors and the police are often the first responders in mental health crises. Those crises give the church the opportunity to be the church—to demonstrate the love of God to families and fellow believers in their time of need."[1] The church has the mental health crisis at its doorstep, with a figurative army of people who wish to lend a supportive ear, a soothing voice, and a wise word. In contrast, the prevailing belief in North America over the last fifty years has been that mental health concerns should be addressed by the professionals and that mental health care should be funded by third-party payers such as insurance companies. For example, it is commonly recommended that when people experience depression or anxiety, they should work with therapists, counselors, psychologists, psychiatrists, or social workers to address those issues.

As trained psychologists and counseling professors, we believe the role of mental health professionals is more important today than ever. Trained clinicians capable of understanding mental health science are in great demand. But rather than advocate for more resources directed toward the professional caregivers, we are calling for clinicians to work within the community context. The number of people looking for therapy is too great for the cadre of existing professionals. Instead, the clinician must become an educator, supervisor, consultant, and

---

[1]Ed Stetzer, "How to Assess the Mental and Relational Health Needs in Your Church," in *The Struggle Is Real: How to Care for Mental and Relational Health Needs in the Church*, ed. Tim Clinton and Jared Pingleton (Bloomington, IN: WestBow Press, 2017), 2.

adviser. The profession must partner with the community to meet the need. As the need for mental health care grows, the nature and delivery of care must grow as well.

Figure 1 illustrates the current model of mental health care. The large rectangle in the lower portion of the diagram contains three components of need: Serious Mental Illness, Any Mental Illness, and Personal/Relational Need. The first two levels of need are diagnosable conditions identified in the fifth edition of the *Diagnostic and Statistical Manual of Mental Disorders* (DSM-5), the manual of mental

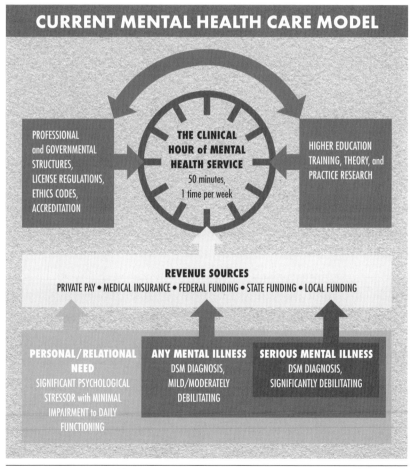

Figure 1. The current mental health care model

health disorders published by the American Psychiatric Association. There are about 157 distinct conditions described in the 2022 edition. These can be acute (think intensity) and chronic (think long-lasting). Or they can be mild/modest and fleeting. But there are significant impairments in life functioning. The third and largest component in the block, Personal/Relational Need, represents significant painful issues or experiences that are challenging and require attention, but they do not impede a person's capacity for daily functioning. These people get up, go to work, and care for others, but they remain in pain.

The smallest rectangle in the lower block, Serious Mental Illness, represents the most acute need. This includes people who are diagnosed with life-debilitating mental illnesses—schizophrenia, dementia, and in some cases, substance-dependence disorders, bipolar I, and major depressive disorders. These diseases prevent a person from engaging in normal and common life experiences. Treatment likely includes medication, psychotherapy, and at times, hospitalization.

The second level of mental illness, incorporating a larger portion of the population, is Any Mental Illness, identified in the middle of the figure. This represents any DSM-5 diagnosable conditions that are serious and impede life functioning. These would include most mood disorders, anxiety disorders, and disorders in childhood, such as the range of attention deficit disorders.

Finally, the largest block represents the Personal/Relational Needs. Most everyone at one time or another experiences life stress, personal adjustments, family crisis, and marital/relational conflict. They frequently seek intervention and support from professional mental health providers. There is not a medical condition per se, but the issues are significant, and good counsel is a valued intervention, for example when individuals experience change, such as a career transition; grief, as in the loss of a loved one; or marital/family tensions.

Now move to the middle tier in the model: revenue sources. This is how the services identified in the lower portion are funded.

Regardless of the nature of the need, the intervention is usually delivered through a mechanism such as private health insurance; public mental health care such as Medicaid; state/community-funded mental health services, which are often paid as block grants to not-for-profit agencies; and self-payment. Most every need, from schizophrenia to adjustment to the demands of life in a new community, is funded through some source within the mental health care economic model. In almost all cases, the clinician is a master's or doctoral-level mental health professional, compensated through one of these means.

The top tier in the model, the circle, is the intervention structure, the clinical hour. While there are many types of interventions, such as hospitalization, group therapy, animal-assisted therapies, and so on, most that are funded by the mental health economic system using the clinical hour. It is usually a fifty-minute session with a licensed mental health care professional, be it a counselor, social worker, marriage and family therapist, or psychologist.

The rectangle to the right of the intervention structure represents the institutions of higher education. They train clinicians and conduct research on the clinical effectiveness of the interventions they develop and prepare students to deliver. The rectangle to the left of the intervention structure represents the professional organizations and state oversight boards. These institutions set the standards for training, determine and enforce ethical parameters, and create licensing laws to operate as a mental health professional within the agency's jurisdiction.

The sheer size, scope, and prevalence of people in need has created the demand for a massive intervention system. The funding challenge to meet it is so large that it must somehow be "managed." This term has become synonymous with the control of costs, and the most effective way to control costs is to restrict practice and the accessibility or quality of care. The necessity for cost controls and limitations of service dominates the conversation regarding service provision. The professional literature reflects opinions regarding the intrusion of managing the financial strains between clinicians and clients. Tjeltveit writes of this issue:

> A science-informed, collaborative relationship for the purpose of improving the well-being of a client can be seen as nothing but a business relationship involving the contractual exchange of money among several parties, management by a third party, and a commodity: psychotherapy. That change in language illustrates a process I call the "commodification" of therapy, an ugly word befitting an ugly transformation. . . . Likewise, counseling psychologists can (and should) treat their clients as persons of worth even if managed care accountants think of them only as consumers whose use of an expensive health care commodity must be managed.[2]

Both the church and the counseling profession typically view the relationship with those who are suffering with the highest regard. Both respect the idea that those who seek care are people in pain. The church and those in Christian mental health care even go so far as to inextricably link the idea of human care to God. Individuals, marriages, and families are tied tightly to the center of our existence as beings created in the *imago Dei*. Therefore, this issue of too many people in need at a cost out of reach for many because of the absence of suitable providers is much more serious than an excessively long grocery story line or a supply chain shortage that delays a birthday gift for a friend. Mental health provision carries a moral weight that should prompt us to create innovative solutions.

Yet instead, we easily go to causation and blame. We ask, "How did we get here? Why is this the case? What is the cause for the pervasive decline in care and the exacerbation of need?" We turn to political ideologies and theological or philosophical commitments. Depending on who you're talking to, the answers to these questions might include:

---

[2]Alan C. Tjeltveit, "There Is More to Ethics Than Codes of Professional Ethics: Social Ethics, Theoretical Ethics, and Managed Care," *The Counseling Psychologist* 28, no. 2 (2000): 245.

- the breakdown of the family
- economic inequality
- the removal of God and our Christian origins from our national dialogue
- personal failings and lack of discipline
- absent fathers
- institutional racism
- the media
- sin
- Republicans
- Democrats
- _____ (any number of other reasons)

And so, we fight. It's a conflict that Christian thought leader and author Rodney Clapp identified decades ago and summarized as though he could see it today:

> The postmodern discovery is that the great guiding light of reason, when seen through the prism of different cultures, diffracts and divides into competing lights. The underlying faith and hope of modernity have been shattered so that we truly live in times of "religious crisis." That is, there is not widespread agreement on what is our ultimate good, the common end or goal of our society. And we now know that reason cannot stand above and apart from the fray to provide a common good. Consequently, we fight endlessly over abortion, over homosexuality, over what genuine justice is, over the meaning of family itself.[3]

Seeking consensus on the root causes is vital before we move toward finding a solution, as emphasized by Clapp. Many of us, perhaps including yourself, have witnessed the perpetual disputes that arise when this step is bypassed. To facilitate genuine change, we

---

[3]Rodney Clapp, *Families at the Crossroads: Beyond Tradition & Modern Options* (Downers Grove, IL: InterVarsity Press, 1993), 23.

must prioritize dialogue over dominance. It's crucial to enlighten rather than impose, to propose rather than mandate. We should extend an invitation rather than exert pressure. Above all, we need to exemplify the potential of harmonious collaboration between faith communities and professional mental health practitioners in nurturing holistic human care.

We can create a solution for an expanding problem. But we can't change the culture by remaining in a culture war mentality.

An Alternative Plan of Action

In 1956 Ray Kroc was operating a couple of small hamburger stands when he was confronted with a life-changing idea—that he wasn't in the hamburger business. He was in the real estate business. That idea led to the creation of the McDonald's empire. Kroc realized that there was something bigger than hamburgers in the franchise business: land. In similar ways, the focus of this book is bigger than mental health care delivery. It's about culture—engaging, changing, and ultimately, creating a different culture.

For many people, culture is the battlefield where ideas are contested, and the side that generates maximum force controls the decision-making. The church has engaged in this battle, and over time its identity has become increasingly political. This is not to say that the church should not be involved in the political process. Rather, it is to suggest that when we consider how mental health can be reconstructed to include the church as an essential copartner, our battlefield mentality will likely interfere with, rather than contribute to, our success—unless we conduct ourselves differently.

Several Christian thinkers offer us a helpful framework for understanding culture. Rather than seeing it as the opposition with whom we will do battle, Paul Gould suggests that the church is to "*resurrect relevance* by showing that Christianity offers plausible answers to universal human longings. And she works to *resurrect hope,* creating new cultural goods and rhythms and practices that reflect the truth, beauty, and goodness of Christianity."[4] Some have challenged us to think of culture and power as part of how we live faithfully to our calling. Culture is the rules, expectations, rubrics, or structures we use to create something else. Andy Crouch writes, "*Culture is what we make of the world.* Culture is, first, the name of our relentless, restless human effort to take the world as it's given to us and make something else."[5]

Couples, families, clans, and ethnic groups form culture to define the rules of life together. Culture is created in every human context. We can say, "Where two or three are gathered, there is culture." Culture provides the unwritten rules that define and clarify how one navigates life in the classroom, the sandbox, the cafeteria, the office, and even the bus. Google's culture is characterized by Ping-Pong tables, emphasizing a high value on creativity. In decades past, IBM Blue was a culture—businesslike, responsible, and powerful. Each church, each athletic team, and each home develop a unique culture.

Mental health professions also have a culture. Those cultures consist of standards and expectations by and for those who are competent to address mental health issues. This culture is evident in professional organizations, ethics codes, and laws pertaining to licensure, billing, and practice. Schools participate in this culture by creating curricula that define how the next generation of culture bearers is educated. The publishing industry participates in the culture as it creates products for sufferers and caregivers to use. These structures were created to define and navigate our mental health culture. When an issue emerges, individuals engage the culture to address it. They

[4]Paul M. Gould, *Cultural Apologetics: Renewing the Christian Voice, Conscience, and Imagination in a Disenchanted World* (Grand Rapids, MI: Zondervan Academic, 2019), 24, emphasis added. Gould credits the term "resurrecting relevance" to S. Michael Craven, *Uncompromised Faith: Overcoming Our Culturalized Christianity* (Colorado Springs, CO: NavPress, 2009).
[5]Andy Crouch, *Culture Making: Recovering Our Creative Calling* (Downers Grove, IL: InterVarsity Press, 2013), 23, emphasis added.

make an appointment with a counselor or listen to a podcast by a psychologist. Each of these are cultural tools designed to address a problem.

By many measures, our culture of mental health care treatment created by clinicians and insurance companies, and supported by government agencies has been extremely effective. Treatments promote change, medications work, and research continues to advance our knowledge. The culture and the professionals who have created and work within it are extremely effective.

Still, there is just too much work to do. Recall the thesis of the chapter: to meet the mental health demand within the United States using our current models of care, we need to train hundreds of thousands more clinicians to serve millions more who suffer from the full spectrum of mental health disorders at a cost of billions of dollars per year.

The culture that we have created around a fifty-minute session with a licensed professional possessing a doctoral or master's degree and thousands of hours of supervised experience is time intensive and extremely expensive. This culture permits each clinician to see about two hundred different clients per year. It is common for the therapist to see those clients for about ten sessions. Seeing 200 people about ten times is about 2,000 hours per year, which is typical for a therapist's annual workload. But the data suggests that there are some twenty million people each year who do not receive the mental health services needed. With these numbers, the problem is obvious. Graduate programs can't train the number of additional therapists needed for those people. Insurance companies and federal and state social service providers cannot pay for that number of sessions. Our resources are swamped. In our current system, we are indeed stuck.

Friendship with Those on a Similar Path

Across the country there's a burgeoning peer movement that's connecting churches with the people in their community who are suffering from mental illness, along with their families and loved ones.

Pastor Brad Hoefs, the founder of Fresh Hope for Mental Health, is convinced that the answer to living with long-term illness is the friendship of those on a similar path.

"A peer can make all the difference talking to another peer," he said. "Talking about what works for them, what helped them and being there for them can be a major factor in that person being better."

Hoefs founded Fresh Hope in 2009 after his own bipolar relapse and inability to find a support group that offered him hope around his diagnosis. Instead, he found himself becoming more discouraged about the prospects for living well with his disease.

"You start to become who you hang out with. You learn how to be chronically ill, let the diseased part of your brain become your identity," he said. "Intuitively, I knew that wasn't good."

Fresh Hope has since grown to include more than eighty support groups in the United States and internationally. It trains and certifies group facilitators who receive recommendations from their pastor. Family members are also welcome. The meetings are free, and Fresh Hope offers separate groups for teens and those dealing with specific issues, such as losing a loved one to suicide.

Lucy is a Fresh Hope leader who has trained facilitators in the Latino community. She acknowledges the tough cultural taboo that still exists around mental health.

"It's like—don't air your dirty laundry," she explains. Often, that means minimizing symptoms or seeking out a general practitioner instead of a psychiatrist or therapist. Finances are often another hurdle as is the fear of deportation in the United States.

For Lucy, Fresh Hope has made all the difference, giving her a vision for a full, rich life living with her diagnosis.

That vision has come from watching her Fresh Hope peers in an online group enjoy their lives and live them with purpose.

"The first thing that struck me," she said, "was there was this group of people—all of them had a mental health diagnosis and all of them were thriving."

Building a New Mental Health Culture: Working with Resistance

If cultures are created to respond to need, then they can be formed with intention. But when new needs arise that require a culture change, there is resistance from those who have established and who benefit from the current cultural practices. Changing a culture requires strong leadership.

The adage from American folklore is that if you build a better mousetrap, the world will beat a path to your door. The creator of that adage is not referring to having a rodent problem and the need for an effective remedy. Rather, they're saying if you build tools that meet the needs of a culture better than the tools that have been in use, those in need will find you. Good ideas form new cultures. The movie version of this concept is "If you build it, they will come."[6]

This brings us back to Andy Crouch and his concept of culture making. According to Crouch, "The only way to change culture is to create more of it."[7] When culture changes, it is because some new tangible tool or system becomes available to a wide enough public that it begins to reshape their world. For cultural change to happen, something new displaces, to some extent, existing culture. "So if we seek to change culture, we will have to create something new, something that will persuade our neighbors to set aside some existing set of cultural goods for a new proposal."[8]

---

[6]Phil Alden Robinson, dir., *Field of Dreams,* Universal Pictures, 1989.
[7]Crouch, *Culture Making,* 67.
[8]Crouch, *Culture Making,* 67.

However, before we can seek to change a culture, we must first look at some common mistakes people—Christians, in particular—tend to make when attempting to effect change. Crouch identifies four inadequate responses to cultural needs that keep us stagnant and stifled in the face of problems.

1. *Condemning culture*. This is an "everyone is talking about the weather, no one is doing anything about it" argument. Churches see widespread disarray and continuing decline in key wellness and spirituality indicators, and view the current solutions as inadequate. They then create alternative programs geared toward serving their own congregations and have minimal impact on the culture outside the church. Crouch writes,

> If all we do is condemn—especially if we mostly just talk among ourselves, mutually agreeing on how bad things are becoming—we are very unlikely indeed to have any cultural effect, because human nature abhors a cultural vacuum. It is the very rare human being who will give up on some set of cultural goods just because someone condemns them. They need something better, or these current set of cultural goods will have to do, as deficient as they may be.[9]

2. *Critiquing culture*. Crouch's second problematic response concerns the intellectualization of any cultural phenomenon. This is most evident by the media talking heads who are paid to entertain their audiences by talking about how actions or measures taken in a given situation are insufficient. In Crouch's words, "The best critic can change the framework in which creators do their work—setting the standard against which future creations are measured. But such analysis has lasting influence only when someone creates something new in the public realm."[10]

3. *Copying culture*. Copying culture occurs when people mimic large portions of a culture but alter certain subpoints to make it more

---

[9]Crouch, *Culture Making,* 68.
[10]Crouch, *Culture Making,* 69.

acceptable to a subgroup. One example is church-sponsored Halloween events where candy is distributed out of the trunks of cars or trucks in the church parking lot. They have copied aspects of Halloween celebration, but it's removed from the neighborhood context where people can engage with other children and parents as they walk the dusk-lit streets in costume. When it comes to mental health, churches can create mental health ministries for themselves, but if they stop with self-service they deny the Great Commission impact of Christian calling (Mt 28:16-20). As Crouch notes, "When we copy culture within our own private enclaves, the culture at large remains unchanged."[11]

4. *Consuming culture.* The church has historically aimed to influence societal shifts by endorsing boycotts, often opting out of one cultural facet in favor of another. Think back to the times when bowling alleys, movie theaters, and nightclubs were in the crosshairs. Perhaps our most notable attempt at this strategy was during the temperance movement. However, upon reflection, even that effort had its flaws and shortcomings. Effecting change through this method hinges on the collective decisions of large groups of people, a task easier said than done. Also, as Crouch writes, "It should not be too surprising that consumption is an ineffective way to bring cultural change, because consumption is completely dependent on the existence of cultural goods to consume in the first place."[12]

Creating Culture

Crouch believes that culture is created and re-created as a result of forming products to meet a new need. The new product and the new culture around that product address the need better than anything that currently exists. Creative culture making requires maturity—reflecting the capacity to engage the culture, to steward it, and to exercise the discipline for transformation.

---

[11]Crouch, *Culture Making,* 69.
[12]Crouch, *Culture Making,* 72.

If there is a constructive way forward for Christians, it will require us to recover these two biblical postures of cultivation and creation. And that recovery will involve revisiting the biblical story itself, where we discover that God is more intimately and eternally concerned with culture than we have yet come to believe.[13]

In the cultivating and creating of culture, humility must abound. "Cultural goods cannot be imposed—they can only be *proposed*. How the public responds is never fully in anyone's grasp—and that is as true for parents serving chili as for presidents declaring war."[14] Society doesn't "need" us to save it from itself. We run the risk of being cast as preachy holier-than-thous who seek to make life decisions for others. Guilt is a horrible motivator toward change. Rather, mental health professionals are cultivators of the human care culture. We implement sound, empirically grounded techniques toward human care. And we are creators—able to imagine ways to deliver the service to critical masses of people who need it.

The mental health need is the call to creative solution making, a proposal that the existing structures of the profession collaborate with the existing structures of the church to address suffering. One group has the resources of knowledge. The other group has the resources of mission. We submit that the Christian counselor, psychologist, therapist, or social worker is the link between these two groups.

Crouch concludes:

> We enter the work of cultural creativity not as a people who desperately need to strategize our way into cultural relevance, but as participants in a story of new creation that comes just when our power seems to have been extinguished. Culture making becomes not just the product of clever cultural strategy or the natural byproduct of inherited privilege, but the astonished and grateful response of people who have been rescued from the worst that culture and nature can do.[15]

---

[13]Crouch, *Culture Making,* 98.
[14]Crouch, *Culture Making,* 98.
[15]Crouch, *Culture Making,* 227.

When It's All Said and Done

Here is where we are: our mental health needs are growing at an exponential rate. We see evidence of a new culture emerging from within the church to address it. The professional mental health culture should support innovative expressions of mental health ministry because the church can contribute in ways the professional culture cannot due to the size and expense of current models of care. We believe that current and emerging Christian mental health professionals are key to the future of care because of their common commitment to both church and clinic.

The partnership between church and clinic is symbiotic, benefiting both through mutual goals. The church has resources, both human and structural, to address the mental health need in a way that the profession cannot. But the church lacks the technical expertise to plan, implement, manage, assess, and improve its programs and services in mental health ministry. The Christian counselor, the community of thousands of trained caregivers who share in the mission of Jesus to a needy world, stand in both the community of mental health professionals and the community of faith. In order for the church to "retool" itself, however, the community of Christian mental health professionals must be prepared to lead.

Figure 2 is a visual depiction of how the church and the mental health clinic could collaborate in delivering care. The model is like the one presented earlier in this chapter. The lower third is unchanged. There remain three levels of mental health need: Serious Mental Illness, Any Mental Illness, and Personal/Relational Need.

The middle third, the funding source, suggests that there are two emerging sources of funding for care. The middle rectangle remains unchanged, the continued use of health insurance to fund professional clinical care. Around it is a gray rectangle that represents a ministry-funded endeavor for human care. Much of the workforce might be volunteers, but it will have a strong presence of mental health professionals who can advise, consult, train, evaluate, and supervise the ministry.

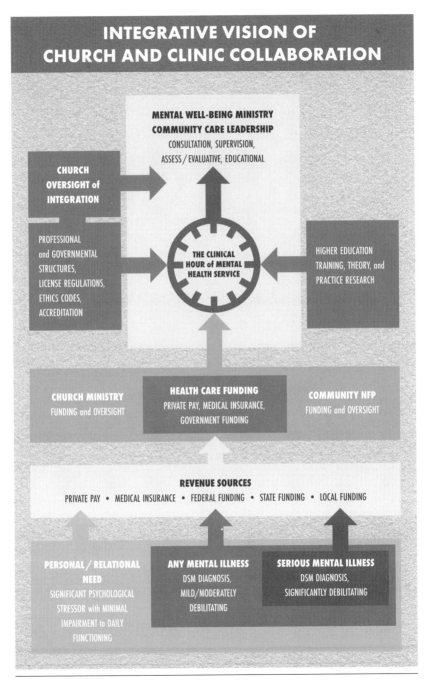

Figure 2. The integrative vision of church and clinic collaboration

Finally, the top third of the model contains a smaller "clinical hour" circle. This represents a reduction in the reliance of the mental health profession to deliver services to all the mental health needs. Emerging around the mental health professional is the larger box. The model suggests that mental health care can be conducted in a clinic-ministry collaboration. Outside entities such as higher education, professional societies, and licensing boards exist and contribute as they have historically. The uniqueness is that the church, the profession, and the Christian mental health provider recognize the new culture and create appropriate rules, oversights, ethical provisions, and services that can deliver the interventions to the population, all while maintaining the church's and clinic's unique identities.

Conclusion: Change, Resistance, and Vision

"The only constant in life is change,"[16] Heraclitus said. It seems that there is one thing that remains, resistance to movement or change. This chapter is a call to leadership during resistance. Need forms the environment for innovation. In the next chapter we will define the need by presenting the data demonstrating an advancing mental health crisis worldwide. We see evidence of need response emerging in churches everywhere. The grassroots solutions are preemptive changes in response to the demands occurring in every church community. But addressing the need, which affects millions, with responses that assist dozens is insufficient. The change needed is institutional. The church, meaning the culture created by those with a shared "kingdom vision," is in a unique position, carries a common mission, and possesses the physical and human resources to contribute to this change.

Leaders are needed to change the existing mental health institutions into structures capable of addressing the depth, width, and height of human need. Christian mental health professionals, professors, and

---

[16]As quoted by Plato in *Cratylus* 401d.

university administrators who prepare the next generation of Christian clinicians and researchers, and students who respond to the call to service within the mental health vocation and ministry are the ones to lead this change. Toward this end, Andy Crouch writes:

> Perhaps a new generation of leaders will arise who want to build for posterity, to plant seeds that will take generations to bear fruit, to nurture different forms of culture that will be seen as blessings by our children's children. If we are serious about flourishing, across space and through time, we will be serious about institutions.[17]

Questions for Reflection

1. In what ways do you see evidence within your church of attempts to condemn, critique, copy, or consume culture?

2. In the sidebar about Jess, she shared believing that her story was bleak, that her mental health condition would be a lifelong struggle, and that there would be no place in the church for her to experience acceptance and ministry fulfillment. What would be Jess's experience if she were to attend your church?

3. Consider the problem we have identified: to meet the mental health demand within the United States using our current models of care, we need to train hundreds of thousands more clinicians to serve millions more who suffer from the full spectrum of mental health disorders at a cost of billions of dollars per year.

   If you had all power and all authority to fix this issue, in the church or within the current mental health system, what would you do?

4. Consider the example of Fresh Hope. How is the traditional mental health model similar to or different from a faithful and true friend?

---

[17] Andy Crouch, *Playing God: Redeeming the Gift of Power* (Downers Grove, IL: InterVarsity Press, 2013), 188.

The Hurrier I Go,
the Behinder I Get

UNPACKING THE SURGE IN MENTAL HEALTH CONCERNS

IN THE OPENING CHAPTER, we delineated a pressing issue and proposed a potential remedy. We highlighted the burgeoning crisis in mental health care, emphasizing the dire need for innovative systems. We further underscored the imperative for Christian leaders, who are proficient in human care disciplines, to helm the change by harnessing the strengths of the Christian church.

In this subsequent chapter, we will delve deeper into the evidence supporting the aforementioned crisis. The data at hand reveals a worrying upsurge in psychopathology diagnoses over the past two decades. The COVID pandemic only exacerbated these mental health concerns, intensifying existing issues and spawning novel challenges. Given the trajectory, it's a grim prospect to anticipate any significant improvements in the post-COVID landscape.

Understanding the sheer magnitude and intricacy of the current demand for mental health services is vital, especially given the glaring mismatch with the profession's capacity to cater to these needs. The foundations of psychology and counseling are undoubtedly robust, but, alarmingly, despite strides in therapeutic techniques and medicinal interventions, the incidence rates of virtually every diagnostic category in mental health—spanning across age brackets, socioeconomic statuses, ethnicities, and regions—are skyrocketing at a pace that outstrips our capability to provide adequate care.

Before delving further, it's imperative to issue a brief caveat. Numerous theories abound regarding the root causes of this surge: from the disintegration of familial structures, systemic racism or sexism culminating in economic disparities, to the curtailment of school prayers or the hegemony of a single political faction in governmental branches. We are not venturing into the territory of causation here—that's a comprehensive subject worthy of its own separate volume. Our focus, in this context, is solely to elucidate the evolving landscape of mental health requirements, thereby laying the groundwork for strategic recommendations to counteract this burgeoning crisis.

Is the Problem Really Getting Worse, or Does It Just Seem That Way?

It is a common belief that mental health is getting worse, both individually and collectively. You hear comments such as "People are all getting crazier" at neighborhood gatherings, in conversations at the barbershop or nail salon, and from many pulpits. Phrases such as "What is this world coming to?" "This is not like it was in our day," and, "It's never been this bad" are common. And most everyone has someone in their circle they're worried about, whether related to anxiety, depression, or even more serious concerns. It is natural to think that the state of mental health in our society is in decline, or even in a free fall, and that it is caused by social ills and historic injustices.

Our social networks and 24/7 news seem to confirm this. We see angry, funny, bizarre, and very sad human behavior every day on social media. From a wide circle of friends, suffering is brought close to us: the suicide of a neighbor, the addiction of a cousin, the hospitalization of a son or daughter for eating disorders or major depression, the coworker facing overwhelming fear. Is it worse or has our awareness increased because of advanced communication and networking?

Indeed, it is worse.

As is commonly attributed to the White Rabbit in *Alice in Wonderland*, he captures the situation well when he says, "The hurrier I go, the behinder I get." The data indicates that we have invested more and more in mental health care. This is not a problem that has been ignored by society or communities. Mental health care has been a priority effort with federal, state, and local governments, private insurance, not-for-profit organizations, and individuals who use their own funds to pay for treatments. The tremendous benefits are obvious: the stigma of seeing a professional counselor is not eliminated, but it is greatly reduced. We have treatments for virtually every mental health issue with demonstrable effectiveness. The success of such interventions is accepted by the vast majority of the population. There is respected science behind our care. Mental health care has arrived.

Yet despite all our progress, we are getting "behinder" and "behinder." In 1986, total dollars spent on mental health services—everything from hospitalization to medicines to outpatient treatment—was $32 billion. SAMHSA reports that figure increased to $171.7 billion in 2009 and to $280.5 billion in 2020. That is a ninefold increase in thirty-four years.[1] As a culture, we spend slightly less on mental health care than the entire GDP of Finland or Denmark. This money is well spent. It is unimaginable to think where we would be without counselors, psychologists, therapists, social workers, and psychiatrists helping people navigate mental health disorders. Care professionals at every level are passionate to bring relief to those in pain.

---

[1] Substance Abuse and Mental Health Services Administration, "Projections of National Expenditures for Treatment of Mental and Substance Use Disorders, 2010-2020" (2014): iii, https://store.samhsa.gov/sites/default/files/d7/priv/sma14-4883.pdf.

But even with the efforts of an army of mental health professionals dedicated to these causes, the need has only continued to grow. We see this in rising addiction and suicide rates, levels of depression and anxiety, divorce and family dissolution. So, we are indeed "behinder" and "behinder." Let us show you how far.

Mental Health in the United States

First, let's understand what we mean by "mental disorders." They are biologically, sociologically, physiologically, and spiritually influenced patterns found in the way we act, think, and feel. Within the medical vernacular, the DSM-5 defines a mental disorder as

> A syndrome characterized by clinically significant disturbance in an individual's cognition, emotion regulation, or behavior that reflects a dysfunction in the psychological, biological, or developmental processes underlying mental functioning. Mental disorders are usually associated with significant distress in social, occupational, or other important activities. An expectable or culturally approved response to a common stressor or loss, such as the death of a loved one, is not a mental disorder. Socially deviant behavior (e.g., political, religious, or sexual) and conflicts that are primarily between the individual and society are not mental disorders unless the deviance or conflict results from a dysfunction in the individual, as described above.[2]

In the pages ahead we'll examine the prevalence of disorders described broadly, then examine five areas of concern that draw most of our resources and are identified as medical/health crises by the World Health Organization and the National Institutes of Health. These are Anxiety Disorders, Depressive Disorders, Suicide, Substance Abuse/Addictions, and Childhood Disorders.

---

[2]American Psychiatric Association, *Diagnostic and Statistical Manual of Mental Disorders*, 5th ed. (Washington, DC: American Psychiatric Association Publishing, 2013), 20.

Trauma and the Church:
Helping Vets and First Responders

Trauma, emerging from parental neglect in childhood to near-death experiences from traffic accidents, is a root cause of many psychological needs. REBOOT Recovery provides a Christian, faith-based curriculum for those who've survived military or first responder trauma, as well as their families.

Evan and Jenny Owens launched the nonprofit in 2012. In her job as an occupational therapist working with members of the military, she noticed that patients were finding help for their mental and physical health but not their spiritual issues.

"We ended up having families together for dinner," says Evan. Gathered in small groups around a table, they quickly realized the power in shared trauma. "We'd say, 'let's get all these families together because they're telling the same type of stories and having the same types of experiences.'"

Since then, REBOOT Recovery has trained more than 1,500 leaders online. These facilitators lead twelve-week classes that include a teaching video and group discussion.

Justin is a REBOOT facilitator who says it's making a night-and-day difference for those who attend. An Army vet, he deployed to Afghanistan and then Iraq. "I was a 'crisis Christian,'" he says, describing his faith for many years.

When he left the service, he lost his way, slipping into depression. A friend urged him to join a veterans support group, and there he came to deeper understanding of his faith. In time he felt called to ministry and landed on the staff of a church that offers REBOOT for veterans and first responders.

Justin says the group's safe environment brings comfort and healing for those accustomed to bottling their pain. "We're just here for them to talk, and the biggest thing I've seen is them being able to talk and get stuff off their chests," he said. Many have spent years being told they were weak if they tried to get help. It's why some still arrive via the church's back door.

Justin's church has quickly built a reputation for its ministry. "I'll get calls, 'Hey I've never met you. I don't go to your church. Can I come and talk with you?'" he says.

Many of these calls come from those who know someone in a REBOOT group. "Veterans are very word of mouth. If someone gets help, they tell others," he says.

When groups end, the church provides aftercare, which includes regular open-invite meals. "If someone's had a hard week, we're just there to help them," says Justin.

Evan and Jenny Owens say several hundred churches have facilitated the REBOOT courses. The churches typically cover the cost of course materials and sometimes meals and childcare as well.

REBOOT post-program surveys show graduates have significant improvement in anxiety and depressive symptoms, social isolation, and sleep issues.

Overall Mental Health Concerns

There has been a steady decline in well-being in the United States over recent decades. Ed Higgins, a professor of psychiatry at the University of South Carolina, describes this trend as

> one of the "inconvenient truths" of mental illness. Suicide rates per 100,000 people have increased to a thirty-year high. Substance abuse, particularly of opiates, has become epidemic. Disability awards for mental disorders have dramatically increased since 1980, and the U.S. Department of Veterans Affairs is struggling to keep up with the surge in post-traumatic stress disorder (PTSD). . . . The toll of mental disorders had grown in the past two decades, even as other serious conditions became more manageable.[3]

Higgins is not the only one to report that things are worse. Wall Street agrees. Health care economics indicate that as the demand for

---

[3]Edward Higgins, "Is Mental Health Declining in the U.S.?," *Scientific American*, January 1, 2017, www.scientificamerican.com/article/is-mental-health-declining-in-the-u-s/.

treatment increases, the price will climb. To profit from rising prices, companies involved in mental health care are seen as "good buys" for investing. Harris Williams and Company is a multinational investment firm that produces research advising financial organizations where money is to be earned and lost. Their 2022 report indicates that the demand for mental health services is increasing simultaneous to the decline in mental health services. Citing data from Mental Health America 2022, they state:

> Behavioral health conditions, including substance use disorders (SUDs), eating disorders (EDs), and mental health disorders, are a significant issue across age groups that continues to worsen. This trend has only been exacerbated by the COVID-19 pandemic causing increasing isolation, anxiety, and health issues for individuals and their loved ones. For example, an estimated 47.6 million individuals report having a mental health disorder, with 45% of people experiencing a negative mental health impact due to COVID-19.[4]

Other investment advisers note that the lack of availability of care throughout the United States for behavioral health conditions has created a serious demand. It is estimated that 24.7 percent of adults with a mental health disorder report an unmet need for treatment, a percentage that hasn't declined since 2011.[5] And nearly 1 in 3 youths with major depression is living without mental health treatment.[6]

Similarly, Edgemont Partners, an investment bank that provides guidance for entrepreneurs seeking to invest in health and mental health care, projects that mental health demand will increase spending through the first quarter of the twenty-first century. Their projection

[4] Whit Knier, James Clark, and Taylor Will, "Behavioral Health: Unmet Demand Highlights Growth Opportunity," Harris Williams, November 3, 2022, www.harriswilliams.com/our-insights/hcls-behavioral-health-unmet-demand-highlights-growth-opportunity.
[5] Maddy Reinert, Theresa Nguyen, and Danielle Fritze, "The State of Mental Health in America 2022," Mental Health America (October 2021), https://mhanational.org/sites/default/files/2022%20State%20of%20Mental%20Health%20in%20America.pdf.
[6] Knier, Clark, and Will, "Behavioral Health."

data suggests the mental health demand in 2025 will expand by nearly 1/3 in just ten years, from $19.7 billion to $28.6 billion.[7]

Finally, FutureWise found that the demand for services will grow exponentially between 2020 and 2027, while the providers of services decrease or are unable to match the rate of growth, they also report few additional funding sources to meet the need and compensate the caregivers.[8]

There is a sad but stark reality to these investment projections. Increased "opportunity" for investors means an increase in suffering for families and communities. More money to be made suggests that the presence of need is increasing. This is like a call to invest in Band-Aids or pain relievers because there are more skin scrapes and headaches. These reports are ominous for those who provide care or those who train providers as they forecast storm clouds on the horizon. Wall Street predictors have determined that serious mental health needs are increasing and that they cannot be met using the current levels of funding, methods, and mental health providers.

Crucial Areas of Mental Health Need

While the economic indicators predict the rising need, the prevalence indicators within each area of mental health also show growth beyond our current capacity to render care. We present data in five crucial areas of mental health need. They are Anxiety, Depression, Suicide, Addictions, and Childhood Disorders. In each area, we find that our capacity to address it is stretched and strained.

Anxiety. Treating anxiety presents an enormous challenge. It is the most common mental health condition. The Anxiety and Depression Association of America (ADAA) reports that 40 million adults, about

[7]Edgemont, *Accelerating Investor Interest in Mental Health,* July 17, 2020, www.edgemont.com /insights/accelerating-investor-interest-in-mental-health/.

[8]FutureWise, *Behavioral Health Market by Component, by Delivery Model, by Function, by End-User and Region: Industry Analysis, Market Share, Revenue Opportunity, Competition, and Forecast 2023–2031,* www.futurewiseresearch.com/healthcare-market-research/Behavioral-Health -Market/3410.

18 percent of the population, and an additional 31 percent of adolescents and children have some form of anxiety diagnosis.[9] A 2020 report by the American Psychological Association cites similar statistics.[10]

Biblically, anxiety is recognized as a human trait that requires nuanced understanding. Paul declares with power and conviction that we should "not be anxious about anything" (Phil 4:6) and that we should release our anxiety by prayer. Peter instructs us to "Cast all your anxiety on him because he cares for you"(1 Pet 5:7). Yet to the Corinthians, Paul reports that "apart from other things, there is the daily pressure on me of my anxiety for all the churches" (2 Cor 11:28 ESV). Anxiety is that which pulls us to care, act, and respond to injustice. But the call to concern can be a trap that dominates, controls, and leaves us defeated.

Anxiety is essential in small portions. It makes us better at just about everything. Anxiety can also make us healthier—more focused, disciplined, and joyful at most everything we do. It motivates us to perform our best, challenges us to strive beyond our reach. This type of anxiety prompts and prods us all to strive for excellence. Without it, mediocrity or apathy would rule most of us. This is Paul's anxiety that he carries for others. Think of this anxiety as a favorite pet, a lap dog. Your life is better because of his or her presence. It's a pain which produces goodness.

But at other times, anxiety isn't our loyal best friend. It is an unwelcome nuisance—the pet that is out of control. It is as if this anxiety barks endlessly, chews on your favorite running shoe, or scares your guests with a growl. Rather than a best friend, this is a significant burden. This anxiety does not prompt us to become better. It distracts

---

[9]Anxiety and Depression Association of America (website), Anxiety Disorders—Facts and Statistics, accessed July 21, 2023, https://adaa.org/understanding-anxiety/facts-statistics.

[10]American Psychological Association, *Stress in America™ 2020: A National Mental Health Crisis* (2020), www.apa.org/news/press/releases/stress/2020/sia-mental-health-crisis.pdf.

us from the good and causes us to waste precious resources on worry, apprehension, and fear. Because of this anxiety, we don't apply for that job and don't ask a potential friend to have lunch. This anxiety prompts us not to try, not to take risks, not to lean into opportunity. While this anxiety is a frustration, it is not a disease, just an irritant that must be managed. This anxiety distracts our attention and robs us of our joy. This is the anxiety of Philippians 4 or 1 Peter 5.

And there is another, more ominous form of anxiety—neither the beloved nor the irritating family pet. It's a wolf, and it bites. This level of anxiety, in the form of panic disorder, post-traumatic stress disorder, obsessive-compulsive disorders, simple, social, and agoraphobias, is a disease or disorder. This anxiety can shut a person down, obliterating the ability to interact with others. You can't escape it. This anxiety shuts us down or keeps us indoors. Anxiety disorder is a ruthless carnivore.

The combined class of anxiety disorders is the most common mental health concern. Somers and colleagues reviewed forty-one international studies between 1980 and 2004. They found that around the world, anxiety disorders—the wolf at the door type of anxiety— would affect about 11 percent of adults in the previous year and about 17 percent of adults over their lifetime. They conclude that "across studies, anxiety disorders were approximately twice as prevalent among women. . . . Overall, the results suggest a burden of illness that eclipses the capacity of specialized mental health service providers."[11] In simpler terms, they're saying that anxiety has become so widespread that the world's mental health resources just can't keep up. Compared to international trends, anxiety in the United States is more prominent. According to the National Institute of Mental Health, nearly one-third of adults will experience it at some time in their life. About 20 percent of all adults will fight anxiety this year,

---

[11]Julian M. Somers et al., "Prevalence and Incidence Studies of Anxiety Disorders: A Systematic Review of the Literature," *The Canadian Journal of Psychiatry* 51, no. 2 (2006): 110.

along with 30 percent of all adolescents.[12] Kessler and colleagues found that only about one-third of those with anxiety disorders will ever seek treatment. Those who do usually wait ten years before seeking help from a doctor or counselor.[13] The ADAA indicates that our anxiety disorders make us three to five times more likely to go to the doctor for concerns other than anxiety; in other words, we are more likely to get sick and feel sicker.[14]

Anxiety appears to occur more often in women than men—about two times as much. But among young adults, the data for both men and women suggest anxiety is on the rise. The rise appears to be both steady and constant.[15]

Duffy, Twenge, and Joiner report that anxiety among college students rose 24 percent between 2011 and 2018.[16] Scheffler and colleagues reported similar trends, but with anxiety levels more serious: "Between 2008 and 2014, the rate of anxiety grew steadily for college students ages 18 to 26. Both men and women experienced large relative increases in diagnoses over this time, with women's diagnoses rising about 47.2% and men's about 53.2%. The overall rate rose by about 48.4% between 2008 and 2014."[17]

Combining these findings, forty million of us and our friends are clinically anxious, the type that makes us feel sick and immobilized. And we will carry this burden for ten years before we get help. Our research data

---

[12]National Institute of Mental Health (website), Any Anxiety Disorder, accessed July 21, 2023, www .nimh.nih.gov/health/statistics/any-anxiety-disorder.shtml.

[13]Ronald C. Kessler et al., "Childhood Adversities and Adult Psychopathology in the WHO World Mental Health Surveys," *The British Journal of Psychiatry* 197, no. 5 (2010): 378-85.

[14]Anxiety and Depression Association of America (website), Anxiety Disorders—Facts and Statistics, accessed July 21, 2023, https://adaa.org/understanding-anxiety/facts-statistics.

[15]R. Scheffler, R., D. Arnold, H. Qazi, J. Harney, L. Linde, G. Dimick, and N. Vora, "The Anxious Generation: Causes and Consequences of Anxiety Disorder Among Young Americans: Preliminary Findings," Berkeley Institute for the Future of Young Americans (website), 2018, https:// youngamericans.berkeley.edu/2019/11/the-anxious-generation/.

[16]Mary E. Duffy, Jean M. Twenge, and Thomas E. Joiner, "Trends in Mood and Anxiety Symptoms and Suicide-Related Outcomes Among US Undergraduates, 2007–2018: Evidence from Two National Surveys," *Journal of Adolescent Health* 65, no. 5 (2019): 590-98.

[17]Richard Scheffler et al., "Anxiety Disorder on College Campuses: The New Epidemic," Berkeley Institute for Young Americans (website), April 2019, https://youngamericans.berkeley.edu/wp -content/uploads/2019/12/Anxiety_Disorder_on_College_Campuses_UCB_Study_FINAL.pdf.

indicates that today there are about twenty-five million adults—more than all the people who live in Florida or New York—who are carrying a very heavy weight.[18] It slows them down, exhausts them, and robs them of joy, spontaneity, and peace. It disturbs families, blocks the ability to work, and locks people in a mental prison of fear and isolation.

Depression. We all know depression as that pervasive sense of sadness. Artists have sung and painted it as the color blue. Looking at Van Gogh's *Starry Night*, one is captivated by its swirls of dark navy blue. The painting cries out in despair. Or hearing B. B. King playing a call-and-response pattern over a twelve-bar scheme where his voice and his beloved Lucile both resonate with the sadness and oppression of life as one who has "got the blues."

Like anxiety, depression is experienced by degree. The mood or feeling of dread and emptiness is common. For some, the disorder of utter despair can completely overpower even the strongest will. NIMH data informs us that about seventeen million adults and three million adolescents between ages twelve and seventeen experience this knock-you-down level of depression in their lifetime.

Compton and colleagues, in their studies on alcohol consumption, gleaned important findings on depression. They analyzed the results of the National Longitudinal Alcohol Epidemiologic Survey (NLAES) 1991–1992 and the National Epidemiologic Survey on Alcohol and Related Conditions (NESARC) 2001–2002 and compared the change. They found that the "prevalence of past-year major depressive episode in total samples increased significantly from 3.33% in 1991–92 to 7.06% in 2001–02. Furthermore, in nearly every age, racial-ethnic, and sex subgroup examined, significant increases in rates of depression were observed over the past decade."[19] This was the number

---

[18] Anxiety and Depression Association of America (website), Anxiety Disorders—Facts and Statistics, accessed July 21, 2023, https://adaa.org/understanding-anxiety/facts-statistics.

[19] Wilson M. Compton et al., "Changes in the Prevalence of Major Depression and Comorbid Substance Use Disorders in the United States Between 1991–1992 and 2001–2002," *American Journal of Psychiatry* 163, no. 12 (2006): 2142-43.

for the general population. For subjects who had a history of substance abuse occurring in the past year, the depression prevalence in 1991–1992 was 9.97 percent, and it increased to 15.06 percent in 2001–2002. Among women, the prevalence of depression with comorbid substance use disorder in 1991–1992 was 13.23 percent, and it rose to 25.41 percent in 2001–2002.

Finally, Compton et al. investigated the prevalence of depressive episodes occurring in the past year of those who did not report any co-occurring substance use. They found that across gender, race, and age, the 1991–1992 prevalence was 2.76 percent, and in 2001–2002 it rose to 6.23 percent. They found significance at nearly every age, ethnicity, and gender group.

Compton and his team wondered the obvious: What is causing the depression increase? They concluded the following.

> Since such a rapid change cannot be explained by genetic causes, attention in future research should be drawn to environmental changes that have taken place during the past decade. Further elaboration of changes in historical and cultural factors, marital stability, health insurance status, household composition, psychiatric and medical comorbidity, and composition of the labor force and other economic indices are necessary to begin to understand rising rates of major depression.[20]

Their final idea is pertinent to every chapter in this book:

> *If the prevalence of depression continues to increase as it has over the past decade, demand for services will increase dramatically in the future and may outstrip the capacity of service delivery systems.* In any case, clinicians can expect to encounter depression more frequently in their practices, especially among young adults.[21]

Drawing similar conclusions, Mojtabai and Jorm analyzed data from surveys conducted between 2001–2002 and 2011–2012, a plurality

---

[20]Compton et al., "Changes in the Prevalence of Major Depression," 2146.
[21]Compton et al., "Changes in the Prevalence of Major Depression," 2146, emphasis added.

of studies assessing millions of subjects. They found that in the United States, 15.1 percent of the population reported modest psychological distress, and 3.1 percent reported severe distress. These percentages were similar when controlled for sex, age, and race, and they held stable over time. As to the prevalence of major depressive disorder, they found that 7.0 percent, or about 25,000 people from a large sample of more than 300,000, reported having met the criteria for depression in the past year.[22] This is slightly higher than the percentage found by Compton et al.[23]

Finally, Mojtabai and Jorm found that subjects reported a 22 percent increase in psychiatric medications and a 33 percent increase in seeing a mental health professional over the twelve-year survey span. And 4.9 percent reported an unmet mental health need from the full sample, while from the subset of subjects who were receiving any form of mental health treatment, their unmet need perception was 18.9 percent. These percentages appeared to be stable over time.

They conclude by comparing expected effects of psychiatric interventions and medications compared to interventions and treatments of heart disease. They write:

> The expectation to see a decrease in the prevalence of distress of depressive symptoms with increase in treatment seeking is not unjustified. Increase in the use of statins has led to significant reduction in population cholesterol levels. Similarly, growth in treatment of hypertension has led to better control of this illness. *Yet there is not clear evidence that expansion in the treatment of mental disorders or psychological distress has led to reduced prevalence or incidence of these conditions.*[24]

In one other comprehensive study, Twenge examined depression rates among 6.9 million adolescents, young adults, and adults between

---

[22]Ramin Mojtabai and Anthony F. Jorm, "Trends in Psychological Distress, Depressive Episodes and Mental Health Treatment-Seeking in the United States: 2001–2012," *Journal of Affective Disorders* 174 (2015): 556-61.

[23]Mojtabai and Jorm, "Trends in Psychological Distress."

[24]Mojtabai and Jorm, "Trends in Psychological Distress," 559, emphasis added.

1982 and 2013. She stated, "Americans in the 2000s-2010s (vs. the 1980s-1990s) were likely to report depressive symptoms, especially psychosomatic symptoms, but were less likely to overtly admit to depression or report suicidal ideation. . . . This pattern of findings was most pronounced among girls and women."[25] The study also found that twice as many high school students now seek treatment for mental and emotional issues. Her conclusion: "Overall, the rate of depressive symptoms among Americans remains unacceptably high."[26]

While a significant portion of the data indicates rising rates of depression, there are some findings that suggest otherwise. Specifically, Olfson et al. observed a decrease in the demand for depression treatment. Their national survey showed a decline from 71 percent in 1987 to 60 percent in 1997.[27] Further research by Marcus and Olfson pointed to an even sharper drop, with the demand falling to 43 percent by 2007.[28] It's important to note that these figures represent shifts in treatment rates, not the actual prevalence of depression. A key factor possibly influencing these numbers is the increasing reliance on antidepressant medications in place of traditional psychotherapy. Simply put, as medications become more effective and widely used, there seems to be a reduction in overt depressive symptoms and presentations.

A final reflection that gives pause is the potential impact of the COVID-19 pandemic on our collective mental well-being, particularly concerning depression levels. The full ramifications of COVID on our psyche might remain veiled until midcentury, giving current students time to progress through their education and navigate a post-COVID environment. But preliminary signs are concerning. A study spearheaded by Juan Bueno-Novitol at Hospital Universitario

---

[25]Jean M. Twenge, "Time Period and Birth Cohort Differences in Depressive Symptoms in the US, 1982–2013," *Social Indicators Research* 121, no. 2 (2015): 450.

[26]Twenge, "Time Period and Birth Cohort Differences," 452.

[27]Mark Olfson et al., "National Trends in the Outpatient Treatment of Depression," *JAMA* 287, no. 2 (2002): 203-9.

[28]Steven C. Marcus and Mark Olfson, "National Trends in the Treatment for Depression from 1998 to 2007," *Archives of General Psychiatry* 67, no. 12 (2010): 1265-73.

Miguel Servet in Zaragoza, Spain, undertook a meta-analysis of studies on adult depression globally during the pandemic's initial six months. Their findings were startling. Instead of the expected depression prevalence of 4 to 6 percent, they found a staggering pooled prevalence of 25 percent, suggesting a sevenfold surge. While this surge might not reflect the ultimate increase, it is evident that a significant uptick is imminent, and in due course, we'll gain clarity on the new prevalence rates.[29]

We can say that most of the evidence suggests that depression is rising and that the slope of growth jumped profoundly due to the COVID-19 pandemic. Where our depression rates settle in the next ten years remains to be seen, but no one offers much hope that depression levels will be better. Most expect depression to increase rapidly because of COVID isolation. Such was the findings of Ettman and colleagues who reported in 2020 that

> prevalence of depression symptoms was more than 3-fold higher during COVID-19 compared with the most recent population-based estimates of mental health in the US. This increase in depression symptom prevalence is higher than that recorded after previous mass traumatic events, likely reflecting the far more pervasive influence of COVID-19 and its social and economic consequences than other, previously studied mass traumatic events. Again one must be cautious in interpreting data to see what is there rather than seeing what one anticipates and expects.[30]

Suicide. You would think that it would be relatively easier to calculate suicide compared to other mental health issues because death is so final and absolute. But it is not as easy as counting. In the data, there are three ways to calculate suicide rates in the population: age,

---

[29]Juan Bueno-Notivol et al., "Prevalence of Depression During the COVID-19 Outbreak: A Meta-Analysis of Community-Based Studies," *International Journal of Clinical and Health Psychology* 21, no. 1 (2021): 100196.

[30]Catherine K. Ettman et al., "Prevalence of Depression Symptoms in US Adults Before and During the COVID-19 Pandemic," *JAMA Network Open* 3, no. 9 (2020): 10.

period, and cohort. The age calculation is relatively simple. For example, each year, how many nineteen-year-olds committed suicide? We can compare nineteen-year-olds in 1974 with those in 2014, and so on. Another way to calculate suicide is by period, such as between 1990 and 1999, how many suicides occurred? This measure demonstrates that we are not in the period of highest suicide; that was in the 1930s when the crude suicide rate was over fifteen per year per 100,000 people. Nor are we anywhere close to the lowest period; that would have been World War II, and again in the late 1950s when the period rate was below ten per 100,000.[31] We also can compare the cohort rate where you follow groups of people through their lifetime—such as the WWII generation (those born around 1920–1925) or those born between 2000 and 2005 who are young adults as we approach 2025.

Phillips offers a thorough picture of suicide progression and digression since our depression era to the middle of the Obama presidency using all three of these methods of measure.[32] The presentation of her data is confirmed by Stone et al. and by Curtin, Warner, and Hedegaard's National Center for Health Statistics.[33]

To summarize the prevalence of suicide, there are about 45,000 suicides per year in the United States. It is about twice as common as murder. The overall combined "crude" suicide calculation, which includes all ages, races, and sexes, has fluctuated between ten and fifteen per year per 100,000 people since the Depression. To consider it by sex, it has ranged from four to seven suicides per 100,000 for women and fifteen to twenty-five per 100,000 for men. During the 1960s, prevalence rates remained stable, around eleven per 100,000 overall (seventeen for men and five for women per 100,000). Then from the early 1970s to the mid-1980s,

[31]Deborah M. Stone et al., "Vital Signs: Trends in State Suicide Rates—United States, 1999–2016 and Circumstances Contributing to Suicide—27 States, 2015," *Morbidity and Mortality Weekly Report* 67, no. 22 (2018): 617.

[32]Julie A. Phillips, "A Changing Epidemiology of Suicide? The Influence of Birth Cohorts on Suicide Rates in the United States," *Social Science & Medicine* 114 (2014): 151-60.

[33]Sally C. Curtin, Margaret Warner, and Holly Hedegaard, *Increase in Suicide in the United States, 1999–2014* NCHS Data Brief, no. 241 (2016).

prevalence rates steadily climbed. They peaked for women in 1972 at about six per 100,000 and for men in about 1985 at about twenty per 100,000. They gradually declined for both men and women until 1999— about four for women and seventeen for men per 100,000. Since the turn into the twenty-first century, suicide rates have increased, back to about five and twenty for women and men (respectively) per 100,000.

While that overall summary is not good news, it shields the scary part. When Phillips looked at suicides among adolescents and early adults, she found that among males, the suicide rates for adolescents (15-19) in 1940 and 1960 was about five per 100,000. For young adults males (20-24), it was about the same. However, in 1980 and 2010, the frequency of adolescent males committing suicide jumped to twelve per 100,000, and for young men, it leaped to twenty to twenty-five per 100,000.[34] Wang, Yu, Wang, Bao, Gao, and Xiang (2016) confirmed this trend in their study of the data that looked primarily at suicide prevalence by sex, age, and race.[35] If this trend holds, it indicates that suicide will continue to rise in future generations, and will be more prominent in age groups as they advance in years.

Addictions. Gerald May laid the groundwork for us in understanding addiction prevalence. "I am not being flippant when I say that all of us suffer from addiction. Nor am I reducing the meaning of addiction. I mean in all truth that psychological, neurological and spiritual dynamics of full-fledged addiction are actively at work within every human being."[36] So, with May's concept of addiction in mind, the prevalence rate has been extremely stable for centuries and looks to remain stable for quite some time. It is 100 percent. We are creatures of habit. But the nature of the habits we rely on have varying capacities for good and harm. We are all addictive beings, but we can

---

[34]Phillips, "A Changing Epidemiology of Suicide?"

[35]Zhenkun Wang et al., "Age-Period-Cohort Analysis of Suicide Mortality by Gender Among White and Black Americans, 1983–2012," *International Journal for Equity in Health* 15, no. 1 (2016): 1-9.

[36]Gerald G. May, *Addiction and Grace* (San Francisco: Harper & Row, 1988), 3.

separate the person who is addicted to spearmint gum from the person addicted to opioids or tobacco or pornography. One addiction might promote tooth decay (in fifty years) and another could kill you tomorrow! We all understand the idea of addiction, but the demons to which we become ensnared differ in their cruelty.

Let's begin the examination of substance abuse addictions with some good news and some very bad news. Drug use among adolescents shows decline or no increase in every category. But the death rates from drug overdose continue to increase at an alarming rate.

First we note the decline in drug use. Data produced in 2019 by the Institute for Social Research at the University of Michigan surveyed more than 40,000 eighth, tenth and twelfth graders. They report that historic measures of drug use, illicit drugs, synthetic drugs, marijuana, and tobacco smoking showed decreases, but innovative deliveries of tobacco and vaping showed a significant increase in use, especially among eighth graders.[37]

Furthermore, the National Institute on Drug Abuse at the National Institutes of Health indicates that adolescent drug use, be it alcohol, marijuana, heroin, cigarettes, or pain killers, has been declining over recent years. It's not accurate to say that we are "winning the war on drugs," but the usages of some drugs for adolescents is declining.[38]

The Behavioral Health Barometer, a SAMHSA publication of drug use prevalence published in 2020, indicates that marijuana use for both males and females in each age group has been in decline since the early 2010s.[39] These findings appear to be holding true for states

---

[37]L. D. Johnston, R. A. Miech, P. M. O'Malley, J. G. Bachman, J. E. Schulenberg, and M. E. Patrick, *Monitoring the Future National Survey Results on Drug Use, 1975–2019: Overview, Key Findings on Adolescent Drug Use* (Ann Arbor: Institute for Social Research, University of Michigan, 2020), https://deepblue.lib.umich.edu/bitstream/handle/2027.42/162579/FINAL.pdf?sequence=1.

[38]National Institute on Drug Abuse, "Most Reported Substance Use Among Adolescents Held Steady in 2022," December 15, 2022, https://nida.nih.gov/news-events/news-releases/2022/12/most-reported-substance-use-among-adolescents-held-steady-in-2022.

[39]Substance Abuse and Mental Health Services Administration, *Behavioral Health Barometer: United States, Volume 6: Indicators as Measured Through the 2019 National Survey on Drug*

where marijuana is legal for adult recreational use. While there are ample studies that show the benefit and harm to society regarding pot legalization, it does not appear to have caused a rapid increase in the drug's use among teens.

The cigarette use data among teens ought to make every high school health teacher proud. Tobacco use is falling substantially among teens, both males and females, and in every racial group. Smoking is not cool. And yet, vaping is. The data informs us that we should be optimistic . . . and concerned. The optimism lies in the fact that nicotine addiction, as we have known it for generations, is dropping. The two-pack-a-day habit fought by grandparents, parents, and those of this generation appears to be far less common today. To youth, smoking tobacco does not have the drawing power it once did. However, innovations in nicotine delivery do appeal to the young. Vaping, with all its various names (e-cigs, e-hookahs, mods, vape pens, vapes, tank systems, electronic nicotine delivery systems [ENDS]), will vaporize nicotine, marijuana, and/or other flavors into the lungs as it is inhaled.

While the good news about addiction is very good news, there remains a lot of bad news. Opioid addiction is not just bad, it's ugly. The literature suggests two trends: First, the addiction occurrence from prescription pain medications—the drugs you and I receive after knee surgery or getting our wisdom teeth removed. These procedures hurt a lot. The pain medicines—called analgesics—are very strong and your body adapts to them quickly. For many, even after the pain is gone, the craving for the medication remains. As the medical and legal restrictions on pain medicines have increased, making their abuse more difficult, the increase in nonmedical opioids, particularly heroin use, has grown sharply. Heroin is cheaper and

Use and Health and the National Survey of Substance Abuse Treatment Services (Rockville, MD: Substance Abuse and Mental Health Services Administration, 2020), www.samhsa.gov /data/sites/default/files/reports/rpt32815/National-BH-Barometer_Volume6.pdf.

easier to get because the neighborhood dealer doesn't care about the person, only the profit.[40]

The second trend and most drastic effect of the opioid increase is that more people are dying from this addiction—a lot more. *JAMA* reports that there were about 65,000 drug overdose deaths in 2017. Two-thirds of them were opioid-related deaths. These deaths have doubled since 2010. NIDA reports that combined opioid overdose deaths (that is, prescription opioids and synthetic opioids such as fentanyl) occurred about 7,000 times in 2001. This rose to 21,000 deaths in 2011. In 2021 there were more than 80,000 deaths reported.[41]

This dramatic increase in opioid addiction has also led to an increase in people seeking treatment. The number of individuals enrolled in opioid treatment programs increased by 132 percent between 2011 and 2015. This drastic uptick places the entire country on a type of opioid alert. The numbers in 2019 show unnerving current prevalence rates: 11.4 million people misusing opioid medication, 2 million people with a diagnosable disorder, and more than 800,000 adults addicted to heroin.

The US Counsel on Foreign Relations summarized our current crisis with opioid addictions succinctly, saying, "Fentanyl and other opioids are fueling the worst drug crisis in the history of the United States. More than 1,500 people per week die from taking some type of opioid, according to the National Center for Health Statistics, making opioids by far the leading cause of fatal overdoses in the country."[42]

---

[40]Christopher M. Jones, Emily B. Einstein, and Wilson M. Compton, "Changes in Synthetic Opioid Involvement in Drug Overdose Deaths in the United States, 2010–2016," *JAMA* (2018):1819-21. doi:10.1001/jama.2018.2844

[41]National Institute on Drug Abuse, "Drug Overdose Death Rates," Trends and Statistics, June 30, 2023, https://nida.nih.gov/research-topics/trends-statistics/overdose-death-rates#:~:text=Overall %2C%20drug%20overdose%20deaths%20rose,overdose%20deaths%20reported%20in%202021.

[42]Claire Kobucista and Alejandra Martinez, "Fentanyl and the U.S. Opioid Epidemic," Counsel on Foreign Relations (website), April 19, 2023, www.cfr.org/backgrounder/fentanyl-and-us -opioid-epidemic.

To summarize, we see a stabilization of many forms of consumption in substances such as alcohol, weed, and cocaine. The opioid addiction, fueled by abuses of prescription and synthetic opioids often produced internationally and smuggled into the country, remain epidemic in concern.

Childhood disorders. We can be apathetic about looking at data regarding adult anxiety prevalence. We can say, "Yeah, adults must be responsible for their behavior." When it comes to kids, however, people tend to sit up and take notice. We are more likely to fight for them. Well, put the gloves on.

Let's begin with a startling piece of information: Olfson, Blanco, Wang, Laje, and Correll compared two four-year periods—1995–1998 with 2007–2010—and found the number of children treated for mental health issues in outpatient settings such as community clinics and private practices doubled.[43] Twice as many kids showed up for counseling in 2010 as they did in 1998. This means that far more counselors were busy working with kids than they had been twelve years earlier. Furthermore, we know that if kids have diagnoses treated by mental health professionals, it is because of a "functional impairment, which substantially interferes with or limits the child's role or functioning in family, school, or community activities" (DSM-V). The federal government mandates that we can't diagnose kids just because their parents are frustrated with them for not making their beds or not doing their schoolwork on any given day. Rather, we diagnose children only when they are not "making it," that is, they are failing in school, with friends, or at home.

Olafson et al. examined the broad trends in mental health care among children and adolescents. They looked at the use of outpatient mental health services over the past twenty-plus years, and they found that psychotropic medication prescribed to children and adolescents

---

[43]Mark Olfson et al., "National Trends in the Mental Health Care of Children, Adolescents, and Adults by Office-Based Physicians," *JAMA Psychiatry* 71, no. 1 (2014): 81-90.

increased at rates similar to the increases in children receiving psychotherapy. Stimulants (commonly used to treat ADHD) increased from 4.0 percent to 6.6 percent. Antidepressants increased from 1.5 percent to 2.6 percent. Finally, antipsychotic medications rose from 0.2 percent to 1.2 percent.[44]

Autism Spectrum Disorders (ASD) and Attention Deficit Hyperactivity Disorders (ADHD) are both increasing and have become part of our mainstream language to describe child behavior. One only needs to use the phrase "on the spectrum" to capture an understanding of an individual child's behavioral pattern.

In 2023 the CDC reported that about one in thirty-six children had an ASD. This is compared to about one in 150 in 2000.[45] Van Narden Braun and associates examined the annual rate of increase for ASD in the city of Atlanta between 1996 and 2010. They report that there was a 269 percent increase from 4.2 per 1,000 children in 1996 to 15.5 per 1,000 in 2010. Average annual increases were about 9.6 percent during the fifteen-year span measured. They found that this change was slightly higher for boys compared to girls, and it was slightly higher for minority groups, but the drastic increases were common across sex and racial differences.[46]

As to ADHD, Children and Adults with Attention-Deficit/Hyperactivity Disorder (CHADD) reports child prevalence in 1997 to be 6.1 percent. About twenty years later the percentage of children diagnosed with ADHD had risen to 10.2 percent. These trends are highest among white children. Hispanics are substantially less likely to be diagnosed, with black children in the middle. The shape of the

---

[44]Mark Olfson, Benjamin G. Druss, and Steven C. Marcus, "Trends in Mental Health Care Among Children and Adolescents," *New England Journal of Medicine* 372, no. 21 (2015): 2029-38.

[45]Centers for Disease Control and Prevention, Data and Statistics on Autism Spectrum Disorder, April 4, 2023, www.cdc.gov/ncbddd/autism/data.html.

[46]Kim Van Naarden Braun et al., "Trends in the Prevalence of Autism Spectrum Disorder, Cerebral Palsy, Hearing Loss, Intellectual Disability, and Vision Impairment, Metropolitan Atlanta, 1991–2010," *PloS One* 10, no. 4 (2015): e0124120.

rise in diagnoses is similar across races.[47] Likewise, Rowland reports that 2007 data from National Health Interview Survey found about 7 percent of four- to seventeen-year-olds had an ADHD diagnosis.[48] The CDC gathered data between 2003 and 2007, and their findings showed an increase of 62 percent, from 9.6 percent to 15.6 percent.[49] Rowland's 2015 study showed outcomes similar to the CDC report placing ADHD prevalence at 15.5 percent.[50]

Conclusion

The purpose of this chapter is to provide evidence that the concerns most people observe informally are indeed serious and require action.

Pescosolido and colleagues looked at the same information that we have been examining and suggested that our current treatment methods are part of the problem. They note that as the population increases its mental health need, trust of and reliance on the medical system decreases. According to Pescosolido and team, the response to address the many disorders has been a clinical/medical solution, rooted in the assumption that if these painful matters of life are seen as medical conditions the stigma would be reduced, and people would be more willing to receive help. But they found that when public opinion of mental health disorders (schizophrenia, depression, alcohol dependence, etc.) is presented as disease or a medical condition, stigma and resistance to treatment increases.[51]

What appears to have been mistaken is the assumption that global change in neuroscientific beliefs would translate into global reductions

---

[47]"General Prevalence of ADHD," Children and Adults with Attention Deficit/Hyperactivity Disorder, https://chadd.org/about-adhd/general-prevalence/, accessed July 22, 2023.

[48]Andrew S. Rowland et al., "The Prevalence of ADHD in a Population-Based Sample," *Journal of Attention Disorders* 19, no. 9 (2015): 742.

[49]Rowland, "Prevalence of ADHD," 749.

[50]Rowland, "Prevalence of ADHD," 748.

[51]Bernice A. Pescosolido et al., "'A Disease Like Any Other?' A Decade of Change in Public Reactions to Schizophrenia, Depression and Alcohol Dependence," *American Journal of Psychiatry* 167, no. 11 (2010): 1321-30.

of stigma. . . . It is our contention that future stigma reduction efforts need to be reconfigured or at least supplemented. An overreliance on the neurobiological causes of mental illness and substance use disorders is at best ineffective and at worst potentially stigmatizing.[52]

They argue that the medicalizing of mental health disorders like the ones we have described in this chapter places them out of the individual's and family's sense of control and management. If depression is a medical condition in the same way that high blood pressure is a medical condition, then I or we can't fix this ourselves. We need a professional. Someone with expertise, education, a diploma, a white coat, and letters (lots of letters) after their name. And, beyond that, it's going to cost money. Goodbye to the summer vacation and eating out, and welcome to medical bills. Indeed, Pescosolido and her team suggest that there are a great number of people who are in free fall with their symptoms, and more are joining in the descent.

This is the glum chapter—the one that presents the evidence and begins to build the argument that change is needed. As members of the profession and professors who have prepared Christian counselors, pastors, and psychologists to care for others, we carry a motivating hope: help is within reach for millions who experience severe pain. But to relieve the suffering of children, adolescents, and adults who are represented by the numbers found in this chapter, we must think differently about the conditions and how we help people change. We need the good folks in white coats, but that's not all. We also need the church.

The Power of a Meal

A CBS News 2014 report on parents of children with mental illnesses identified a particularly painful sign of the stigma and lack of awareness these families often face. Gathered with a group of mothers in

---

[52]Pescosolido et al., "A Disease Like Any Other?" 3127.

Connecticut, anchor Scott Pelley asked how raising their children is different from raising a child with a physical illness. The mothers responded in unison: "casseroles."

For years, many congregations have provided a meal ministry to families with new babies or someone who is recovering from surgery. It's easy to organize, it's tangible, and it connects people in deep and meaningful ways. No wonder the mothers Pelley interviewed coveted it. For them, a pot of chili or spaghetti, salad, and bread sticks would have validated their pain and suffering and let them know that they were seen and supported. Instead, they felt ignored, abandoned, and shamed when no one added their family's name to the list.

Mental health advocate Amy Simpson has also zeroed in on the power of casseroles, calling mental illness "the no-casserole illness" in her book *Troubled Minds: Mental Illness and the Church's Mission*. She notes that while churches can be quick to support people with physical problems, they often pull back from those suffering with their mental health.

Simpson, whose mother was diagnosed with schizophrenia while she was growing up, explains, "When the church is silent to a person in crisis, it can sound remarkably like silence from God."

This kind of stigma is often observed by the Christian mental health professionals in the community who understand both their patients' needs and the attitudes in the local church. When child psychiatrist Dr. Steve Grcevich first opened his practice, he discovered that the parents of his patients were literally going to great lengths to avoid being seen entering his office. In *Mental Health and the Church*, Grcevich explains that his practice occupied prominent space in a bank building located at one of the community's busiest intersections. He would later discover that many families arrived for appointments with their children after having parked in a nearby grocery store parking lot and trudged across a large grassy area. They made the trek in all kinds of weather to access Grcevich's office. The reason for their time-consuming roundabout? The hope of avoiding detection as mental health patients.

Today Grcevich is the founder of Key Ministry, which provides re-sources and consulting for churches that want to create welcoming environments for these families. He's found that it's much easier for them to attend regularly when congregations take proactive steps to accommodate their children.

Questions for Reflection

1. As you read through this chapter, the numbers might seem stag-gering. To better understand the scale and impact, relate these statistics to your personal experiences. Within the context of your family, community, or place of worship, what observable trends can you identify? How would you describe the senti-ments or concerns expressed by educators, parents, law en-forcement officials, and community advocates?

2. Consider the multifaceted reasons behind the surge in mental health needs. Can you pinpoint a confluence of factors con-tributing to this increase? Reflect critically on the interplay of these factors.

3. In the statement by Pescosolido et al. (2010) that "the current solution is part of the problem," what underlying message do you discern? What might they be implying about prevailing ap-proaches to addressing the issue?

4. The sidebar highlights the profound impact of simple gestures, like sharing a meal. Think about someone in your immediate circle—whether in your community, place of worship, neigh-borhood, or family—who often extends gestures of kindness, such as offering meals, gifts, or sending heartfelt messages. In what ways do their actions parallel the efforts of a mental health worker in offering comfort and support?

PART 2

The Evolution
of Integration

IF YOU ARE TO ASK ANY PROSPECTIVE student seeking admission to a counseling or psychology program from a faith-based institution about why they chose to study in a faith-centered program, the answer will probably be "integration." They desire to be both Christian and compassionate, theological and psychological. They want to be in the church and be mainstream. Students want to pursue careers in mental health disciplines while allowing their faith to inform their conceptualization, diagnosis, and treatment. They aim to harmonize the elements of clinical practice with the diverse components of their faith, and vice versa.

The next two chapters will consolidate ideas around integration and offer direction for the future. But let's be clear what it means. Robert Noyce and Jack Kirby were the first to bring the word *integration* to the mainstream. They were electrical engineers, not counselors. They solved a problem of tubes in in our televisions and radios. All electronics ran by using very large vacuum tubes. They looked like light bulbs. A radio used to have dozens of tubes, that's why they were the size of a dresser. They just didn't work well. They were hot. They broke easy. And they took up a lot of space. A computer using vacuum tubes would be the size of a small house. Noyce and Kirby each designed new forms of electronic circuits. The parts were made of the same material, such as silicon (hence the origin of the moniker "Silicon Valley" where all this work was occurring). Circuits could be made very small and very powerful and very fast. They were all made from one piece. These new circuits were called integrated circuits because everything fit together as a single piece. To be integrated is to be cut from the same silicon wafer. When it comes to faith and psychology, to be integrated is to be cut from the same cloth; everything fits, matches, and belongs.

The evolving nature of integration demands more than becoming secure in one's faith while interacting within the secular profession. Rather, it means collaborating with the secular profession as to the characteristics of human need and implementing demonstrated interventions to bring about healing, transcending the need to simply defend or blend faith into practice, and fostering a seamless connection between spiritual and psychological healing.

History serves as a mirror, reflecting ourselves and our collective actions. An apt representation of this idea is found in the compassionate and integrative behavior exhibited by Christians during the second century CE, specifically in the year 165 CE. The Roman Empire was stricken by a cataclysmic plague that decimated its population. The widespread contagion, likely smallpox or perhaps measles, claimed an estimated 10 million lives, with daily deaths in the city of Rome peaking between 2,000 and 5,000. The scale of devastation was such that about 10 percent of the Empire's population succumbed to the disease, forever branding this period as Galen's Plague, named after the renowned Greek physician who journeyed to Italy to document and combat this formidable illness.

Amid this crisis, many sought to escape the virulent grasp of the disease by deserting the infected cities. This led to a catastrophic void in aid for those who were sick, rendering them utterly helpless, save for one group: the Christians. Emblematic of their spirit of integration, they willingly stepped into the role of caregivers, operating under a mission steeped in selfless service to society's most vulnerable. The absence of medical knowledge about smallpox in biblical texts did not deter them. Instead, their unwavering commitment to Christ's teachings impelled them to learn and practice medicine to ameliorate the suffering around them.

The emperor at the time, Julian, was known for his hostility toward Christianity, earning him the title Julian the Apostate. Yet even he couldn't help but recognize the selfless work of the Christians. He penned, "The impious Galileans, in addition to their own, support ours, it is shameful that our poor should be wanting our aid."[1] This recognition underscores the profound impact that the integrational actions of the Christians had on society. Their endeavors serve as a historical testament to the power of integration, exemplifying how compassionate outreach and unity can bring about immense positive change even amid the gravest crises.

As the convergence of faith and psychology continues to mature, the church must be prepared to act in a way that no other institution can. We aspire to be integrated in our care for others. We can combine the best of both Christian faith and modern psychology, ultimately becoming a powerful force for healing in a world desperately in need of it.

[1]Quoted in Rodney Stark, *The Rise of Christianity: How the Obscure, Marginal Jesus Movement Became the Dominant Religious Force in the Western World in a Few Centuries* (San Francisco: HarperSanFrancisco, 1997), 84.

Integrating Integration

MENTAL HEALTH CARE has a very large sufficiency problem, and the church can help. The need is great. The cost is high. The capacity to train professionals in adequate numbers is stretched. The evidence suggests that an alternative to the current model of care is required.

So, where do we start? Integration. For Christian psychology, Christian counseling, biblical counseling, pastoral counseling, and all the other iterations of faith-based therapy, the foundation is integration. It is the DNA of faith-based practice. If the delivery system is to change, we must think anew about what it means to integrate the Christian tradition with the mental health profession. We believe that the changes occurring in how human suffering is addressed demand that we integrate well. Further, we believe that the integration required now is distinct from the integration of a previous generation. In this chapter, we will examine the practice of our integration—both the church to the clinic, and the clinic to the church.

A Metaphor of Christian Integration

We can understand the experience of Christian mental health and the broader culture through a metaphor. We have created the story of Alicia, a child of divorce. She anticipates major life change as she approaches high school graduation. Her dilemma is told in the first

person as she lived out a commitment to parents who could not rec-
oncile life with each other.

> I am my parents' daughter—both. When they divorced when I was
> nine, my brother, sister, and I had to learn how to live in two houses
> and to adjust to parental expectations. We did it all well, but it was
> hard. My brother sided with my mom. My sister went with my dad. I
> was stuck in the middle. Both Mom and Dad were good to me, and
> they tried to work together . . . most of the time. There was a time,
> before I was born, that they were happy together. And they remained
> committed to me and my siblings. But Mom and Dad couldn't remain
> committed to each other. They each remarried and started other fam-
> ilies. I have half-siblings on both sides. I am part of their families but
> not fully part of either. Maybe because I always had another house to
> go to, it made me not 100 percent part of the house I was in. My life is
> good. But parts were difficult. It's better now compared to how it used
> to be. We all know how not to upset others. But when I go to college,
> I want to be someone different. In each one of my parents' homes, I
> know how I am supposed to be for them. At my mom's house, I must
> be neat and organized. There is always order. At my dad's house, there
> is never structure or plans. No matter where I am, I am adjusting to
> their expectations of me. I must be that person that my mom needs
> me to be and that person that my dad expects me to be. I am in a spot,
> and there is not a lot of room to be different. I am moving to a new
> place in the world, and I want the freedom to become a new adult. I
> may always be "their Alicia," but "my Alicia" is going to become a
> different person. I want to create a new Alicia, not the one split be-
> tween two parents.

When it comes to the story of Christianity and psychology/counseling,
Alicia's story is our story. We are split between two parents, caught
between two disciplines, two traditions, and two ways of thinking.
Our "parents" divorced. We grew up in a "broken home," needing
the support and approval of both the clinic and the church. The

relationship between the mental health professions and Christianity left the Christian practitioner wishing and needing to bridge the space between them.

I (Jim) can recall an Alicia experience when I announced to my faith community that I planned to study counseling psychology at a secular university. To many it was as if I had declared I was making a pact with the devil or was, like Luke Skywalker, being pulled toward the dark side of the Force. I was told by many I respected that if I studied secular psychology I would lose my faith. Such intentions are often received the same way Alicia would be if she told her mom's family that she was going to move in with her dad and his family, the ultimate betrayal. Similarly, one Christian mental health colleague spoke of interacting with other professionals at a national association conference. In the conversation, she let it be known that she teaches at a Christian graduate program. The response of one was, "Really? I am surprised. You seem so smart." The not-so-subtle implication was that affiliation with that "other parent" is an indicator of stupidity. To many, the secularization of the mental health profession produces moral issues irreconcilable with their faith. To others, to identify with a religious program is to adopt fantasy and myth. It is like adults believing in the tooth fairy or the Easter bunny.

But to us, integration is the means through which we can retain the beauty and elegance of our faith with the discipline and practice of human behavioral sciences. Integration seeks to fit all the parts together as a single unit or whole entity. It is to be undivided, as Alicia longed to be. It is to have a single identity or loyalty. It is to have all of yourself accepted as essential and respected. To be integrated is to have a home. Coe and Hall inadvertently use divorce language in their description of the tensions between psychological science and faith. They describe the "unwarranted *split* between the scientific and the religious, the scientific and the moral. The result is bringing together two distinct fields and two distinct methodologies as if reality and methodology were split."[1]

Historically, integration was an attempt by mental health practitioners to live with their secular parent who was once married to their Christian parent. They adopted models to define, describe, and distinguish their purposes. They created methods to practice the discipline of care within Christianity. They tried their best to keep the "family" together, to live in both worlds. Their "divorce" experience is like that of children trying to gain the affection and affirmation of parents who seemingly have little love for the other. They may wish for the two-parent ideal. But post-separation, they live under "mom's" roof for a while and then at "dad's" house. Yet for many there remains a common ambition to bring them together (or integrate), to unite excellence in mental health care and fidelity to the Christian tradition.

The models of Christian integration are descriptions of a split family. Each approach describes an example of how to live in a house divided. Scholars, skilled clinicians, and students sound much like Alicia describing her family. We wrestle with becoming integrated. We know of the tension between loyalty to this parent and loyalty to that parent. We understand the confusion of living with two bickering parents—the church and the clinic—and doubting whether you can be loyal to both of them.

Mental Health and the Pulpit

Jack Graham, a hard-charging Southern Baptist mega-church pastor in Texas, never expected to find himself out of gas and unable to work. But after two decades at the helm of the now 57,000-member Prestonwood Baptist Church in Plano, he received a cancer diagnosis. Surgery followed and then unexpected anxiety and depression.

---

[1]John H. Coe and Todd W. Hall, *Psychology in the Spirit: Contours of a Transformational Psychology* (Downers Grove, IL: InterVarsity Press, 2010), 72, emphasis added.

"I was dealing with something that was life-altering in many ways," he said.

For the first time in his life, Graham began to experience sleeplessness, a loss of appetite, and an inability to read or study. Unable to perform the work he normally thrived in, he took a couple of months off. Still, the symptoms persisted. He went back to work, although he now acknowledges he wasn't ready.

It would take a year before he felt that he was beginning to heal and resume a more normal pace of life.

Bishop Joseph Walker also never saw the depression coming. The energetic thirty-seven-year-old leader of Mt. Zion Baptist, a 29,000-member, multisite church in Nashville, he was overwhelmed by his wife's death from pancreatic cancer.

"I knew I was in a dark place," he said.

He began attending Gilda's Club, a support group for cancer patients and their families. Not only did he find emotional support, he began to learn afresh the stories of those in deep pits, and he realized that in his church, such stories were usually whispered, if they were discussed at all. He also sought out individual counseling despite a cultural taboo that prevents many in his world from even considering it.

"I think there is in the African American community this whole idea— this phobia, this stigma—that if you get counseling you're crazy," he said.

He is now aware that the stigma can especially crush those in the pulpit. Men and women in full-time ministry fear the possibility of professional loss if they acknowledge their need for help. "There's this sense of 'don't tell anybody that you're really struggling with something because you'll never be effective, nobody will ever use you,'" he said.

But Bishop Walker decided to tell his congregation about his experience.

"I was very transparent about my journey and what I had gone through. It opened the floodgates to people talking about their own journeys," he said.

Graham also began speaking publicly about his year of anxiety and depression and in 2019 he preached an eleven-part series titled "Help!" which addressed anxiety, depression, and loneliness, and encouraged people to find a therapist and consider medication when appropriate.

Graham and Walker have a newfound appreciation for those in their pews who are battling with mental health, and they're working to create communities within their churches where such stories don't have to be whispered.

What They Did . . . and How Are We Different?

There are many excellent descriptions of our integration models in text and journal articles. David Entwhistle wrote a comprehensive historical analysis of Christian integration from its inception to the twenty-first century.[2] He distinguished between paradigms and procedures. Paradigms capture the big picture of how something should be represented. Procedures are the techniques used in constructing the paradigm. Paradigms are the whys and the worldviews. Procedures are the "how come" and the "what does it look like?" The model builders and theory thinkers create unique paradigms.

Greggo and Sisemore edited the essential integration text where established paradigms are explained and compared by their originators. After summarizing the unique paradigms of the five views, they concluded that "the overlap of the approaches is more than one might expect, . . . for different theories sometimes lead to surprisingly similar practices."[3] Different paradigms. Similar procedures.

Paradigms or theories transcend time. They have staying power. But procedures and techniques are more closely tied to the direct life

---

[2]David N. Entwistle, *Integrative Approaches to Psychology and Christianity: An Introduction to Worldview Issues, Philosophical Foundations, and Models of Integration* (Eugene, OR: Wipf and Stock, 2021).

[3]Stephen P. Greggo and Timothy A. Sisemore, *Counseling and Christianity: Five Approaches* (Downers Grove, IL: InterVarsity Press, 2012), 199-200.

and times of people in pain. Procedures have to fit into the life experience of clients. The postmodern reality has altered the modern logical-positivistic culture from which the founding ideas of Christian integration were formed. In other words, while our paradigms of integration might stay, our techniques must adjust. The need and function of our integration, both in theory and practice, have changed over the decades. The many social accelerants, such as a pandemic, an economic boom, a political postmodern cultural revolution, a charismatic revival of the Spirit, famine, pestilence, or war, mean the landscape of integration is always changing. Integration must be nimble.

The original models of integration provided the theologically and empirically based paradigms to define Christian mental health practice. They did so to establish a metaphorical beachhead, or a presence within the profession by using the language of the professional culture. Christian integration reflected a cognitive-behavioral approach because in large part it was the paradigm of thought and understanding of the mental health culture. The early purpose for integration was for Christian mental health professionals to demonstrate to each parent that they were legitimate. Christians had to prove to accrediting bodies that Christian psychology, counseling, or other disciplines were valid and acceptable. By and large, that is no longer the primary demand for integration. Alicia has grown up and become her own person.

Neff and McMinn consider the meaning of integration for the millennial generation. They ask the question, "what does integration look like when . . . ?"[4] They are searching for actions, techniques similar to Entwhistle's procedures mentioned earlier. They refer to integration as needing to become "embodied." For them, integration is not a concept or an idea but a person.

---

[4]Megan Anna Neff and Mark R. McMinn, *Embodying Integration: A Fresh Look at Christianity in the Therapy Room* (Downers Grove, IL: InterVarsity Press, 2020), 3.

The call for embodied integration has existed for decades. Siang-Yang Tan and Eric Scalise called for the inclusion of theory and skills with an integration that is "intrapersonal," that is, it must be focused on a Christlikeness as its key dimension.[5] Neff and McMinn have expanded the call.

> The language of integration has been the written and spoken word. We write books and articles, talk together at conferences, teach our classes with our required textbooks and written paper assignments. This has been a cognitive, intellectual endeavor for the most part, and pneumatology (the study of the Holy Spirit) is not easily contained in words and intellectual concepts as other theologies may be.[6]

So, while we observe, think, and create new procedures, we must also think about the paradigms or the theories on which they are built. The Christian mental health theory and practice integration of the twenty-first century contains broader applications that the original theories. They must address the needs of a more complicated world and attend to more challenging applications of Christian integration. We must answer the question raised by Neff and McMinn, "What does a twenty-first-century Christianity/psychology integration look like?" We observe the embodiment of this integration and its evolution as the church positions itself as a pivotal provider.

In with the Old . . . and in with the New Too!

Existing integration models are not dead languages with expired usefulness. As Entwistle has argued, these paradigms have staying power. They are alive, active, and essential to the understanding of being Christian in the mental health profession. They are the grammatic rules that define and structure our language. Our thoughts about the creative work of the trinitarian Father, the redemptive

---

[5]Siang-Yang Tan and Eric Scalise, *Lay Counseling: Equipping Christians for a Helping Ministry* (Grand Rapids, MI: Zondervan, 2016), 145.
[6]Neff and McMinn, *Embodying Integration,* 225.

work of the trinitarian Christ, and the advocacy work of the trinitarian Spirit are defined through our integrative models. Coe and Hall affirm the value of the past, while recognizing that integration change is in the air. "Clearly there is evidence of change on the horizon for how a new generation of Christian psychologists, standing on the shoulders of their predecessors, are looking into more holistic, relational, and experiential models for relating psychology to faith."[7] The change that they foresaw appears to reflect Entwistle's description of a paradigm that undergirds new procedures, which reflect current needs.

Neff and McMinn use a grammar metaphor to describe our future. "What if integration was more a verb than a noun? Imagining these possibilities calls us to locate and embody integration in the person of the psychotherapist more than in the pages of a textbook or journal article."[8] Think of paradigms as nouns and procedures as verbs. This distinction is of parts and processes. Nouns, as parts of integration, are arguable facts, the positions, the Christian worldviews, which can be measured next to other worldviews. Nouns include the veracity of Scripture, the condition of human depravity, and divine grace. Nouns are things we can debate, measure, and prove, such as the principled reality that humans are made in the image of God and the acknowledgment of sin, grace, judgment, and redemption. Nouns are things. They have substance. Our early integration models were things. They were the raw materials by which a Christian mental health professional designed their craft, built their identity, and justified their legitimacy before secular boards and professional guilds. Early integrationists had to prove themselves to a skeptical profession. (It is probably true that nouns are just as important today as they ever were. But that argument will be made later in this chapter.) The integration "nouns" were measurable proof. And they remain.

---

[7]Coe and Hall, *Psychology in the Spirit*, 73.
[8]Neff and McMinn, *Embodying Integration*, 5.

Yet Neff and McMinn's question also remains. "What if integration is a verb?" Their question imagines action to be a companion to substance because verbs bring action to nouns. The integrative literature, the classroom instruction, and the Christian conference symposia have tended toward the essential philosophical, theological, and theoretical concerns. But students seldom were able to see integration, experience integration, or have a clear sense of what a counselor does to demonstrate integration. It was like an article on the shelf rather than a way of being. Prior to Neff and McMinn's grammar metaphor, others expressed the same core concern. In 1979 Carter and Narramore identified the product/process characteristics of integration. They called for seeing "verbs" such as self-awareness, humility, openness to learning, and acceptance of the unknown as virtues.[9]

Randall Sorenson wrote of the need to integrate the "experiential verb" with creativity and thoughtfulness. He authored two articles in which he cast the ten lepers in Luke 17 in an allegorical morality play like Bunyan's *Pilgrim's Progress*, saying he

> [recast] them for my purposes here as ten invented characters who represent different but common responses to the notion that integration is something indivisibly, irreducibly, and fundamentally personal. It is my thesis that it is all too easy for those of us who write professional articles or publish books on integration to run from this notion much as the lepers ran from Christ.[10]

Sorenson's thesis is that Christian integration is worship and intimacy with God. He said, in his era, that integration is a verb.

Because of the need to establish Christian mental health within the secular professions, there rose a necessity to make the beauty of integration into a formal code, a noun. It was essential to define Christian

---

[9]John D. Carter and Bruce Narramore, *The Integration of Psychology and Theology: An Introduction* (Grand Rapids, MI: Zondervan, 1979).

[10]Randall Lehmann Sorenson, "The Tenth Leper," *Journal of Psychology and Theology* 24, no. 3 (1996): 197-211.

integration as a measurable product to compare product outcomes. This was and remains an essential aspect of any program seeking external accreditation. Sorenson summarized the process then, and it remains essential today.

Much of the integration taught was theoretical classroom content. This is not to disparage the vital role that a sound grasp of theoretical principles has both for good clinical practice and for the enterprise of integration. Students voiced a concern, however, that they could go through their entire doctoral program with very little exposure to direct clinical data on how the faculty actually practiced what they taught, particularly pertaining to what integration looked like clinically.[11]

The core elements or "nouns" of integration serve as the foundational ingredients for the Christian clinician. However, as recognized by Neff and McMinn, Carter and Narramore, Sorenson, and numerous other scholars—and likely echoed by many students—there's a need for something deeper. The "verbs" of integration encapsulate the yearning to witness the master clinician's adeptness, as they skillfully draw from Jesus' teachings and exemplify his life, weaving a tapestry of healing through their artistry.

The process of integration is the result of internalization of the biblical text, theological understanding, worldview clarification, and skill amalgamated into professional life. It's as though students are saying, "I understand the function of each thing. But can you show me how to put them all together? I have learned the parts, but I want to know how to combine them into an agent of care." Like Alicia, all of us long to live as integrated people, having reconciled our parts into a single identity, and to engage both parts with elegance. It is, as Bouma-Prediger describes,

> the attempt to live out one's faith commitment as authentically as possible in everyday life, including one's *vocation or professional life....*

---

[11]Sorenson, "The Tenth Leper," 207.

The aim of this type of integration is internal harmony or consistency between faith commitment and the way of life. In other words, the task is to live in accordance with one's *faith commitment and worldview*.[12]

The harmony between faith and life is the essence of Christian integration.

If Integration Is an Action Verb, Then What Is Its Action?

If there is a verb that contains both the psychology and theology of the twenty-first century, an action word that depicts the integrated thought of our work as clinicians and our work as Christ followers, it is the verb "to attach." Specifically, it is the action of one person attaching to another person, thing, idea, identity, or ultimately, to God. Attachment forms relationships. We are relational beings. In both Christianity and therapy, attachment is everywhere. Integration calls us to think theologically about attachment psychology and to think psychologically about attachment theology. Revisions and reconstructions of how we "do" mental health within the church must be grounded in our theology and psychology integration. Alicia desired to be attached to both mother and father. So do we.

Let's start with theology. The late theologian Stanley Grenz makes a powerful observation: "Of the various significant developments in theology over the last hundred years, none has more far-reaching implications for anthropology than the rediscovery of the doctrine of the trinity."[13] Such a bold declaration! To suggest that no other development has had as profound an impact in the last hundred years is truly remarkable.

He concludes his assertation by stating:

The stampede to the relationality inherent in the social model of the Trinity has crossed traditional confessional divides. But the commitment

---

[12]Steve Bouma-Prediger, "The Task of Integration: A Modest Proposal," *Journal of Psychology and Theology* 18, no. 1 (1990): 27, emphasis added.
[13]Stanley J. Grenz, *The Social God and the Relational Self: A Trinitarian Theology of the Imago Dei*, vol. 1 (Louisville, KY: Westminster John Knox, 2001), 3-4.

to a theologically oriented social personalism has also brought together proponents of otherwise quite diverse, even disparate theological projects. Hence, feminist and liberation theologians close ranks with each other and with evangelical, philosophical, and process colleagues in suggesting that God is best viewed as the social Trinity.[14]

Voices emerging from Christian psychology cast a similar claim. Hathaway and Yarhouse trace the historical trajectory of psychological and theological integration, which they call integrative projects, and land it squarely on the Trinity:

> A profound implication for the integrative projects arises from the character of a Trinitarian God. . . . Despite the complex developments in Trinitarian thought over the centuries, orthodox accounts of the Trinity make it clear that reality must be ultimately understood in personal rather than impersonal terms.[15]

Their statement is worthy of pause and consideration. Note the use of *profound*. These authors are not inclined toward hyperbole or exaggeration. They do not declare too many things as being profound. Therefore, we would be wise to be attentive to it. The profound idea—that is, the deep, sincere, and thoughtful meaning—is that God is relational.

It's easy to skip past the importance and significance of a relational God. The relational characteristic means that God (singular) is persons (plural), and the persons of God engage both with one another and with created persons. The core characteristic of the triune God's attached relationality is articulated clearly by Jesus in John 13 and the following chapters of Jesus' final discourse. Chapters 13 and 14 show us God's intra-relational attachment. Jesus begins to describe the attachment between the Father and the Son, saying, "Now the Son of Man is glorified and God is glorified in him. If God is glorified in

---

[14]Grenz, *Social God and the Relational Self*, 5.

[15]William L. Hathaway and Mark A. Yarhouse, *The Integration of Psychology and Christianity: A Domain-Based Approach* (Downers Grove, IL: InterVarsity Press, 2021), 37.

him, God will glorify the Son in himself, and will glorify him at once"
(Jn 13:31-32). Then in chapter 14, Jesus addresses the Holy Spirit's role
in the attachment. "If you love me, keep my commands. And I will
ask the Father, and he will give you another advocate to be with you
forever—the Spirit of Truth" (Jn 14:15-17).

Here is the profound integration concept implied by Hathaway and
Yarhouse: Christian faith integration begins with God acting, loving,
engaging (note all the verbs) with God.[16] Jesus' trinitarian context of
"As the Father has loved me" (Jn 15:9) is followed with his expectation
of our conduct toward one another: "My command is this: Love each
other as I have loved you" (Jn 15:12). The theological verbs of Christian
integration are to conduct ourselves toward one another in the way
that God engages in relationship with God.

In the mental health, counseling and psychology dimension, attachment has emerged as the twenty-first-century psychodynamic
intervention. Hall and Maltby describe the historical developments
of attachment. It began with the original sex-drive-based Freudian
psychoanalysis at the onset of the twentieth century. Subsequently,
multiple theories emerged in the post-Freudian era by Anna Freud,
Melanie Klein, W. R. D. Fairbairn, John Bowlby, and D. W. Winnicott,
among others. Initially, attachment theory focused on infant matu-
ration within developmental psychology. Then, in the latter part of
the twentieth century, explicit empirically based psychotherapy
emerged. "This emerging clinical modality . . . has developed largely
due to contemporary innovations in attachment theory in which
theoretically driven research and psychoanalytic therapy have reen-
gaged in significant dialogue."[17]

Ultimately, Hall and Maltby describe the characteristics of relational attachment as the capacity to coordinate thoughts, behaviors,

---

[16]Hathaway and Yarhouse, *Integration of Psychology and Christianity*, 37.
[17]T. W. Hall and L. E. Maltby, "Attachment-Based Psychoanalytic Therapy and Christianity: Being-in-Relation," in *Christianity and Psychoanalysis: A New Conversation*, ed. E. Bland and B. Strawn (Downers Grove, IL: InterVarsity Press, 2014), 185.

and especially emotions through self-regulation. Self-regulation is learned and managed through relationships with others. This "being with" orientation "corresponds well to the image of God in human beings and the view of growth and healing as a relational process."[18]

A powerful point of contact between the theology of trinitarian relationship and psychological attachment theory is Karl Barth's theological anthropology. The essence of Barth's view is "God is a being in relation with himself as Father and Son in the Spirit, so the human essence is reflected in the being of the man Jesus, a man who lived his life in encounter with God and others."[19] Daniel Price ties Barth's trinitarian theology with psychological attachment theory through object relations theory.

> The analogical relationship between Barth and object relations is reinforced by Barth's insistence that in the human being we see a reflection of the love expressed within the triune God and poured out in the divine-human covenant. Hence human beings are by nature beings who encounter one another: I with Thou, mutually conditioning one another's being and shaping one another's destiny.[20]

With attachment as the action verb of faith integration, we now can ask two questions. First, how does trinitarian attachment influence the human relationship with God? And second, how does trinitarian attachment influence our human response to each other? The answer lies in three great ideas drawn from historical Christian theology regarding the caregiver's response to those in need because of the Father's, Son's, and Spirit's care toward human creation. The three are *coram Deo*, the Latin term representing the Father's presence in the lives of individuals; *Immanuel*, the Hebrew term representing the Son; and *Parakletos*, the Greek term representing the Holy Spirit.

---

[18]Hall and Maltby, "Attachment-Based Psychoanalytic Therapy," 215.
[19]Daniel J. Price, *Karl Barth's Anthropology in Light of Modern Thought* (Grand Rapids, MI: Eerdmans, 2002), 16.
[20]Price, *Karl Barth's Anthropology,* 227.

Coram Deo: Attached to the Father

Coram Deo is to conduct our lives mindful that we are in God's presence. The term was very important in the early church and the Reformers. The Latin phrase was taken from Jerome's Vulgate in Psalm 56:13 where David declares, "For you have delivered my soul from death, yes, my feet from falling, *that I may walk before God* in the light of life" (emphasis added). *Coram Deo* is to act in every moment with the understanding that we are in the presence of God. The phrase literally refers to something that takes place in the presence of, or before the face of, God. "To live *coram Deo* is to live one's entire life in the presence of God, under the authority of God, to the glory of God."[21]

The biblical text describes the Father in whose presence we stand. Eric Johnson recognizes two paternal qualities of the Father toward human creation. The first is that the Father shows his *bounty,* and the second is that the Father shows his *communion.* Creation shares (communion) in the Father's blessing (bounty). "This union places believers 'in the Beloved' (Eph. 1:6), so that believers are themselves 'holy and beloved' (Col 3:12), that is, loved by God in a way that corresponds analogically to the Father's love for his 'beloved Son' with whom he is 'well-pleased' (Mt 17:5; Lk 3:22)."[22]

Three responses to *coram Deo* are crucial to our work as mental health care providers and crucial for any person who seeks to live rightly with God, humanity, and self. Attachment to God the Father elicits particular responses, verbs consistently articulated in the biblical text and in the history of human care. They are to be humble before God, to fear God, and to rejoice in the presence of God. Each corresponds to the idea of God as our Creator, our Judge, and our Savior.[23]

---

[21]R. C. Sproul, "What Does 'Coram Deo' Mean?," November 17, 2021, www.ligonier.org/learn /articles/what-does-coram-deo-mean.

[22]Eric L. Johnson, *Foundations for Soul Care: A Christian Psychology Proposal* (Downers Grove, IL: InterVarsity Press, 2007), 395.

[23]David Powilson, "A Biblical Counseling View," in *Psychology and Christianity: Five Views,* ed. Eric L. Johnson (Downers Grove, IL: InterVarsity Press, 2010).

First, *coram Deo* declares that God is our Creator, and we are the created. This calls us toward humility regarding the precious work that is done as therapists, psychologists, counselors, and caregivers. It is not by us, as we are but clay (Is 64:8); rather, the valuable work done as "clay" is to show that the "all-surpassing power is from God and not from us" (2 Cor 4:7). Isaiah's vision of being in the presence of God produces a humble meekness: "Woe to me!" (Is 6:5). But that humility of self-realization is followed not by withdrawal from God but selection by God and a willingness to go and serve: "Then I heard the voice of the Lord saying, 'Whom shall I send? And who will go for us?' And I said, 'Here am I. Send me!'" (Is 6:8). *Coram Deo* is our motivation to empathize with the suffering in God's created order and with the pain of the individual who, like us, longs to be connected to the gaze of God.

Second, out of our humility toward our creator comes fear, for God is our judge. In the biblical text, *coram Deo* produces a response that is not understood in the twenty-first-century English vernacular: the fear of the Lord. The Old and New Testaments are replete with examples of those who were awed in the presence of Creator God—they feared for their lives. The awe displayed by Moses is the archetypal image of fear toward God when standing in his presence.

> And the LORD said, "I will cause all my goodness to pass in front of you, and I will proclaim my name, the LORD, in your presence. I will have mercy on whom I will have mercy, and I will have compassion on whom I will have compassion. But," he said, "you cannot see my face, for no one may see me and live." (Ex 33:19-20)

Solomon instructed his son to "Fear the LORD and the king" (Prov 24:21)—a message that should never dismiss the fact that the dad writing the proverb to his son was the king! Our democratic minds have never had to really "fear the king" as was needed for survival in other eras. In our age, political authorities work for us as our elected representatives. Yet *coram Deo* declares that in the presence of God, we experience fear as someone utterly powerless in the presence of another. Powerlessness before God is an essential model to those who seek counsel in a state of powerlessness over their pain and their circumstances.

Finally, *coram Deo* is a source of joy. Fear in God's presence is followed by humility in God's presence, culminating in joy in God's presence. Having been told by an angel of God that she will bear a child, Mary displays this trajectory from awe and humility to joy and then exuberant hope.

Mary said:

"My soul glorifies the Lord,
    and my spirit rejoices in God my Savior,
for he has been mindful
    of the humble state of his servant.
From now on all generations will call me blessed,
    for the Mighty One has done great things for me—
    holy is his name.
His mercy extends to those who fear him,
    from generation to generation. (Lk 1:46-50)

The *coram Deo* of embodied integration is the response verb of attachment to God the Father. It is to do good work as distinct and beyond doing good works. C. S. Lewis made this distinction in an overlooked essay, "Good Works and Good Work," found in *The World's Last Night and Other Essays*. The two are related but distinct. Lewis explains Jesus turning the water into wine at the wedding of Cana. He notes that he did a good thing (good works). He was empowered, commissioned, and ordained to do good works, to alleviate suffering, to bring good news to the lost, and to declare the presence of God in their midst. He also did work that was good, referring to its creativity, quality, and purpose.

Good works are things like tithing or serving those in need. They are quite separate from one's work. And good works need not be good work, as anyone can see by inspecting some of the objects made to be sold at bazaars for charitable purposes. This is not according to our example. Nor is the neglect of goodness in our work, our job, according to precept. The apostle says everyone must not only work but work to produce what is "good."[24] When our Lord provided a wedding party with an extra glass of wine all around, he was doing good works, but also good work; it was a wine worth drinking.

To do good work is to act in response to being in the presence of God. This good work is in reciprocity of God's bounty and communion with us and particularly with sufferers who come to sit with us. In the practical, experiential way, *coram Deo* can be a rehearsed discipline. We engage the action through intentional practice. *Coram Deo* is to be like the psalmist David living out his good work:

> Where can I go from your Spirit?
>> Where can I flee from your presence?
> If I go up to the heavens, you are there;
>> if I make my bed in the depths, you are there.
> If I rise on the wings of the dawn,
>> if I settle on the far side of the sea,
> even there your hand will guide me,
>> your right hand will hold me fast.
> If I say, "Surely the darkness will hide me
>> and the light become night around me,"
> even the darkness will not be dark to you;
>> the night will shine like the day,
>> for darkness is as light to you.
> For you created my inmost being;
>> you knit me together in my mother's womb.

---

[24]C. S. Lewis, *The World's Last Night, and Other Essays* (New York: Harcourt Brace Jovanovich, 1973), 71.

I praise you because I am fearfully and wonderfully made;
  your works are wonderful;
  I know that full well. (Ps 139:7-14)

Immanuel: Attached to the Son

Our attachment to God the Father is experienced and articulated as
coram Deo. As the Father and Son remain in reciprocal relationship
so also are we engaged with the Son. The second concept of trinitarian
relationship is contained in the word *Immanuel*. Most every Christian
knows the meaning: "God with us." At Christmas, we sing "O Come,
O Come, Emmanuel." The harmony has a haunting tone. "O Come,
O Come, Emmanuel, and ransom captive Israel."[25]

Matthew refers to Isaiah 7–8 by connecting the birth of Jesus with
the messianic deliverer (Mt 1:22-23). Judea was under siege. Oppression was in the air. The people lived in terror and were secretly
searching for rescue, escape, and freedom. "God with us" was Isaiah's message of hope. The deliverer will come. The gospel declaration is that God became present on earth. Matthew takes the
historical and symbolic story of Isaiah and shows how it has been
fulfilled in Immanuel.

With its culmination at the cross, "God with us" must be the core
of Christian integration for the mental health professional. Paul describes the Christians as regents or ambassadors—those who represent the king. "We are therefore Christ's ambassadors, as though
God were making his appeal through us" (2 Cor 5:20). The lived integration begins with an understanding that God is with us, and we
are to represent that presence. Pope Benedict wrote that "God is not
distant. God is Immanuel. God with us. He is no stranger. He has a
face, the face of Jesus."[26] While *coram Deo* places us in the presence

---

[25]Raymond F. Glover, *The Hymnal 1982 Companion*, vol. 1 (New York: Church Publishing, 1995), 56.

[26]Pope Benedict XVI, "Urbi et Orbi" (Christmas address, December 25, 2010), www.vatican.va /content/benedict-xvi/en/messages/urbi/documents/hf_ben-xvi_mes_20101225_urbi

of God, like the high priest standing before God in the Holy of Holies, Immanuel places God, the person of Jesus, in humanity's presence. Johnson writes, "In the life of Jesus the glory of God was specially articulated to humans. He was *the* Sign of God expressed on earth."[27]

Clients who bravely reach out for counseling services often grapple with feelings of isolation, bewilderment, and despair. Such calls don't typically originate from those who feel grounded and satisfied. Instead, they arise when vital relationships or resources fail to offer guidance through life's complexities. These individuals, overwhelmed by emotional, behavioral, or cognitive challenges—whether it's depression, anxiety, anger, angst, compulsion, or obsession—find themselves hindered, unable to lead fulfilling or even functional lives. In their moments of utmost vulnerability, they reach out, seeking a lifeline.

One of our essential tasks as integrative mental health professionals is to consider Immanuel, "God with us," in those who come to see us. For most, the idea of Immanuel is lost in the anxiety, the depression, the trauma. "God with us" is a concept outside awareness because of the enormity of pain. Our trinitarian theological tradition is that God is with us, and God is good. We understand this in the intellectual sense: "Yes, I know God is with us and God is good in general, but I don't know that God is with me, and God is good to me." In the presence of anxiety, trauma, loss, despair, or depression, it is easy to lose the idea that God is good to me. Immanuel, "God with us," in the relational space between clinician and client demonstrates the goodness of God. In Christian integration, we bring the hope of Immanuel into the counseling space.

The essence of trinitarian integration is God with us. Therapy is a declaration of "God with us." Immanuel is God embodied. The

---

.html#:~:text=Dear%20brothers%20and%20sisters%20listening,face%2C%20the%20face%20of%20Jesus.

[27] Johnson, *Foundations for Soul Care*, 268.

message from Matthew declaring Immanuel is a message of hope. For integration to be embodied, it must reflect characteristics of the trinitarian act of presence. The most powerful Christian integration theme is the embodiment of hope—that God is indeed with me. Embodiment begins with Immanuel.

Parakletos: Attached to the Spirt

To the sufferer, we convey Immanuel. Before God, we stand *coram Deo*. Combined, we embody the presence of God—expressed to our Creator and to one another. But the physical body of Christ was historical, limited to a space and time that are not ours. Therefore, we experience the presence of God through the dynamic work of the Spirit, the Paraclete (the English term deriving from the Greek *Parakletos*).

To the client, we represent the presence of God as Paraclete. In John 14, Jesus identifies the Holy Spirit as the one who advocates or comes alongside to support and strengthen. "But the Advocate, the Holy Spirit, whom the Father will send in my name, will teach you all things and will remind you of everything I have said to you. Peace I leave with you; my peace I give you. I do not give to you as the world gives. Do not let your hearts be troubled and do not be afraid" (Jn 14:26-27).

The third emerging concept from an integrated theological/psychological attachment is captured in the term *Paraclete*. We know this as the title of the Holy Spirit, as in John 14 when Jesus said, "I will ask the Father, and he will give you another advocate to help you and be with you forever—the Spirit of truth" (Jn 14:16-17). The Greek word *parakletos* has many English translations. The most common meaning is advocate, comforter, or counselor. We note with fascination that every description/translation of the word *parakletos*—to bring comfort, to counsel, to advocate, to guide, to teach— is a word woven into the identity of mental health professionals. They are the central tenets of our mental health professional selves.

Psychologists, LPCs, psychiatrists, LMFTs, and LCSWs are counselors, comforters, advocates, guides, and teachers. The single word in the Greek lexicon to describe the trinitarian activity of the ongoing presence and relationship of God within humanity—*parakletos*—is translated into the multiple identities on which our respective professions are built.

It's essential not to conflate the Holy Spirit's role as "God within us" with our responsibilities as caregivers. While we are not divine, our training guides us to emulate the actions that God employs to provide care to others. Integrated counselors serve as a beacon in the lives of those in pain, acting as ambassadors of the Divine Trinity. With an embodied integration, the mental health professional, through the church, will have the freedom to return to one of its primary historical functions—literally to be the paraclete with others. We believe that the future of our integration is to be the community of saints who are called as ambassadors to humanity—to represent the quality and character of God, indwelled by the Holy Spirit—the one who serves in the absence of the King.

The United Identity

We return to Alicia who introduced our ideas through her split identity as a child caught between pleasing two parents. Imagine her as able to articulate an identity that permits her to draw from her heritage of both parents while also accepting that there are aspects that may still be unreconciled. Similarly, the Christian practitioner draws from the theological heritage as well as the mental health heritage to form a definition of self. We carry the identity and image of the trinitarian God who aspires to engage a culture in a way consistent with the Great Commission (Mt 28:18-20) and the Great Commandment (Mt 22:34-40). The Great Commission provides the content for the Christian counselor, and we use psychological science to declare gospel truth. The Great Commandment is how we are to conduct ourselves in the delivery of that message.[28] Our love for our neighbor is a reflection of our love for God, God's love for us, and ultimately, the internal love that God displays toward the trinitarian self.

Christian practitioners can speak to both the church and the profession. We have the knowledge and the skills needed as provision to both church and culture. Let's consider, then, how you might live in relationship with both "parents."

From our Christian parent, the counselor carries a history, tradition, and experience that contributes to the formation of an adult faith identity. Such a grounding assists one in being secure, principled, and clear as to life values, core virtues, and purposed vision. More specifically, the counselor who draws from an intrinsic, lived experience of knowing the love of God can draw from the deep resources of their soul to exhibit love for the wounded and the wounder. The identity of the counselor's Christian parent can become the essence of personhood.

Simultaneously, the influence of the professional parent also forms an identity that contributes to character formation. Developing the identity of a human helper suitably equipped to render care to people facing complicated problems is an essential skill. Compassion and knowledge generated by faith and training become an effective force. It is the task of every Christian clinician to allow the professional identity to inform one's faith identity with knowledge and skill generated by the mental health disciplines, and to permit the faith identity to inform one's professional identity with meaning. The person who has mastered a body of knowledge and is unambiguous as to her identity is both smart and secure.

In acknowledging the value of both allegiances, one may accommodate one at the expense of the other as though they are distinct

---

[28]P. Douglas Small, "The Great Commitment: Prayer and the Great Commission," in *The Great Commission Connection*, ed. Raymond F. Culpepper (Cleveland, TN: Pathway Press, 2011).

sources of identity. It is easy to separate a Christian identity from a clinical identity, especially when the originators of the clinical theory or approaches have negated or even ridiculed the Christian identity. Sometimes our mental health field has so promoted the importance of one's professional identity over and above the value and benefit of our faith identity that to many, the faith identity is seen as having no value and no purpose. Family psychologist Froma Walsh pushed back on that idea, identifying a crucial absence in the practice of human care when she wrote, "Most families and couples who come for therapy or counseling are seeking more than symptom reduction, problem solving, or communication skills; they are seeking deeper meaning and connections in their lives."[29] She is advocating that our parents (the theoretical and the theological) be joined in our care for families, couples and individuals.

Like Alicia and her commitment to exhibit loyalty to both parents, Christian counselors want to hear the call of God and then respond faithfully to it. They wish to demonstrate faith integration as a verb, an idea or truth formed into action. It is not a framed degree on the wall. Rather, integration is a manner of existence through which everything else enters, is influenced, and then exits. Christian counselors wish to be attached to God the Father, Son, and Spirit, who is caring for creation, is reconciling human suffering, and is a comforting presence amid pain and evil. The passion for care is propelled by an intense commitment to be about something greater than any individual can be.

As Alicia seeks connection with her other parent, so the counselor seeks to be trained in the most advanced science of human care and to exhibit excellence in treatment assessment, diagnostics, and intervention for individuals, groups, couples, and families. From one parent we derive mission, and from the other we derive method.

---

[29]Froma Walsh, "Integrating Spirituality in Family Therapy," *Spiritual Resources in Family Therapy* 2 (2009): 31.

Why Do We Need Psychological Science to Care for Those in Need?

If the church is to be about fulfilling the mission of God through the presentation of the gospel, then it must utilize the most sophisticated knowledge base and resources to accomplish its purpose. For our purpose, the gospel presentation focuses on our calling to equip the church to deliver knowledge, training, disposition, and skill toward the mental health needs of others, that is, to attend to suffering that emerges through the human experience. To accomplish the ministry of human care, those who extend the gospel must understand and possess specific skills in relationship formation.

In psychology we know that someone must be competent in assessment and diagnosis. We know that counselors must be capable of creating complex treatment strategies. Because we are proposing some type of triaged care—with experts attending to the most complicated situations, and fundamental or straightforward concerns to be addressed by lay counselors—the discipline of supervision must be employed.

We know that mental health care will have some form of attachment, but what is the structure to be? How does one care in response to trinitarian *coram Deo*, Immanuel, and Paraclete? What are the procedures, the steps, and the processes? The revelation from the biblical text leads us to truth. It does not, however, provide the particulars, such as whether a clinician should address a person's suffering by increasing or decreasing counselor accessibility when a client shows patterns consistent with borderline, narcissistic, or histrionic personalities.

It is here that we respect the contribution from the other parent. The mental health scholarship has produced profound information regarding the neurobiology, psychology, and sociology of human suffering. We have learned much regarding the workings of the brain and how it engages in relationship to create safety and form purpose. We know a great deal about the workings of our bodies, how our unique personalities interpret circumstances and respond to them, and how our interactions with others affirm and alter our perception of safety and danger, approach or avoidance, security or anxiety. Equipped with such knowledge, the counselor can apply it to address stress, trauma, pathogens, social-familial dysfunction, and typical and atypical human growth and development. The social sciences of psychology, counseling, and therapy research provide us with crucial content to direct the action verbs of Christian integration. Psychological research informs the church as to how it can be most effective.

Assessment/diagnosis: Determining the sufferer's need. Abraham Maslow is credited with saying, "I suppose it is tempting, if the only tool you have is a hammer, to treat everything as if it were a nail."[30] Maslow's statement reflects the truth that when our understanding of mental health need is narrow, then our solutions, interventions, and efforts to heal will be narrow as well. Ministers and lay counselors are vulnerable to seeing everything through their paradigm of sin and salvation. Similarly, mental health professionals are vulnerable to seeing need predominantly through a stimulus-response model. Both those in ministry and those in mental health must answer the question "What are we dealing with in this person, couple, family, or group?" and consider the biological, psychological, sociocultural, and spiritual factors that could be influential. Churches and ministries will continue to need the expertise of the Christian mental health professionals trained in the language of mental health care, capable of conducting clinical, behavioral, psychological, and projective assessments, and proficient in interpreting the assessment data to form a diagnosis for a person seeking support. Only then can the church or ministry decide whether that person is best served within the ministry context or with a referral to a therapist. Churches and ministries need mental

---

[30]Justine Harris, book review of *The Psychology of Science—A Reconnaissance*, by Abraham H. Maslow, *Canadian Journal of Counselling and Psychotherapy* 1, no. 1 (1967): 15.

health expertise to discern the nature of the suffering and the path forward.

Treatment: Responding to the sufferer's need. Leaders in churches and clinics working collaboratively to address suffering are tasked with answering the question "What are we going to do to help?" Both the church and the clinic make essential contributions. The church will treat the pain through access to the trinitarian response to God and adherence to the principles of truth put forth in the biblical text. The Christian caregiver seeks to be the *hospitality* provider, as exemplified by the parable of the Good Samaritan (Lk 10:25-37). The parable is a template meant to challenge the status quo of "religious folk" by demonstrating a response of both compassion and action. Jesus suggested that the Good Samaritan "had pity on him." The Greek word for "pity" here does not mean "I felt sorry for you." Rather, it means to be moved with compassion. To this traveler, the scene was gut wrenching and prompted action, although the cost of time and resources was substantial. The motive and manner of the Good Samaritan is worthy of consideration. Our clinical/economic models do not have space for this type of practice. Indeed, it is very poor capitalism. We must acknowledge the obvious: it would be impossible for the Samaritan, good or otherwise, to attend to *everyone* in this manner. The parable cannot mean that each person must meet the needs of everyone they encounter. The story and any economic system would collapse. It does, however, mean that at times, as in the case of the Good Samaritan, we must attend to others without regard for self-interest or personal gain.

In 2006 the American Psychological Association created a task force to examine the use of "evidence-based practices." It confirmed that "psychological services are most effective when responsive to the patient's specific problems, strengths, personality, sociocultural context, and preferences."[31] The tone of the report may, to many,

---

[31] APA Presidential Task Force on Evidence-Based Practice, "Evidence-Based Practice in Psychology," *The American Psychologist* 61, no. 4 (2006): 284.

reflect the behavior of the priest or the Levite in the parable as it defines and determines the characteristics of care. They fully supported the use of evidenced-based practices as the backbone of psychological science. But Wampold, Goodhart, and Levant also reached further. Their perspective suggested that it is not a narrow, rigid application of rules. Rather, it allows for a broader range of approaches and applications. They found that it

> allows psychologists latitude to deliver treatment tailored to individual needs and to offer innovative methods, or creative combinations of methods, that *take into account differing theories, traditions, clinical circumstances, patient characteristics and values, and the evolving nature of science.* However, the psychologist is responsible for ensuring that the services he or she delivers are safe and effective.[32]

While they are not specifically referring to faith-based mental health interventions, it applies to the possibility of counselors and churches collaborating in providing effective care for the suffering. This is such a unique and desperate time when society needs what the church can offer. The church in turn must offer hope via the message of Jesus linked with human excellence found in the best practices, disciplined interventions, and efforts to benefit the recipient. Caregivers who carry the love of God and the discipline and accountability of the mental health professions serve with a powerful pedigree.

Supervision: Guiding and discipling the provider with advancing methods and insight. The greatest contribution for the mental health professional in the future may likely be found in the delivery of supervisory services. Supervision has emerged in the mental health field as a discipline within the discipline. Good supervision is distinct from good counseling. It is defined by Loganbill, Hardy, and Delworth, creators of one of the most utilized models of counselor development, as

---

[32]Bruce E. Wampold, Carol D. Goodheart, and Ronald F. Levant, "Clarification and elaboration on evidence-based practice in psychology," *American Psychologist* 62, no. 6 (2007): 616.

"an intensive, interpersonally focused one-to-one relationship in which one person is designated to facilitate the development of therapeutic competence in the other person."[33] Watson elevated the specialty of supervision into a discipline of Christian integration by aligning Christian virtues with both the supervisory learning journey and the development of clinical competencies. Think of it as a form of discipleship tailored for the compassionate caregiver. She proposes, "Clinical supervision at its best can be understood as an educational experience that forms the character of supervisees to help them withstand the challenges of contemporary clinical practice. By integrating the interdisciplinary literature on virtue and character strengths with clinical supervision methods and spiritual formation practices, a Christian integrative approach to clinical supervision aims to develop clinicians of faith, hope, and love who serve Christ's kingdom with wisdom, justice, temperance and courage."[34]

Ethics: Ensuring a quality of care to protect and support the sufferer. What are the rules to ensure that mental health care delivered in ministry communities is conducted with autonomy, nonmaleficence, beneficence, fidelity, and justice?[35] Some in the church might take issue with our discussion of ethical behavior within the realm of the mental health professions. After all, shouldn't our moral code come from the truth of Scripture and not from the designs of professional organizations? Yes, righteousness, holiness, and morality flow from our theological anthropology—the principles of righteousness applied to human action. In that regard, the church has a historical base of theological and philosophical thought regarding what constitutes moral action. But the mental health profession has addressed

[33]Carol Loganbill, Emily Hardy, and Ursula Delworth, "Supervision: A Conceptual Model," *The Counseling Psychologist* 10, no. 1 (1982): 14.
[34]Terri S. Watson, *Developing Clinicians of Character: A Christian Integrative Approach to Clinical Supervision* (Downers Grove, IL: InterVarsity Press, 2018), 3.
[35]K. S. Kitchener, "Intuition, Critical Evaluation and Ethical Principles: The Foundation for Ethical Decisions in Counseling Psychology," *The Counseling Psychologist* 12, no. 3 (1984): 43-55.

themes, issues, positions, and policies that are worthy of being integrated into human care but that are not necessarily addressed directly in Scripture. These include a process for ethical decision-making (what to do when a situation emerges in which you don't know what to do), informed consent (explaining to those who suffer what to expect through the experience, costs, and limitations of the service), confidentiality (the obligations of the caregiver to protect the information given), record management (how confidential information will be store and guarded so that others do not have access), definitions and qualifications for competent service provision (evidence that the caregiver is capable of addressing the needs of the sufferer), and guarding against dual relationships and conflict of interest (how the ministry will address the multiple layers of relationship that can occur in community).[36]

A Family Reunion?

Like Alicia, we can continue to sift through all that each of our "parents" have taught us. As she need not carry every aspect of her divorced parents' values and lifestyles to fully embrace them as parents, neither do we. Instead, she can cherish the contributions— great or small—made by each parent as they are useful for her in adulthood. So too, the Christian mental health community need not accept some of the worldview implications of the mental health profession to benefit from that heritage. Nor must we improperly exegete a mental health identity from Scripture to validate our existence within the church. We can embrace multiple identities, demonstrating fidelity to our religious traditions and delivering effective mental health care in alignment with our professional standards and expectations.

---

[36]See Alan C. Tjeltveit, "There Is More to Ethics Than Codes of Professional Ethics: Social Ethics, Theoretical Ethics, and Managed Care," *The Counseling Psychologist* 28, no. 2 (2000): 242-52; and Siang-Yang Tan and Eric Scalise, *Lay Counseling: Equipping Christians for a Helping Ministry* (Grand Rapids, MI: Zondervan, 2016).

Finally, we take our longing for connection as something imbued in us by our Creator. We are relational as God is relational. We pursue attachment, intimacy, and communion as God's character reflects it. As God's union in the Trinity is one of giving and receiving, both internally with one another and externally with creation, so are we to reflect these qualities. The concept of integration is more than being able to mix Freud with Billy Graham or to make behaviorism Christian. Integration aims to unify the disparate aspects of the human self into a cohesive whole. While we might not achieve a unity quite like the divine "us," we strive to emulate that paradigm.

Questions for Reflection

1. Consider the metaphor of Alicia and her divorced parents as a parallel of the Christian mental health worker who seeks identity in both faith and the profession. In what ways does the metaphor fit for you? Where does it fail or come up short? Is there a better metaphor that you could use to describe your desire to be true to both callings?

2. How do you see the characteristics of divine attachment, intimacy, and communion reflected in your own relationships and interactions? In what ways can you better emulate the reciprocal giving and receiving found in the divine union of the Trinity, both in your personal connections and your interactions with the world around you?

3. How can we blend the principles of historical theology and psychology in a way that's understood and relevant to the broad culture, to the local community, and during therapeutic sessions?

4. The term "mental health" does not resonate with everyone. What kind of language might be appropriate for your community?

4:00

Word and Deed

*We must learn to regard people less in the light of what they
do or omit to do, and more in the light of what they suffer.*

DIETRICH BONHOEFFER, *LETTERS AND PAPERS FROM PRISON*

IN THE PREVIOUS CHAPTER we introduced you to the fictional
Alicia. The metaphor of her journey is one of difficulty. So is ours.
She must amalgamate the contributions received from her mother
and father and recreate them into a mission, a purpose, and a life task.
Our journey as Christian mental health professionals is to integrate
the contributions of two important sources of truth: the trinitarian
God as revealed in the biblical text, and the truth found in creation
and discovered or learned by the application of the creative intelligence endowed by God to us.

In part one we described a crisis of need. The demand for care has
outpaced the capacity to deliver care with the current system. This
crisis creates opportunity. Transition paves the way for origination
and creativity. The emerging need forms space for exploration, innovation, and application of new ideas. A new application of integration is one of them.

The Christian clinicians partnering with churches are free to address unmet needs. There is space for the gospel to be received

through the medium of human care. But our integration must be more cogent, creative, and constructive than the theoretical paradigms within an academic context. The concept of integration must be understood and exercised beyond the place where theory meets theology. If we seek to impact society, then our integration must move from an internal process to an external one. Our integration must be an articulation. We must speak it, show it, and touch people with it.

Alicia must do more than discover her voice. She must speak it—and so must we.

Bridge-Building Between Counselors and Pastors

Eric Johnson has a vision for a new generation of counselors who begin with a rich understanding of the Christian faith, particularly the healing properties of the Gospel, Christian meditation and a close relationship with God from which they interpret contemporary psychology and psychotherapy and incorporate all that is compatible with their faith. In doing so, he believes they can strengthen relationships with their local pastors and create theologically and clinically informed interventions to meet the needs of their communities.

Johnson is a Christian psychology professor at Houston Christian University who taught Christian counseling for seventeen years at The Southern Baptist Theological Seminary.

He's working on a Christian Transformational psychology, describing it as right in between the integration approach and the Bible-only approach.

"We're saying, 'hey, both sides are bringing something to the table that's valuable. Let's sit down and talk.'"

To that end, he's developing curriculum that will train licensed professional counselors to do what he calls "Christ-centered therapy" with Christian clients.

"They're going to be able to make the case to pastors in their community that 'sending folks to me will be value-added. What I do in the counseling room, for example, is deeply compatible with what you teach and preach at church,'" he said.

Johnson acknowledges that many pastors who support biblical counseling will be skeptical at best of such therapy but he believes there's a large group of pastors that see the validity of much of modern psychology and psychiatry merging with biblical wisdom.

He's also seen that therapists who are weak in their understanding of theology are often unable to persuade local churches of the value of their work, let alone defend it.

Johnson cites one mega-church whose elders dismantled their church-based clinical counseling agency after attending a biblical counseling training that viewed any approach with a clinical orientation as heresy.

"Some of the problem was caused because the therapists were, for the most part, only clinically trained," said Johnson. "They were doing therapy with members and they didn't talk about Jesus, they never brought the Bible into it and so they played into these stereotypes that these church leaders had been given by the Bible-only ideologues, so the therapists couldn't really dispute the criticism."

Johnson says it could have played out differently if the therapists had more theological training.

"I can imagine a scenario where they had been able to respond and say 'oh no, on the contrary, I work out of a Christ-centered background that's clinically informed,'" he said. "That would have gone a long way to mitigating the criticism if not making the critics back off and say 'we didn't realize it wasn't clinical only but it was more nuanced, and based on a Christian worldview.'"

Johnson is developing more theologically and biblically based training seminars for those who are already licensed.

"It would be sort of like a skill set or a knowledge base as if you were learning how to do EMDR or DBT," he said.

It would not only strengthen the ability of counselors to relate to Christian clients but it could build a stronger bridge between Christian therapists and the church.

A New View of Worldview

The work of integration has been about worldview. The prevalent view of Christian thinking in our era has been that "we are our worldview" and that our integration models emanate from it. This is stated by Entwhistle when he writes, "The worldview with which you were raised, modified to whatever degree by your experiences and personal reflection, has tremendous implications for your view of psychology and integration. A well-thought-out Christian worldview is a precondition for effective integration."[1] Entwhistle and others see the fundamental components of a Christian worldview to include the understanding of creation, fall, redemption, and glorification/culmination.[2]

Worldview is a noun. It is like a lens through which we see everything. It is also much more: "A worldview is not only a view of the world, but a way of life in the world. It not only tells one what is (the factual situation), but also what ought to be done (the normative direction to be taken) in order to be able to walk the way."[3]

Charles Colson was influential in leading the worldview discussion in the broader Christian culture in the late twentieth century. He drew his ideas from Francis Schaeffer, among others.[4] Both men had a dualistic style in their worldview presentation. Correct worldview equals a Christian one. An errant worldview equals a humanistic or secular one. As a result, they lost potential depth by articulating Christian worldview as a single idea or position, when in fact Christian worldviews are as complicated as our theologies.

---

[1]David N. Entwistle, *Integrative Approaches to Psychology and Christianity: An Introduction to Worldview Issues, Philosophical Foundations, and Models of Integration* (Eugene, OR: Wipf and Stock, 2021), 76.

[2]Mark A. Yarhouse and James N. Sells, *Family Therapies: A Comprehensive Christian Appraisal* (Downers Grove, IL: InterVarsity Press, 2017).

[3]Bennie J. Van der Walt, "Sharing an Integral Christian Worldview with a Younger Generation: Why and How Should It Be Done and Received?" *In die Skriflig* 51, no. 1 (2017): 1-11.

[4]Francis Schaeffer, *How Should We Then Live? The Rise and Decline of Western Thought and Culture* (Wheaton, IL: Crossway, 1983).

Most people pick up presuppositions from their family and surrounding society, the way that a child picks up the measles. But people with understanding realize that their presuppositions should be *chosen* after a careful consideration of which worldview is true.[5]

While Schaeffer drew great attention to Christian worldview, and Colson accelerated it, Christian psychologists used worldview arguments to create a new approach to the discipline of psychology. Christian psychology became a unique application within the professional discipline. Many argued that Christian psychology was distinct from psychoanalysis, behaviorism, or cognitive or humanistic psychology because of a different explanation of origin and purpose of existence. Worldview made it different. Of course, worldview thinking is prevalent outside of Christian circles. It has a rich tradition among social scientists in anthropology and social work, and has eventually become prevalent in psychology. It is not exclusively Christian. Koltko-Rivera examined the full extent of worldview in psychology. He defined it as

> a way of describing the universe and life within it, both in terms of what is and what ought to be. A given worldview is a set of beliefs that includes limiting statements and assumptions regarding what exists and what does not (either, or in principle), what objects or experiences are good or bad, and what objectives, behaviors, and relationships are desirable or undesirable. A worldview defines what can be known or done in the world, and how it can be known or done. In addition to defining what goals can be sought in life, a worldview defines what goals should be pursued. Worldviews include assumptions that may be unproven, and even unprovable, but these assumptions are superordinate, in that they provide the epistemic and ontological foundations for other beliefs within a belief system.[6]

[5] Schaeffer, *How Should We Then Live?*
[6] Mark Edward Koltko-Rivera, "The Worldview Assessment Instrument (WAI): The Development and Preliminary Validation of an Instrument to Assess World View Components Relevant to Counseling and Psychotherapy" (PhD diss., New York University, 2000), 2.

The Christian worldview was an academic explanation of the way the supernatural world—God—and the natural world—creation— were integrated as the human experience. Christian worldview is our understanding of Trinity and its work in creation, and we know of this work through the physical, biological, and social sciences. Worldview is theology and theory coming together to make new culture. Jonathan Pennington describes worldview not as a raw idea, but as a way of being. His philosophy of Jesus is an idea that brings human flourishing.[7] It's not an academic concept. It is like Ezekiel's revival of the dry bones that now carry life.

Culture emerges out of our worldview. The mental health culture is the thing we create to blend our theory (the thing that we use to understand creation) and our theology (that thing we use to define our worldview). Culture is, according to Andy Crouch, "what we make of the world."[8] Culture is the output of our values. Values don't stay on an intellectual shelf. They are turned into actions, products, positions, and perspectives. A worldview is a cognitive assumption about right and wrong, origins, responsibilities, and entitlements, the sum of which are our values.

Unfortunately, worldview has become a political endeavor: "The task must be to increase the number of Christians working in the realm of law and public policy at levels of government and, short of that, to mobilize popular indignation to pressure politicians to support the policies and laws compatible with Christian principles."[9] The call toward worldview is often a call to political action. Many debates have been fueled over worldviews and the identification and application of how we are supposed to live. The culture has scripted

---

[7]Jonathan T. Pennington, *Jesus the Great Philosopher: Rediscovering the Wisdom Needed for the Good Life* (Grand Rapids, MI: Baker Books, 2020).

[8]Andy Crouch, *Culture Making: Recovering Our Creative Calling* (Downers Grove, IL: InterVarsity Press, 2013), 23.

[9]James Davison Hunter, *To Change the World: The Irony, Tragedy, and Possibility of Christianity in the Late Modern World* (New York: Oxford University Press, 2010), 13.

a *mano a mano* confrontation of worldviews about how the world should be run. We have reduced worldview to conservative or liberal and fight it out on the political stage and dramatize it on news channels. Audiences tune in to learn of the awful things the other side is doing, and the great things our side is seeking.

As our society has separated into a dualistic power struggle, the church has gotten involved, and politics is now tied to the church's identity. Of course, the church should be involved in the political process, but its politics can detract from its primary purpose, message, and identity. We know we have erred when the broader society understands Christianity through a political agenda, not a human care agenda. If we are going to reach the world, our integration around this concept must change.

Worldview drives our mission. It moves us toward a faith/profession articulation "action point"—a verb: to speak one's Christian integration worldview into the creating of products, institutions, and actions that alleviate suffering. Crouch describes his observation of worldview and the call to act:

> The risk of thinking "worldviewishly" is that we will start to think that the best way to change culture is to analyze it. We will start worldview academies, host worldview seminars, write worldview books. These may have some real value if they help us understand the horizons that our culture shapes, but they cannot substitute for the creation of real cultural goods. And they will subtly tend to produce philosophers rather than plumbers, abstract thinkers instead of artists and artisans. They can create a cultural niche in which "worldview thinkers" are privileged while other kinds of culture makers are shunted aside. But culture is not changed simply by thinking.[10]

We hear and accept the call to move integration from the blending of ideas, concepts, and truths of two disciplines toward articulation,

---

[10]Crouch, *Culture Making*, 64.

the expression of voice and action. Our mission as mental health providers called to serve Jesus is to carry out ministry and professional activity. There is need for care utilizing the science of the mental health discipline with the service of Christian ministry. Unlike previous calls to integrate, this is the call to speak, to act, to engage, to bring healing.

Worldview must also move beyond the clinical hour. Most Christian integration emerged from academics whose professional identities were closely tied to clinical disciplines—primarily psychology, but also counseling, marriage and family therapy, and social work. Their task was to make the clinical hour as defined and managed by the profession into a Christian experience. Integration was the blending of Christian truth with the scientific method of empirical evidence. But in adopting the science of the professional mental health disciplines, we also adopted their economic culture. This culture was built around the clinical hour. If a client attends a session with a clinician it will almost always involve a fifty-minute experience that is billable to an insurance company. The clinical hour is the focal point of mental health provision. Though not typically stated in this manner, the task has always been to take the secular therapeutic hour, with all its valuable content in understanding human processes, and turn that hour into an experience of Christian redemption.

Integration for the counselor was to place the Christian narrative into the therapeutic process that was defined by the mental health profession. Christian integration has been, in practice, a process of turning "their" therapeutic hour into a fifty-minute "Christian" experience. The profession's economic model was infused with Christian content, tone, emphasis, or influence. The counselor had to be thoughtful regarding worldview and skillful in professional practice. But the need for aid by a large segment of society demonstrates that the clinical hour, even when conducted through a Christian integrated format, is insufficient to meet the demand and need.

Getting Through Dark Days with Friends at Church

For years, Nancy believed that her depression was her fault. "I always thought I needed to get my act together and this depression would not keep on happening," she said. She had received care at several psychiatric hospitals and remembers "pretty dark and lonely" days.

After someone at her church suggested a Grace Alliance group, she went to her first meeting and found a spark of hope. "I felt relief mainly because I was in a very accepting atmosphere," she said. "I didn't have to put on a good face. I just sensed that people there—we're all in a similar boat and we could be real," she said. Nancy stayed and eventually became a leader.

The Grace Alliance offers a unique support environment. It's focused on a discipleship experience for anyone who wants to improve their emotional and mental health while building their faith in Christ. Its tools include a science-based topical curriculum with scriptural insights for those with a diagnosis or experiencing symptoms, and a separate one for their families. There's also a basic curriculum, called THRIVE, for people who want to pursue overall mental and emotional wellness.

Like Nancy, Katie has facilitated Grace groups for years but for different reasons. Katie is a caregiver. Her daughter, now in her early thirties, received a bipolar diagnosis at age thirteen. Katie says everything escalated when her daughter was in her early twenties.

"I was told that she's probably going to be diagnosed with schizophrenia and I need to prepare that she couldn't work full time," she said. "It was like a living death sentence. It was shocking, and I was not prepared."

Although she enjoyed a strong friend group, no one else was living what Katie and her family were experiencing, which included multiple hospitalizations for their daughter as well as homelessness and jail time.

To compound the family's pain, well-meaning friends gave hurtful advice, says Katie. Some of them encouraged her to pray more, change her parenting, or blame her daughter's 's "sin nature." Others told her she needed prayers for deliverance and for demons to be released.

One friend told her about the Grace Alliance, and she found a group. It was an hour away, but Katie was desperate.

Both Katie and her husband found the comfort and community and understanding they so badly needed. "They all had similar stories," she said. "To hear them share—it was incredible. We just felt so not alone. We were not isolated anymore. It was just really, really encouraging."

Katie is preparing for a lifetime of off-and-on crises with her daughter. She has already walked through multiple cycles where her daughter moves from medication and stability to no medication and a downward spiral that typically ends with a police interface and hospitalization. She's watched her daughter get kicked out of a private, locked facility and burn other bridges in the mental health community in their area, leading her to fear that one day, she will have nowhere to turn.

The Grace group she leads now serves as the community she and the other members need to roll with the rollercoaster of caregiver challenges. They've worked through the curriculum multiple times and still come back to it. "These are things that apply all the time, and they're good reminders," she says.

Joe Padilla cofounded Grace Alliance in Waco, Texas, in 2010 after his wife's mental health journey turned their lives upside down. It led to him leaving his job after twelve years of ministry leadership. Even after seeking professional and ministry counsel for years, they saw no improvement in her health. Grace Alliance was born out of his research into neuroscience, psychology, and biblical and theological studies.

Padilla is committed to the long-term journey of mental health patients and their families like Nancy and Katie. But he's also committed to what he calls the "basic life is hard" crowd. The COVID pandemic elevated the conversation in this group that is attracted to more of a wellness model. They're coming to the Grace website for content via its blogs and looking for tools and tips around mental resilience, agility, and endurance. Grace's THRIVE curriculum connects science and faith for those who see themselves having a hard time but who don't identify with "mental health" and may never seek out a therapist or pursue medication.

Padilla's goal is to make it easy for people to start peer groups using the Grace curriculum and training. They can meet in church settings, homes, online and even on Instagram Live. "This is a long game. We're thinking about innovation over the next ten years. How do we engineer this in a cultural way?" he asks. He hopes that churches will see mental health as a growth opportunity and look for ways to partner with community resources.

Building a Better Cultural Product

Articulation is to speak the spiritual disciplines, the Christian virtues, the embodiment of the trinitarian God to humanity, and to do so with an understanding of what it means to "give your life away." That is the clear mission of the Christian counselor who seeks to live as the embodied gospel to the world. We aim to become the skilled articulators—ones who are adept at confronting the effects of suffering with eternal hope. But that hope must have a delivery system, a method of transmission, a language, and a code of action required for application. The science of psychology and all disciplines of learning are useful, even essential, to that mission.

We affirm Neff and McMinn in their effort to connect psychology and mental health practice under the mission Dei of the church, and in citing David Bosch to explain the foundation or purpose:

> Mission Dei has helped articulate the conviction that neither the church nor any other human agent (read psychology/counseling) can ever be considered the author or bearer of mission. Mission is, primarily and ultimately, the work of the Triune God, Creator, Redeemer, and Sanctifier, for the sake of the world, a ministry in which the church is privileged to participate. Mission has its origin in the heart of God.

God is a fountain of sending love. This is the deepest source of mission. (Bosch, 1991, p. 392)[11]

From the origin of the integration movement to the present, our mission has expanded. Originally Christian psychology or like disciplines were not accepted by the professions or by the church. Our original integration mission was to create a philosophical, logical, theoretical model of therapy that was drawn from empirical science applied to the theological and ministry functions of the Christian church. We were very successful, as evidenced by the Christ-centered academic programs that received accreditation to train psychologists, therapists, and counselors: Fuller, Rosemead, Wheaton, George Fox, Azusa Pacific, Cal Baptist, and others that accomplished that in psychology. Similarly, Denver Seminary, Regent, Evangel, John Brown, Asbury, Liberty, and many more were institutional leaders in counseling. (Our sincere and humble apology to the hundreds of leaders who were once our students and whose institutions were not mentioned in this list. We see all of you!) Now there are over sixty Christian institutions that are professionally accredited in a mental health discipline throughout the United States. It is wrong to suggest that the mission to maintain strong Christian programs is over, as with every new accrediting board, the need to justify our existence and demonstrate our competence remains a continual effort. On top of that continuing mission is now, more than at any time in our modern professional era, the call to exhibit an applied integration. An integration that is a verb. We seek worldviews that are spoken into an action word exhibited in churches, in ministries, and in private practices. It is the articulation of our integration.

The articulation of our mission might draw from psychology. It and all bodies of knowledge exist to undergird the caregiver to

---

[11]Megan Anna Neff and Mark R. McMinn, *Embodying Integration: A Fresh Look at Christianity in the Therapy Room* (Downers Grove, IL: InterVarsity Press, 2020), 190-91.

assist in the restoration of the person with their Creator. Articulation involves permitting the outcomes of empirical science addressing human behavior to be manifested in the value, vision, and conduct of human care. The biblical text has much to offer on how we are to articulate our integration. We are to prioritize this concept Jesus called the kingdom of God. We are to seek the interest of others above the interest of self. We are to alleviate suffering for all, but especially the vulnerable and unprotected. We are to care for God's creation as its appointed stewards. We are to love justice, seek mercy, and walk humbly with our God. That is the articulation of our integration. The verb. We are to live out the commands and commissions of the Bible, which depicts Christians providing extraordinary care toward others, emanating out of their faith in Jesus and considering eternity.

We see articulation in the parable of the Good Samaritan. The sufferer receives attention regardless of rank or ethnicity or ability to compensate. This spiritual discipline or value of care is presented as a norm for any who follow Jesus. In this case, the Samaritan had his plans disrupted and he accepted inconvenience as he went about making interventions for one who could not repay him. The text does not define the specific practices of care—how wounds were bound, how health was restored, how care was provided. The methods applied would have been in keeping with the medical theory and knowledge of the day. The healing oils and ointments applied would have been derived from the science of the era. Though rudimentary compared to our day, the care offered combined the best science with the presence of compassion.

Similarly, psychological practices emerging from the science of human behavior can indeed inform the way the church and the followers of Jesus live out their calling today. The emphasis is on applied interventions, coming from science, offered with the compassion of those who would be Jesus to the needy. Paul takes the specifics of the

Good Samaritan parable and turns it into application: "Let us not become weary in doing good, for at the proper time we will reap a harvest if we do not give up. Therefore, as we have opportunity, let us do good to all people, especially to those who belong to the family of believers" (Gal 6:9-10).

Do not grow weary of doing good. The Samaritan challenged the existing culture and created a new one. The story redefined the meaning of doing good. "Good care" becomes a new identity. We can speak to the church and the profession because we carry knowledge and possess skills needed by both. We know good care as defined by our professions. It is empirically validated, and it is set within the limits and boundaries of ethics. It is good. And we know good care as defined by the Gospels and the Epistles. It is the Great Commission and the Great Commandment. It is care that surpasses personal profit and self-fulfillment. It exists, in part, because of a vision for the big picture, the *imago Dei*, the resurrection, and ultimately heaven.

Changing demands prompt a call for a new system of care, and we can respond by offering a new product—a different approach from just the insertion of core Christian concepts within the established practice of the mental health profession. Rather, we see a new concept of human care, a church-drawn mental health ministry in which the practices of the profession—that is, the full content of empirically related conduct—have a presence with the truth of the call of Jesus. The church can use the tools created by the profession to conduct its mission of the "care of souls." Arthur Bonner articulates these values best in his summation:

> For both Christian clergy and mental health professionals, the reemergence of the soul and recovery of the interest in its care offer the possibility for a holistic Christian ministry. Christian soul care that succeeds in reunifying the psychological and spiritual aspects of persons holds the promise of relevance and potency that has often

been lacking in the ministrations of both Christian clergy and mental health professionals.[12]

His statement is even more powerful when we consider that he was writing about the church and the profession in the context of Chiapas, Mexico, and the need for mental health care as a way for the church to minister to the impoverished.

To articulate integration is to embody it as Christian virtue, a personal characteristic of life, a therapeutic intervention tool, and a goal or outcome for professional/ministry engagement. Part three of this book will focus on how we are to teach the articulation of faith in practice. For the remainder of this chapter, we will consider how to demonstrate articulation.

Demonstrating Virtue as Articulation

Psychology is now virtuous. At least it is attempting to be. Virtue has become a prominent research theme and academic agenda. As a topic of scholarship, it attracts some of the best minds. Since the formation of the positive psychology movement in the 1990s, Martin Seligman and others have led an intense examination of the components of human excellence or virtue. Positive psychology focuses on human strengths as opposed to a focus on deficits. "The message of the positive psychology movement is to remind our field that it has been deformed. Psychology is not just the study of disease, weakness, and damage; it also is the study of strength and virtue."[13] Tangey notes that the evaluation of virtue as a valued human behavior has been intentionally avoided in the past. "Mainstream psychology steered clear of such value-laden topics as religion, virtue, and morality. In their zeal to establish psychology as a bona fide science, psychological scientists

---

[12]Arthur Bonner, *We Will Not Be Stopped: Evangelical Persecution, Catholicism, and Zapatismo in Chiapas, Mexico* (Parkland, FL: Universal Publishers, 1998), 14.

[13]Martin E. P. Seligman, "Positive Psychology, Positive Prevention, and Positive Therapy," in *Handbook of Positive Psychology*, ed. C. R. Snyder and S. J. Lopez (New York: Oxford University Press, 2002), 4.

embraced notions of objectivity and fact. . . . Virtues as a group have been relatively neglected in psychology."[14] Now, private foundations and government-sponsored organizations are resourcing millions of dollars to understand the effect and impact of virtue.

To the Christian, virtue is easy to imagine because there is a clear telos, or goal, toward which we strive. We are to become somebody. Our theological term is *sanctification*. Simply stated, it is the process of getting better—better at being more like Jesus. Never perfect. Never in our own strength. But still a movement toward a goal because of the presence of God the Holy Spirit dwelling in us. To be virtuous is to be like Jesus. "An understanding of human virtue assumes a common belief in the chief end of human existence. . . . Christians remain called to know and live according to that purpose and to cultivate those qualities that allow us to fulfill that calling with excellence."[15]

Without having Christian mental health integration in mind, Chatraw and Swallow Prior identify the purpose of those who attend to human care: to live the call to care for others with excellence, in the way that Jesus would have them act. While the science of mental health provides essential knowledge, the virtue of Christian maturity permits that raw understanding to emerge beyond fact into a life-breathing and life-providing phenomenon. To articulate the integrated reality of mental health, creation, and the identity of the Creator is to live out James 3:17: "But the wisdom that comes from heaven is first of all pure; then peace-loving, considerate, submissive, full of mercy and good fruit, impartial and sincere."

The articulation of our integrative practice is our lived and breathed experience with a restorative Trinity. As Neff and McMinn reveal, integration is more

---

[14]June Price Tangney, "Humility," in *Handbook of Positive Psychology*, ed. C. R. Snyder and S. J. Lopez (New York: Oxford University Press, 2002), 411.

[15]Joshua D. Chatraw and Karen Swallow Prior, *Cultural Engagement: A Crash Course in Contemporary Issues* (Grand Rapids, MI: Zondervan Academic, 2019), 54-55.

a way of being in the office (and out of the office) than as something we do. To what extent am I aware of God's presence in the complex and challenging work we are doing? How am I being personally formed so that I can communicate God's love in relation to the other? Am I attuned to the present moment, and willing to stay in the moment even when my mind is reacting a million miles a minute toward the latest evidence-based intervention? Ultimately, these are all the questions about being a loving presence with the hurting soul that is sitting with me. They are the questions about recognizing and reflecting—however dimly—the presence of God in our broken world.[16]

While there are dozens of virtues described and modeled in the biblical text, we focus on three: hospitality, justice, and compassion. They exist outside of Christian mental health delivery. But their meaning and application within the context of human soul care make them powerful. To think of them as action verbs—to be hospitable, to be just, and to be compassionate—is to articulate an integration that comes from the church to all those God loves.

Be Hospitable

It may surprise you that the first virtue of Christian integration we name is hospitality. You might not think of it as integration, but more like a person who makes delicious tacos and is quick to invite others to join them in their backyard; it's a person who can throw a great party. At first take, that image would be correct . . . but there is so much more. The twenty-first-century mindset of hospitality describes people who are nice, welcoming, friendly, and open to others. Yes, that is hospitality. However, when we dig into the origin of hospitality, we discover a sobering responsibility, which, outside of the Christian tradition, remains rare—even ridiculous!

Integration begins with our capacity to be hospitable in the Christian tradition. The etymology of the original Greek word, *philoxenia*, is

---

[16]Neff and McMinn, *Embodying Integration*, 211.

"the love/friendship of strangers." Few take offense at the idea of "do to others what you would have them do to you." It sounds just, fair, and kind. The Golden Rule is so very pleasant! But *philoxenia*, at times, is not so nice or lovely or pleasant. It carries depth. Sacrificial depth. "In light of Jesus' life, death, resurrection, and return, Christian hospitality is the intentional, responsible and caring act of welcoming or visiting, in either public or private places, those who are strangers, enemies, or distressed, without regard for reciprocation."[17]

The phrase "without regard for reciprocation" might make us all catch our breath. It turns hospitality into something very different from any therapeutic model. It brings therapy to the realm of human care ministry and removes cost as the centerpiece. Unlike the humanistic unconditional positive regard, which is offered in an economic exchange, Christian hospitality is offered because of the *imago Dei*. The care that we saw in the parable of the Good Samaritan was hospitality.

The concept of hospitality was not new in Roman times; it's what you did for "your people"—your family, your clan, and any friend in your social class. The Roman military was the first to create something like what we now call "hospitals," but only for its own people. Even Roman citizens didn't qualify. The church introduced a different hospitality. "One unique feature of the biblical church community was the makeup of its members, for it extended its hospitality to people, regardless of their social, cultural, or economic status. The sacred community, called the church, looked beyond itself, as a sign and instrument of the kingdom of God."[18] This hospitality began a new culture. The care exhibited through the hospitality of the early church was extraordinary, and it engaged the culture in which the church was situated. Millions found refuge from plagues, pestilence,

---

[17]Arthur Sutherland, *I Was a Stranger: A Christian Theology of Hospitality* (Nashville: Abingdon, 2010), xiii.

[18]Charles E. Farhadian, *Introducing World Religions: A Christian Engagement* (Grand Rapids, MI: Baker Academic, 2015), 9.

and war. In the historic Christian tradition, hospitality was the first virtue of integration, intersecting the call of God and the need of the people. "Hospitality . . . always included family, friends and influential contacts. The distinctive Christian contribution was the emphasis on including the poor, and neediest, the ones who could not return the favor."[19] This extreme hospitality could be costly for caregivers, sometimes exposing them to deadly disease. Dionysius, the bishop of Alexandria, wrote about the year 263:

> And now certainly all things are turned to mourning, and everyone is in grief and lamentations sound throughout the city, due to the multitude of the dead and those who are dying day by day. . . . Certainly, very many of our brothers and sisters in their exceeding love and family feeling, did not spare themselves, but kept by each other, and visited the sick without thought of risk to themselves, and minister to them continually, serving them in Christ. So, they died with the others.[20]

In the word *hospitality* we may immediately recognize the connection to *hospital* and *hospice*. To us, hospitals are the great centers of healing. To those in Dionysius's day, they were places where you went to die. In the early church, *hospitality* was also a verb: to sit with the suffering and the dying. Hospitality invites the sick, infirmed, wounded, injured, needy, and lost to enter. While we may think "practice hospitality" means "be nice," it takes on a whole new meaning when we understand "hospitality" as meaning to be a hospital or a hospice. It is to remain in the presence of suffering. The stench of death resides where we practice hospitality, and the early church understood this.

We see the calling to be hospitable in the words of Jesus in Matthew 25:44-46.

---

[19] Christine D. Pohl, *Making Room: Recovering Hospitality as a Christian Tradition* (Grand Rapids, MI: Eerdmans, 1999), 6.

[20] Amy G. Oden, *And You Welcomed Me: A Sourcebook on Hospitality in Early Christianity* (Nashville: Abingdon, 2010), 152-53.

They also will answer, "Lord, when did we see you hungry or thirsty or a stranger or needing clothes or sick or in prison, and did not help you?"

He will reply, "Truly I tell you, whatever you did not do for one of the least of these, you did not do for me."

Then they will go away to eternal punishment, but the righteous to eternal life.

The gravity of Jesus' words might explain why the integration of work in mental health care with Christianity begins with hospitality. Jesus' words should sting. Christian care starts with a full commitment to bring aid, care, and support to those in need. Hospitality says, "As a core component of my love for Jesus, I will care for you." It is not first a business plan, an economic model, or a professional responsibility. (Though it will include a business, be reliant on economics, and be informed by the profession.)

Oden states, "Taken as a feature of Christian life, hospitality is not so much a singular act of welcome as it is a way, an orientation that attends to otherness, listening and learning, valuing, and honoring. The hospitable one looks for God's redemption presence in the other, confident it is there."[21] Hospitality is the conduit for bringing the power of the cross to the clinical moment. It is our faith speaking into our practice.

The distinction between hospitality as being nice and hospitality as sacrifice is possible because of our trust that God is the provider and protector. This allows us to see others through the lens of eternity rather than the lens of immediate self-interest. John Chrysostom wrote of hospitality in the lives of Abraham and Sarah as strangers and sojourners:

But how were they strangers? They had no care for things here. And this they showed not by words, but by their *deeds.* . . . He yielded the first places to others: he threw himself into dangers; he suffered troubles innumerable. He built no splendid houses, he enjoyed no

---

[21]Oden, *And You Welcomed Me,* 14-15.

luxuries, he had no care about dress, which all are things of this world; but lived in all respects as belonging to the City yonder; he showed hospitality, brotherly *love*, mercifulness, forbearance, contempt for *wealth* and for present *glory*, and for all else.[22]

Hospitality is a sacrifice of self for others: spouse, family, church, community, and especially those distant, the stranger, the poor, the one who is incapable of returning fair and equitable compensation. To Augustine, one can be hospitable because our vision is forward toward heaven. "You don't live here as one who will live forever, nor will those to whom you leave it live forever. . . . When we shall have passed away, and we come to that place where we no longer pass away, we may find our good works there."[23]

The practice of mental health care integrated within the Christian tradition is to exhibit hospitality. But hospitality must have boundaries. Care has limits. Without limits, the providers then become those in need because all care providers cannot be perpetually giving. Those who care must also be cared for by others. It is the essence of Boszormenyi-Nagy's relational ethic in contextual family therapy.[24] It declares that loving others, caring for others, is the continual process of giving and receiving. The caregiver must also be the care receiver.

The virtue verbs such as hospitality are to be integrated with the empirical science of how, how much, when, and when not. Giving to others is met by receiving from others. Integration becomes the exercise of care within the limits of human capacity. Biblical virtue sets the content—the character of Christian care. Our mental health scholarship defines the context—the characteristics of the care, the measured effects, the amount, and the direction of care applied. Our

---

[22]John Chrysostom, "Homily 24 on Hebrews 11," trans. Frederic Gardiner, in *Nicene and Post-Nicene Fathers, First Series,* vol. 14, ed. Philip Schaff (Buffalo, NY: Christian Literature Publishing, 1889). Revised and edited for New Advent by Kevin Knight, www.newadvent.org/fathers/240224.htm.

[23]Oden, *And You Welcomed Me,* 45.

[24]Ivan Boszormenyi-Nagy and Barbara Krasner, *Between Give and Take: A Clinical Guide to Contextual Therapy* (New York: Routledge, 2013).

scholarship has identified the effects of unrestrained hospitality in terms such as "burnout" or "compassion fatigue." Tan speaks to the essence of self-care for the effective practice of those who practice hospitality. He writes:

> Self-care for the counselor, however, refers to healthy and wise strategies for taking good care of oneself as a counselor to manage stress well and prevent burnout. . . . It is . . . loving and wise to engage in proper self-care that eventually leads to the helping and healing of others.[25]

Let us suggest a variation to the concept of self-care. The phrase implies the separation and individual autonomy of the caregiver. It implies that the person gives to others, then takes care of self, is restored and then capable again to care for others. Within the contextual family therapy of giving and receiving, self-care would not refer to taking care of yourself but rather being engaged in relationship such that others take care of you. The reciprocity of relational attachment suggests that as one gives through hospitality, he or she must also be the recipient from others of the same hospitality. Caregivers cannot be self-deniers or self-sustainers.

Hospitality must have restraints outlined by ethical limitations that define competent care. Unbounded hospitality is the vulnerability of having purity in one's intent and effort but foolishness regarding method and practices. The empirical evidence and professional standards of ethical care restrain our hospitality in the same way that they serve to restrain an unbridled profit motive. This professional dimension prevents overreach and permits us to care carefully by enforcing ethics that serve to bridle and manage unrestrained "do goodism" in the name of hospitality.

To use a final metaphor to describe hospitality, we often hear the phrase "it's a marathon, not a sprint." In this case, we suggest that

---

[25]Siang-Yang Tan, *Counseling and Psychotherapy: A Christian Perspective* (Grand Rapids, MI: Baker Academic, 2011), 19.

hospitality, practiced with essential restraints of self-care, becomes more like the actions of a sprinter rather than a marathoner. You run hard—as hard as you can—and then you rest. Then once restored, you run again. And you run hard. Followed by rest. And then you run. The mission of hospitable care, with the objective of reducing the suffering of others, is fenced in by research that informs us about how that care might be effectively administered to maximize its effect and extend the caring capacity of the caregiver.

Be Just, Be Righteous

Citing justice as a foundational virtue for mental health care evokes reactivity. The reactivity is grounded in an observation of Miroslav Volf as he wades out into its depths. He notes, "Nobody stands nowhere." By that he means that "we do not argue about justice as disembodied and a-social 'selves' suspended by a sky hook above the hustle and bustle of social conflicts."[26] We all have suppositions, conclusions, opinions, and positions about justice as a mental health construct. Some have argued that the inclusion of social justice in the mental health profession is the ever-elusive "fifth wave" of the profession, placing it as a primary theory of care, along with psychoanalysis, cognitive-behaviorism, humanism, and multiculturalism.[27]

Indeed, the focus on justice is essential, but there are diverse opinions about how justice is applied. Differences about its use, understanding, and application create declarations of injustice by all sides who disagree with all perspectives but their own. Justice can become easy prey to the presumption that there is only one justice, and we all need to be on the same road. Typically, that justice is defined by those in power. Compliance with that common justice is the

---

[26]Miroslav Volf, *Exclusion and Embrace: A Theological Exploration of Identity, Otherness, and Reconciliation* (Nashville: Abingdon, 1996), 207.

[27]Manivong J. Ratts, "Social Justice Counseling: Toward the Development of a Fifth Force Among Counseling Paradigms," *The Journal of Humanistic Counseling, Education and Development* 48, no. 2 (2009): 160-72.

only way for peace to exist within a community. Refusal to comply with it becomes a threat, and threats to justice are unjust. Such threats are a disruption and they disregard peace, commonality, and unity. All this is paramount to a declaration of opposition. It is unjust to be opposed to justice as defined by our group. To oppose our justice is an act of defiance. It is a declaration of "war." And since you by default are declaring war, then I am "justified" in attacking you, denying you, even killing you. This is your just reward for being unwilling to abide by the code of justice, the *one* code.

To speak directly of justice is to reclaim the virtue as a fundamental theme central to the Trinity's redemption of creation. Indeed, the mission of Jesus, the Son, was a mission of justice. But the topic of justice carries an additional complication when discussed within the Christian community, that is, one of contextual understanding. In the New Testament, the word *dikaios* (and related terms) is used a little less than two hundred times. About one-third of the time, translators have selected "justice" as its intended meaning. Most of the time, however, it is translated as the word "righteousness." To most of us, "justice" and "righteousness" mean very different things. Usually, in our way of thinking, justice is associated with the call to fairness, especially fairness before the law. But righteousness carries the connotation of holiness, to be right before God. To the writers of the New Testament, to be just and to be righteous are the same thing. This should cause us to pause and be humbled.

The justice and righteousness articulated by Jesus carries some but not all of the components of today's cultural view of social justice. This should make all of us, regardless of our social-political leaning, squirm. To Jesus, the unjust are the ones who think that they are most justified in declaring who is right and who is wrong, and Jesus' justice exposes their arrogance. The only legitimate response from all is modesty and humility.

Justice/righteousness is a complicated idea that encompasses both physical and spiritual realities. It is not reliant on shared balance, and it is not subject to our respective merit. Roberts describes the Christian notion of justice as a variation from the classic Greek concept and the mental health profession's emphasis on "social justice": "Full human wellbeing would not be achieved by having a society of people who were 'just' only in the strict and narrow sense, nor would an individual flourish if he did not have the virtues that go beyond strict justice."[28] The capacity of Christian justice goes beyond fairness or equality. It is to be more than fair and more than equal. Generosity, mercy, forgiveness, and the previous virtue of hospitality are not provided because of merit or "fair" distribution. Mercy is not just. It is beyond justice. Volf makes this same claim: "To be a follower of Jesus Christ means . . . to affirm that God's justice transcends the cultural construal of justice."[29]

The virtue of justice, displayed in the gospel of Jesus and applied to human care ministries, exists in the will and activity to embrace others. Such an embrace has the capacity to reach beyond the justice of equality, which is limited by the tautology of social justice as fair distribution, exemplified in the statement "all should respect all; none should respect those who do not respect all."[30] Embracing another despite their lack of merit is the very definition of Christian grace.

We can see evidence of this more limited understanding of justice in the literature of the mental health profession and in the historical "in a different voice" phenomenon from the twentieth century, extending into the present. This was a call for individuals to find their "voices"—that is, the right to speak. It was a confrontation of the historic oppression of ethnic, economic, sexual/gender, age, and ability groups that captured our attention. "I will be heard. I will be seen." These were and are the calls of the oppressed for justice.

---

[28]Robert C. Roberts, "Justice as an Emotion Disposition," *Emotion Review* 2, no. 1 (2010): 36-43.
[29]Volf, *Exclusion and Embrace*, 198.
[30]Volf, *Exclusion and Embrace,* 204.

Even David, as king of Israel (e.g., the most powerful in his day), lamented the sense that God had abandoned him, leaving him unheard, unseen, and unprotected.

The right to have a voice is a call to be acknowledged and to receive care. But there is something important missing from the focus on having a voice, something that Boszormenyi-Nagy identified in his development of relational ethic.[31] In our cultural cacophony, everyone seeks to have a voice, declaring "I WILL BE HEARD!" But in doing this, everyone has, in some capacity, defined themselves as the oppressed. There are few, however, who are giving an "ear." Justice requires a voice. And justice also necessitates an ear.

A voice without an ear only leads to frustration, which can balloon into violence, chaos, and, to use Nagy's term, "destructive entitlements." The need for exchange, for giving and receiving, for welcoming gets missed in our discussion of justice. Parties become injured, and they seek justice as an extraction, and it takes the form of power reversal. Likewise, the language of voice without the language of bidirectional listening only rationalizes future injustice.

Indeed, the Christian call to justice is a call to be present or, as Carlos Pozzi has written, a call "to be with." This position is a biblical one, based on the incarnation of Christ. In Christ, God becomes human to be with us. To be with the underserved involves a reciprocal relationship of mutual impact. In this relationship, we are both teachers and students. We are researchers and subjects. To be with requires relationship, not just technique. It requires a deeper understanding of others, walking in their shoes, or looking at things from their point of view. The concept is full of contradiction: the researcher becoming the subject or the teacher learning from the student.

---

[31]Boszormenyi-Nagy and Krasner, *Between Give and Take.*

A theology of accompaniment requires openness to a relationship. However, relationship is interpersonal. It happens among people. One cannot have a relationship with an abstract concept such as "justice" or "the underserved." Working for justice or for the underserved requires a relationship with an underserved person.[32]

Justice brings us back to hospitality and the concept of giving out of self toward another self. Justice requires an active participation, active sacrifice, and active engagement.

Be Compassionate

The most important concept in mental health care, empathy, is not found in the Bible as a primary theme. Instead, there is something better: compassion. Carl Rogers transformed the mental health field by articulating the importance of empathy. He defined it as "the therapist's sensitive ability and willingness to understand the client's thoughts, feelings and struggles from the client's point of view. [It is] this ability to see completely through the client's eyes, to adopt his frame of reference."[33]

Empathy is to enter the emotional realm of another, seeking to experience their emotions and their circumstances as a facsimile of their experience. But for empathy to be effective as a therapeutic tool, more than emotional identification is needed. Research on empathy indicates it "will not be effective unless it is grounded in authentic caring for the client. We encourage psychotherapists to value empathy is both an 'ingredient' of a healthy therapeutic relationship as well as a specific, effective response that promotes strengthening of the self and deeper exploration."[34]

---

[32]C. F. P. Montero and R. S. C. Preussler, "Psychology and Social Justice: Working Towards a Christian Justice-Based Model of Integration," *Journal of Psychology & Christianity* 21, no. 4 (2002): 306.

[33]Carl R. Rogers, *A Theory of Therapy, Personality, and Interpersonal Relationships: As Developed in the Client-Centered Framework*, vol. 3 (New York: McGraw-Hill, 1959), 85.

[34]Robert Elliot, Arthur C. Bohart, Jeanne C. Watson, University of Toronto, David Murphy, "Therapist Empathy and Client Outcome: An Updated Meta-analysis," *Psychotherapy* 55, no. 4. 399-410. https://eprints.nottingham.ac.uk/51119/.

Enter compassion as the third essential aspect of the articulation of integration. Few images from the biblical text are more poignant than Jesus looking over Jerusalem, the city of peace, and weeping as he foretold its destruction: "As he approached Jerusalem and saw the city, he wept over it and said, 'If you, even you, had only known on this day what would bring you peace—but now it is hidden from your eyes'" (Lk 19:41-42).

Compassion is empathy plus engagement. Empathy and involvement. It is to identify with the sufferer and then respond with hospitality and justice. Read how the Gospel writers described Jesus:

- *Matthew 14:14:* "When Jesus landed and saw a large crowd, he had compassion on them and healed their sick."

- *Matthew 15:32:* "I have compassion for these people; they have already been with me three days and have nothing to eat."

- *Matthew 18:27:* "The servant's master took pity on him, canceled the debt and let him go."

- *Mark 6:34:* "When Jesus landed and saw a large crowd, he had compassion on them, because they were like sheep without a shepherd. So, he began teaching them many things."

- *Luke 7:13-14:* "When the Lord saw her, his heart went out to her and he said, 'Don't cry.' Then he went up and touched the bier they were carrying him on, and the bearers stood still. He said, 'Young man, I say to you, get up!'"

In these descriptions of the compassion of Jesus, we see a combination of action and feeling. Paul describes God feeling and acting similarly, saying he is "the Father of compassion and the God of all comfort" (2 Cor 1:3). Compassion originates with God. God felt, then God acted. We display compassion when we act toward others in the way that God has acted toward us. The idea is theological. The practice is psychological. Our science gives us instruction in how we might conduct our compassion with effect, impact, and purpose.

Empathy is among the first concepts taught in counseling skills training. It's a good place to start in understanding articulation. Carl Rogers understood compassion from his childhood, adolescent, and early adult experiences as a Christian. He struggled with sin, hell, and judgment so much that he left his pastoral studies at Union Theological Seminary and went across the street to Columbia and studied psychology. But the compassion of Christianity was never far from his mind. Empathy became its facsimile. Not the original, but close. It is

> to perceive the internal frame of reference of another with accuracy and with the emotional components and meanings which pertain thereto as if one were the person, but without ever losing the "as if" condition. Thus it means to sense the hurt or the pleasure of another as he senses it and to perceive the causes thereof as he perceives them, but without ever losing the recognition that it is as if I were hurt or pleased and so forth. If this "as if" quality is lost, then the state is one of identification.[35]

Neff and McMinn bring to our attention the limitation, the "shortness" of empathy. "Notice that empathy is typically conceived as instrumental. In other words, we see empathy as a therapeutic end of helping a patient become less depressed or anxious, less bound up by shame, and more connected to others. Empathy is a therapeutic strategy."[36]

Empathy and compassion are similar, but not the same. Empathy "puts on the brakes" at the point of deep, personal identification with the one who suffers. Shane and colleagues identified the difference:

> Empathy and compassion were welcomed and valued by patients. Patients felt that empathy and compassion share attributes of acknowledging, understanding, and resonating emotionally with a

---

[35]Rogers, *A Theory of Therapy*, 210-11.
[36]Neff and McMinn, *Embodying Integration*, 86.

person who is suffering. Compassion also added distinct features: action, supererogatory acts, virtuous motivators, and unconditional love, with compassionate responders functioning in an instrumental fashion in the amelioration of suffering. These results are consistent with studies focused on health care providers' conceptualizations of compassion as an intensification of both cognitive and affective empathy coupled with the addition of action aimed at the alleviation of suffering.[37]

Compassion goes further into the journey with the sufferer than empathy due, in part, to empathy's separation as a clinical boundary. Empathy can say, "I feel what you feel," whereas compassion can say, "I will go with you to where your suffering occurs." Compassion can make justice/righteousness more than the entry into a political battle; it becomes a personal journey with another in their grief. Neff and McMinn speak of this depth of integration by referring to it as the outcome of grief and gratitude shared and offered to others. They cite McKee, who wrote:

> The work of the mature person is to carry grief in one hand and gratitude in the other and to be stretched large by them. How much sorrow can I hold? That's how much gratitude I can give. If I carry only grief, I'll bend toward cynicism and despair. If I have only gratitude, I'll become saccharine and won't develop much compassion for other people's suffering. Grief keeps the head fluid soft, which helps make compassion possible.[38]

Compassion is the principle that allows counseling ministry to take a step further than the professional limits will permit. Vivino and colleagues conducted an exploratory examination of therapists who were nominated by their peers as being compassionate. They

---

[37]Shane Sinclair et al., "Sympathy, Empathy, and Compassion: A Grounded Theory Study of Palliative Care Patients' Understandings, Experiences, and Preferences," *Palliative Medicine* 31, no. 5 (2017): 445.

[38]Tim McKee, "The Geography of Sorrow: Francis Weller on Navigating Our Losses," *The Sun* 478, no. 11 (2015): 40.

concluded that "compassion was conceptualized as a process or state of being that connects to the client's overall suffering or struggle and provides the rationale or the impetus to help the client find relief from his or her suffering. In contrast, empathy was conceptualized as being more connected to the process of understanding the client from moment to moment."[39]

The effectiveness of Christian compassion integrated with the discernment and boundaries of professional limitation allows for greater effectiveness as well as the need to exercise caution through supervision and conduct evaluations of the ministry. With a sly degree of humor, Boniface, the eighth century English Benedictine monk wrote to the archbishop of York, Egbert, "I am sending you a cloak, and a towel to dry the feet of the brethren, after you have washed them."[40] The meaning here is that compassion can take our human care efforts beyond what our clinical roles permit, but it comes with responsibility to respect the limits, usually defined by effective research from the clinical profession.

But there is a dark side to compassion. The exhibition of unbridled and unrestrained compassion has produced a powerful and popular theme in the research: compassion fatigue. It also makes the care provider vulnerable to over-involvement, pride when someone improves, and shame/guilt when they do not. Valent described compassion fatigue as the "unsuccessful, maladaptive psychological and social stress responses of Rescue-Caretaking. [The responses] are a sense of burden, depletion and self-concern; and resentment, neglect and rejection, respectively."[41] Compassion can be dangerous without boundaries, limits, and restraints. Charles and Katherine Figley have focused their careers on the issues that cause compassion fatigue among

---

[39]Barbara L. Vivino et al., "Compassion in Psychotherapy: The Perspective of Therapists Nominated as Compassionate," *Psychotherapy Research* 19, no. 2 (2009): 167.

[40]Oden, *And You Welcomed Me*, 197.

[41]Paul Valent, "Diagnosis and Treatment of Helper Stresses, Traumas, and Illnesses," in *Treating Compassion Fatigue*, ed. Charles R. Figley (New York: Routledge, 2013), 26.

caregivers.[42] He also has studied compassion resilience. They refer to this as creating compassion for the compassionate. To apply the findings of resilience, compassion of Christian integration must include, among other things, accountability to others to help set limits of care, separation from the efforts of care provision for restoration, and the conversation around care limits.

Conclusion

For Neff and McMinn, integration as a verb is meant to cause a crescendo.[43] The idea that began as an academic concept now has legs. It moves. It has voice. It speaks and it has hands. It touches.

If integration is a verb, then articulation is our action, and virtues are our tools for action. *Hospitality, justice,* and *compassion* are three nouns that identify how we are to move, to speak, to touch those who suffer. The intent of integration is to be hospitable, to be just, and to be compassionate. Indeed, these are not the only three virtues. We could also talk about mercy, gratitude, kindness, resilience, grace, forgiveness, trust, patience, and more. We invite you to write those books! These chosen three serve as a primer toward engaging those in our care with the model of Christian mental health care.

James Davison Hunter summarizes this integration, writing to Christians of every discipline to act out their professions within the context of their love of Jesus.

> Indeed, there are intellectual, economic, and managerial resources available within the church and among Christians to make a profound difference in every sphere of life—the social welfare of the needy, the environment, education, the arts, academia, business, community formation and urban life and so on; and at every order of magnitude—the local, the regional, the national and the international. This will

[42]Charles R. Figley and Kathleen Regan Figley, "Compassion Fatigue Resilience," in *The Oxford Handbook of Compassion Science*, ed. Emma M. Seppälä et al. (New York: Oxford University Press, 2017), 387-98.

[43]Neff and McMinn, *Embodying Integration*.

invariably mean collaboration, networking, mutual dependence, and institution-building.[44]

Institution building. That is, culture making. The culmination of Christian articulation expressed through our hospitality, justice, and compassion is found in Philippians 2:6-8: "[Christ Jesus], being in very nature God, did not consider equality with God something to be used to his own advantage; rather, he made himself nothing by taking the very nature of a servant, being made in human likeness. And being found in appearance as a man, he humbled himself by becoming obedient to death—even death on a cross."

The history of Christendom is thick with demonstrations of exceptional and profound care as the means to speak the gospel to the culture. The science of the mental health profession can sharpen the effectiveness of that care. But the science of care cannot match the Spirit of care shown by those who see suffering through the lens of resurrection. The vision and the process can be collaborative between the church and the clinic.

Questions for Reflection

1. Reflect on your worldview. What aspects of your worldview lend themselves toward minimizing important ideas? What aspects serve as your strength?

2. Think of the worldview of counseling theories and systems (Freud, Rogers, etc.). Where are you pulled toward resonance or disagreement? What do you do with either pull?

3. Hospitality, justice, and compassion are three important virtues. Where do you see them emerge in your life and practice?

4. We use the term *articulation* as the expression of faith within mental health care. How is that similar to or different from integration?

---

[44]Hunter, *To Change the World*, 271.

PART 3

Navigating the Way Forward

I F A NEW CULTURE IS CREATED, then we must get there. We must be about building the infrastructure for it to happen. Consider the words of King David: "He heals the brokenhearted and binds up their wounds" (Ps 147:3). As God's hands on earth, we must learn something about wound care if we are to be about binding wounds. And if the church is going to be about this care on a scale far greater than what it is today, we must prepare existing and emerging professionals and pastors to operate in the new culture. People must be trained to meet the needs coming through our church doors. Leaders must train people to carry out the vision and to address the problems with integrity, excellence, and professionalism, and within established ethical guidelines. Naming the current state and condition (part one) is the easy part. Casting a theological vision for the gospel and the clinic (part two) is more challenging. Addressing the challenge (part three) is the hard part. Here we will consider how to prepare clinicians to meet the need.

Innovation always emerges spontaneously. Where problems exist, creativity follows. We see the problems, and we see seedlings of innovation emerging in churches large and small. Our task is to place ourselves in front of the change to be ready when society catches up. This is true for any human need and cultural transformation. Charles

Taylor understood this. In his time, he saw the future and determined to be in front of it. He was ready when "change sent him a telegram." He saw the need before everyone else. He placed himself in the path where change was going to occur. Rather than being stuck on the ground, he determined solutions that got above a problem of his day, and others who followed his ingenuity got us all off the ground, literally.[1]

Charles E. Taylor was born in 1868 in a small farm town in Illinois. As a boy, he fought the soil with a horse-drawn plow. He died in 1956, during the birth of nuclearization and computers.

His life was about travel. In his twenties, marriage took him to Dayton, Ohio. The chatter in Dayton was about a new mode of mechanical transportation: the bicycle! Taylor was fascinated by it. He got a job as a bicycle designer and mechanic. He taught himself metallurgy, taking the knowledge of the blacksmithing trade from horse-drawn agriculture and applying it to create simple machines of steel and aluminum. His employers were impressed with his intelligence and vision for mechanical transportation. Trusting Taylor to run their bike shop, they turned their interests toward building human kites. They believed humans could fly. In 1903, Taylor got a telegram from his bosses, Orville and Wilbur Wright, who were in North Carolina. They were testing their flyer and found that the engine they purchased was too heavy for their plane. They couldn't get it off the ground. They needed him to turn all his attention to designing, casting, and constructing an engine that was both light and powerful. Their request was incredible: stop making bicycles and make an engine that is both powerful and light enough to fly and bring it to us . . . now! Taylor had read about Henry Ford and the German designer Karl Benz and the emerging technology of gasoline-powered engines but had never made one. Within six weeks, he was on a train to Kitty Hawk with an

---

[1]Howard DuFour and Peter Unitt, *Charles E. Taylor, 1868–1956: The Wright Brothers' Mechanician* (Dayton, OH: Prime Digital Printing, 1997).

aluminum cast twelve horse-power engine that weighed 151 pounds. He had built it in the repair shop of the Wright Cycle Company. We all know of Orville and Wilbur, but without Charles Taylor, they would only be known for flying very large kites and gliders.

Taylor saw the world from the perspective of a horse, then a bicycle, and then spent fifty years helping people fly. As the culture around him shifted to address the challenges of that day, he shifted with it. But to do so meant he had to "retool," both literally and figuratively. He knew about horses and plows, but he had to learn about gears and cranks and steel tubing. As soon as he mastered the bicycle, he had to learn about pistons and pushrods. The emerging culture required new knowledge and new ways to implement that knowledge. With each shift, from horses to bicycles to airplanes, he mastered new content, developed new skills, and found new applications. So must we.

This section has four chapters to address how to prepare Christian clinicians and churches to meet the need of the culture using the ministry context of the church. There are four knowledge/skill areas likely needed in the new mental health culture. These are not new avenues or realms of knowledge. Rather, they are areas that have not been prioritized in Christian counselor training and development. They have been in the periphery, but they must be brought to the center of our training. Future Christian counselors working with churches in full-service community care will need new knowledge to be effective. Each area will serve as a topic in this chapter. They are (1) biblical theology and Christian thought, (2) supervision, (3) consultation program evaluation, and (4) ethics and economics.

To "fly" in the twenty-first century we must have a diversified skill set. The clinical hour will only be part of the work. We must now travel at speeds that Charles Taylor's parents never dreamed possible, but Charles himself did! Just as he shifted his learning focus, we must also shift focus in order to become equipped to meet the new need. Professors and institutional leaders must think about how to prepare students for advanced aeronautics, not Conestoga repair, and emerging students and current professionals must develop their skill set to fly, not to canter.

One final word: in these chapters we do not give attention to the essentials of clinical competence. The ability to assess, diagnose, and treat mental health disorders should remain key to the training of Christian mental health professionals. That is unchanged. The story of Charles Taylor should not be taken to suggest that what we have been doing is not to be part of the future of counseling work, as in we are no longer building bicycles but are making airplanes instead. Clinical acumen remains the central organizing skill of the professional in the future. There is no less of a need to produce great therapists. Rather, the emphasis shift is a broadening and diversifying of how great therapy is delivered within church ministry contexts. Therapists must become great teachers and mentors as they manage others with less formal training, without advanced degrees, and without state or provincial endorsed licenses to practice. If we are going to arrive at our destination, we're going to have to fly, not pedal.

5:00

The Foundation of Christian Care

LET'S THINK BIG. Consider what life would be like if a counselor had a caseload of ten thousand clients. Let your head spin with that number: ten thousand. It is typical for a clinician to work with about two hundred people per year. Multiply your caseload by fifty! If you were responsible for that many people, the way you did your work would be different. Centuries ago the church wrestled with a similar question, and came up with a solution. They called it the *cura animarum,* or the care of souls.

The phrase "soul care" is not new to this century. It's not new to the previous century, either, or the one before that. It actually dates back to the thirteenth century when the church was defining the role and responsibility of the pastor. More than one hundred years ago, Fanning wrote of the meaning of soul care within each Catholic church community: "mindful of their obligations as members of a parish to institute and improve the parochial institutions necessary for the proper furtherance of the object of the Church, we shall have the true idea of the cure of souls as intended by Christ and as legislated for in the canons of His Church."[1]

---

[1]William Fanning, "Cure of Souls," *The Catholic Encyclopedia*, vol. 4 (New York: Robert Appleton Company, 1908), www.newadvent.org/cathen/04572a.htm.

"Soul care" referred to the responsibility of the parish priest for the well-being of those within the community. From very early in Christian history the church was the center of human flourishing, responsible for the care of all the souls who dwelled within the sound of its bells. All things pertaining to the life of the community happened at the church. The word *parish* has roots in words focused around community. Life was enhanced through the church. It included birth, death, marriage, education, advice, guidance, and sometimes even food. The church service didn't mean sixty minutes of music, a sermon, and free coffee. It was a reference to where we serve and are served by others.

Likewise, the identity of the Protestant church was connected to being a place of respite for soul, mind, and body. Richard Baxter wrote a manual for pastoral care in 1673, titled *Directions*. In 2018, Lundy and Packer offered an update and revision of a portion of Richard Baxter's *Directions*.[2] Lundy and Packer focus on Baxter's instruction for the care of depression and anxiety. In the preface, Packer wrote: "[We] came to think that a mini-treatise by Baxter that, at its heart, sought to serve the depressed would, if republished in a modern edition, be a valuable resource for pastoral care of depressed persons in today's churches."[3]

The church, both Catholic and Protestant, carried responsibility for the emotional well-being of society as part of its mission. It is time to return to this missional calling, but to do so, we must prepare clinicians to work in church settings. For mental health professionals to have a prominent presence within churches and ministries, counselors must be educated in the text, theology, and history of the

---

[2]The full title of Richard Baxter's work is *A Christian directory, or, A summ of practical theologie and cases of conscience directing Christians how to use their knowledge and faith, how to improve all helps and means, and to perform all duties, how to overcome temptations, and to escape or mortifie every sin: in four parts* (London: Printed by Robert White for Nevill Simmons, 1673).

[3]J. I. Packer and Michael S. Lundy, *Depression, Anxiety, and the Christian Life: Practical Wisdom from Richard Baxter* (Wheaton, IL: Crossway, 2018), 9.

church. *Therefore, the first task in preparing a new generation of counselors is theological training.*

A Pastor . . . a Counselor . . . a Pastoral Counselor?

As our story of Alicia suggests, identity carries powerful meaning. As I (Jim) mentioned earlier, many years ago the Sells family went on a year-long adventure to Honduras for a sabbatical I had been granted from Northern Illinois University. My focus there was on indigenous counseling methods. I worked closely with and under the sponsorship of Iglesia en Transformación in Tegucigalpa, the capital. The church provided an office among the pastors. From that setting I interviewed pastors, counselors, psychologists, and other mental health caregivers. In addition, I worked with the church staff, conducting supervision of therapy and pastoral care. I even preached in very broken Spanish. The first week, Pastor Jairo Sarmiento offered me a "promotion." He said, "In the US you are a professor and a psychologist, but here, with us, you are a pastor!" The new title and role prompted me to rethink how mental health care could be delivered and how mental health clinicians need to be prepared.

At the onset of this chapter a series of essential questions must be asked: Who is the professional mental health provider who works within a church context? Are they a pastor? Are they a clinician? A pastician? A clinstor?

Identity informs the essentials of training. It stands to reason that educational experiences are designed around the identity of the graduates. Engineers need engineer training. Accountants are trained in accounting. In our context we have two identities. Therefore, Christian mental health professionals need to be educated in clinical competence (which they currently are) and theology (which they are not).

It is imperative for the counselor who seeks to impact God's kingdom to be an applied clinical theologian. We must be adroit at the comprehensive and effective application of the biblical text as we serve as ministers of reconciliation, as described in 2 Corinthians 5. Paul declares us to be Christ's ambassadors who seek to apply knowledge of the amelioration of human suffering. Because our identity exists with two clear dimensions, so must our expertise. Stuart Scott puts forth a calling for everyone who seeks to represent Jesus in human care.

> There is an operative conviction that God's Word is relevant to all of life and can be practically applied to every heart and every circumstance of difficulty. While this does not imply that Scripture is the only source of information in the counseling process, biblical counselors are consistent in their detailed biblical analysis of information and in their overwhelming focus on special revelation—the Bible—which alone is infallible and authoritative truth.[4]

Scott identifies two sources of knowledge, consistent with our two identities. Not two opposing truths, nor two opposing identities, but truth found in two locations: the Bible, the revelation of God through his expressed Word; and the created text, the revelation of God through the created order. We must understand the biblical text and competently integrate it with God's revelation of mental health knowledge. Second Timothy 2:15 is a verse we must live out each day in the counseling ministry role. Paul exhorts Timothy to "do your best to present yourself to God as one approved, a worker who . . . correctly handles the word of truth." Counselors will use the biblical text—both directly to reference it with clients and indirectly to influence the way hospitality, compassion, and justice are to be applied. The applied clinical theologian must consider the ways that the role of counselor is a direct extension of the office of pastor.

In describing the educational task of pastors engaged in counseling ministry, Graham and Whitehead describe two objectives for those

---

[4]Stuart W. Scott, "A Biblical Counseling Approach," in *Counseling and Christianity: Five Approaches*, ed. Stephen P. Greggo and Timothy A. Sisemore (Downers Grove, IL: InterVarsity Press, 2012): 157-83.

who serve as clinicians in ministry contexts. First, they need to possess "theological fluency." Second, they need a "traveling theological knowledge."[5] We like their description of tasks used in the context of preparing clinical counselors for work in ministry contexts. In naming theological fluency as a teaching goal, they draw a distinction between it and theological literacy. Theological literacy is to exhibit knowledge of theological ideas through reading, writing, and speaking. Preaching pastors need to possess theological literacy—to be trained in Hebrew and Greek (and, for many, German!), and to have as one's primary work to study Scripture and deliver to the church the fruit of that studying. The goal of theological literacy is to use Scripture for direct persuasion. But the objective of a theologically fluent counselor is softer, less direct, less prophetic, and more pastoral. Theological fluency carries a wide array of knowledge. Doering suggests that "we become fluent when we 'inhabit' our theology as a faith perspective that we use to understand and respond to spiritual and psychological needs. Whereas becoming theologically literate involves learning to think critically, becoming theologically fluent involves formation."[6] The counselor becomes the applied theologian by taking the truth declared from the pulpit as "the Word of the Lord" and placing it into the context of thriving marriages, maturing children, managing tensions between coworkers, regulating emotional reactivity, and controlling habits.

The role of counselor is central to ministry delivery. The research literature reveals that the pastor is and has always been central to mental health access. "Surveys by the National Institute of Mental Health found that members of the clergy were more likely than were

---

[5]Larry Kent Graham and Jason C. Whitchead, "The Role of Pastoral Theology in Theological Education for the Formation of Pastoral Counselors," *American Journal of Pastoral Counseling* 8, nos. 3-4 (2006): 9-27.

[6]Carrie Doehring, "Theological Literacy and Fluency in a New Millennium: A Pastoral Theological Perspective," in *Theological Literacy for the Twenty-First Century*, ed. Rodney L. Peterson and Nancy M. Rourke (Grand Rapids, MI: Eerdmans, 2002), 311-24.

psychologists and psychiatrists combined to have a person with a mental health diagnosis from the Diagnostic and Statistical Manual of Mental Disorders come to them for assistance."[7] This means that the church is the access point for many people seeking help for relief of emotional suffering. That is true now and has been for decades.

But there is another important aspect related to being an applied theological clinician that has to do with clergy competence. Steve Greggo declared in an address to the Evangelical Theological Society that

> there is ample evidence that folks in the pew wish that they could speak with their spiritual leaders and obtain quality help. Research suggests that this preference is strong amongst Protestants, even stronger for regular service attendees, and highest amongst those who hold theological convictions about the priority of Scripture.[8]

Greggo and others report that, by and large, pastors are not trained to be effective mental health caregivers beyond the role of spiritual encouragement. He states,

> Credit hours dedicated directly to counseling in typical MDiv programs are limited (2-4 credit hours or 3 percent of the MDiv degree). A single course cannot train leaders and pastors for the vast range of potential counseling scenarios across cultures. Nor can it provide encyclopedic depictions on how to speak with theological acumen into the range of complexities associated with modern living.[9]

Greggo is correct that pastors cannot sufficiently address mental health needs with only minimal training in interventions. This further points to the need we have been highlighting of bringing professional

---

[7]Andrew J. Weaver et al., "Collaboration Between Clergy and Mental Health Professionals: A Review of Professional Health Care Journals from 1980 Through 1999," *Counseling and Values* 47, no. 3 (2003): 162.

[8]Stephen P. Greggo, "Counseling Care and Evangelical Pastoral Leadership: Implications for Seminary Education," 5. Talk presented at the Evangelical Theological Society Conference, Milwaukee, WI, November 2012.

[9]Greggo, "Counseling Care," 8.

mental health care in collaboration with the church. It also highlights a second need, that mental health professionals working in the church must be prepared to serve with theological fluency as described by Doerring. The church needs to increase its capacity to receive those in need, and it must do so by demonstrating competence equivalent to the knowledge and skill of the mental health professions. But the church cannot and should not expand its ministry to incorporate professional mental health care if those taking on the role are incapable of representing the Christian ministry in which they serve. Greggo, writing about the practitioner as an advocate for bioethics, suggests the same conclusion:

> Christians trained in one-to-one helping typically have reasonable mastery of an extensive biblical anthropology based upon the implications of humankind being created imago Dei (Gen 1:27-31; 9:6-7). It is impossible to appropriate any psychological or counseling approach into Christian service without an adequate grasp of this basic doctrine. Therefore, the familiar imago Dei framework is offered initially to establish the basis of human dignity and further as a method to access a range of other useful theological material.[10]

Training Biblical Counselors in the Church

In Oregon, authorities are desperate for help in caring for mental health needs, and rightly so. Waiting lists for therapy and psychiatry can extend suffering for months. The advocacy group Mental Health America has ranked the state as one of the worst in the country when it comes to both prevalence of mental illness and access to care.

This double whammy of a scarcity of caregivers and overwhelming demand has led to a unique partnership between the biblical counseling center at Salem Heights Church and the surrounding mental health and medical community.

---

[10]Stephen P. Greggo, "Applied Christian Bioethics: Counseling on the Moral Edge," *Journal of Psychology & Christianity* 29, no. 3 (2010): 21-22.

Biblical counselor Emily Dempster at Salem Heights Church saw the crisis as opportunity. Dempster and a team of biblical counselors at Willamette Valley—area churches received training and certification through the Association of Biblical Counselors (ABC) via an eight-month class. "Equipped to Counsel" teaches laypeople, pastors and staff how to offer short-term, targeted biblical counsel to address issues like addiction, anger, anxiety, and depression.

Salem Heights has trained hundreds who've attended the class, and the church also offers close to one hundred seventy-five hours of free biblical counseling to the community every month. Dempster says local hospitals and mental health facilities have referred to Salem Heights as their waiting lists overflow.

"We've been able to have a reputation in the community that if someone is open to faith-based counseling they're able to make a referral to us," she said. More than half of those coming through their doors have no affiliation with Salem Heights, which provides an unparalleled opportunity for the church.

"It's really clear what we do and what we're offering, and here we have people that are asking for it and that are asking for help and that are reaching out," said Dempster.

Dempster also can't help but notice how the ministry encourages those who offer counsel. "I love how God's Word is changing not only the life of the people we're helping but also the counselors themselves," she said. "Getting a front row seat to watch God work in someone else's life changes their life."

Demand has grown especially during the pandemic: more couples seeking counseling for their marriages, more anxiety, depression, eating disorders, porn issues, and more youth seeking help.

Salem Heights has developed its own waiting list, and it's one reason the church has become a training center for biblical counselors in the Willamette Valley. Thirty churches and parachurch organizations have sent hundreds for training since Salem Heights began it in 2013. Most receive their certification, a two-year process that Dempster encourages.

"Especially in the Northwest where people don't know what biblical counseling is, it does give them something to stand on to say, 'I've been trained and certified,'" she said.

Salem Heights joins a growing movement to train biblical counselors. The Association of Biblical Counselors has launched twenty-five regional training centers in recent years and is working to launch more.

Executive director Shauna Van Dyke says it's not just lay leaders taking the classes but teaching and executive pastors who feel ill-equipped to meet mental health needs.

"It's not just sermon prep," she emphasizes. "It helps them to see Scripture from the practical point of how to help, how to apply this to not only their own lives but the lives of others."

For Salem Heights, offering free counseling to the community offers the bonus of introducing people to the church.

"We're not going door-to-door saying, 'Do you want to hear about Jesus?' They're coming to our door and saying 'Can you help? I'm hurting. I'm struggling. Can you tell me about the hope that you have?'" explains Dempster. "What a privilege, and what a door to have open!"

The Commission and the Command

Within the pastoral tradition, there are two "greats": the Great Commission and the Great Commandment. Our discussion about Christian theology and the role of the counselor must focus on these two ideas.

The Great Commission is the phrase used to describe the command of Jesus to go and make disciples in Matthew 28:16-20. It reads:

> Then the eleven disciples went to Galilee, to the mountain where Jesus had told them to go. When they saw him, they worshiped him; but some doubted. Then Jesus came to them and said, "All authority in heaven and on earth has been given to me. Therefore go and make

disciples of all nations, baptizing them in the name of the Father and
of the Son and of the Holy Spirit, and teaching them to obey everything I have commanded you. And surely I am with you always, to the
very end of the age."

Hudson Taylor, the pioneer missionary to China, was the first to pop-
ularize the phrase "Great Commission." Through it he introduced us
to an essential concept of care. Though the phrase is used for Christian
missions—as motivation to go to foreign lands—its real focus is on
empowered discipleship, to do the work of the kingdom under the
authority of the triune God. Castleman writes that the idea is "about
the Church's inauguration, identity, and union with Christ to be an
extension of his own life in the world. . . . Like Jesus, we are commissioned to 'do' who we 'are' and that's what makes it GREAT."[11]

Neff and McMinn address the essentiality of the Great Commission
as part of Christian integration: "Mission is located within the activity
of God. The sending of Jesus (by the Father) to a particular culture to
embody and translate the divine message of creation, reconciliation,
and redemption was the consummate mission. Jesus came and infused a particular culture with this gospel of hope and redemption."[12]

The Great Commission clarifies both our boss and our job description. Most enter a graduate mental health program to access to
a career path. It's a good job! But the Great Commission mandate is
for us to consider our work in an elevated context. We are commissioned, and God is our commissioner. We are sent by one who shares
the mission and purpose of the work. The mission of the Father was
the sending of the Son. The mission of the Son in the incarnation
was to reveal the life of the Father. The Spirit's mission is to bear
witness to the Son through the church. The co-missioning suggests

---

[11]Robbie F. Castleman, "The Last Word: The Great Commission: Ecclesiology," *Themelios* 32, no. 3
(2007): 70.
[12]Megan Anna Neff and Mark R. McMinn, *Embodying Integration: A Fresh Look at Christianity
in the Therapy Room* (Downers Grove, IL: InterVarsity Press, 2020), 187. We recommend all to
read their ideas.

that we are joined to a great purpose, the reconciliation and redemption of humanity, with our trinitarian Creator. "Because God is a missionary God, life in fellowship with him takes the objective form of active participation in reconciled and reconciling communities. The life of the community, as such, is not external to the message, but it exists in the act of reconciliation."[13] Such activity within the context of the church creates additional clarity as to our "employer" and our "job description."

Related is the Great Commandment, which comes from the words of Jesus. In Matthew 22:36-40, Jesus is asked by a Jewish lawyer about an idea that every faithful Jew would understand.

> "Teacher, which is the greatest commandment in the Law?"
>
> Jesus replied: "'Love the Lord your God with all your heart and with all your soul and with all your mind.' This is the first and greatest commandment. And the second is like it: 'Love your neighbor as yourself.' All the Law and the Prophets hang on these two commandments."

Jesus is paraphrasing the Shema, the most important prayer of the Jewish people, found in Deuteronomy 6:4-5. They declared it daily. Jesus affirms the importance of the covenant with God to the people of Abraham. But he does not stop with devotion to God. He ties it to people. The phrase "and you shall love your neighbor as yourself" is also an Old Testament command, found in Leviticus 19:18: "Do not seek revenge or bear a grudge against anyone among your people, but love your neighbor as yourself." People didn't give the command to love your neighbor the same daily repetition, focus, and intention they gave the Shema. It's easier to say you love God than to demonstrate that love by expressing it toward others.

In Matthew, Jesus declares a new understanding of the Great Commandment—that we show our love of God by demonstrating love for

---

[13]John G. Flett, "Missio Dei: A Trinitarian Envisioning of a Non-trinitarian Theme," *Missiology* 37, no. 1 (2009): 14.

those whom God loves, our neighbor. These concepts form the basis for our mental health ministry. Hospitality, justice, compassion, and all other virtues are built on these commandments. God's fundamental commissioning is to disciple-making, and the discipleship model also serves as our care model. Therapy is the clinician's modality for loving our neighbor.

The power of the Good Samaritan story is tied to the Great Commandment. In Luke 10:25-37, Jesus responds to an inquirer who posed the question, "Who is my neighbor?" He was asking, "How far does loving one's neighbor actually go?" Jesus' explanation of the Great Commandment will keep us all very busy pursuing the Great Commission. The essence of the work of the counselor is to be the conduit of God's mercy (Lk 10:37).

What Are We to Teach Them?

We take a broad application to Paul's commissioning declaration in Romans 10. "And how can anyone preach unless they are sent? As it is written: 'How beautiful are the feet of those who bring good news!'" (Rom 10:15). The clinician's role as preacher comes from theological fluency, not literacy. Christian graduate schools and seminaries should prepare clinicians for fluency. And for the clinicians who are trained in secular contexts, we suggest individual study, certificate programs offered through professional organizations like the Christian Association for Psychological Studies, the Association for Biblical Counseling, the Charis Institute, and many others.

Christian practitioners must be prepared in three broad domains. First, and most obvious, they must be prepared in the broad range of clinical practice. This skill set is not the focus of this chapter; we hold it as a given, as it exists within the clinical training of each discipline. But it does warrant mentioning that every clinician working in church domains will need to have a broad general knowledge of psychopathology, diagnosis, and assessment. This must include the ability to diagnosis and triage severe mental illness, such as schizophrenia and bipolar I disorders, and the plurality of less frequently occurring disorders, as well as the full range of common diagnoses such as generalized anxiety, major depression, and substance abuse disorders. It is also essential for each to be able to diagnose and create treatment interventions for children, couples, and families.

As to the theological and pastoral training, we see two broad applications: theological knowledge and articulation of integration. Theological knowledge includes five areas of content fluency listed here and then described individually. They are:

- theology: the study of the trinitarian God
- anthropology: humanity, the opus of creation
- hamartiology: sin
- soteriology: salvation
- ecclesiology: the church and its historical application of Christian thought

Theology. We have addressed some aspects of trinitarian theology as it relates to integration. We revisit it here as a curriculum theme.

Theology is the study of the personhood of God—his character, nature, and essence but so much more. The Trinity, as the core identity of God, reveals the nature of God as relational. Tanner states that "the essential social character of human persons is an analogue for the essentially relational character of persons within trinity."[14] Seamands describes the Trinity as the grammar of the Christian faith. "Grammar is a set of rules governing a particular language. . . . [It] enables us to speak rightly about the God who is revealed in Scripture as Father, Son and Holy Spirit."[15] Through understanding the Trinity, everything else makes sense. The trinitarian existence is both self and other and

---

[14]Kathryn Tanner, *Christ the Key*, Current Issues in Theology (Cambridge: Cambridge University Press, 2010), 3.

[15]Stephen Seamands, *Ministry in the Image of God: The Trinitarian Shape of Christian Service* (Downers Grove, IL: InterVarsity Press, 2009), 11.

simultaneously self as other. "Persons and community are equiprimal in the Trinity. . . . Divine persons are not simply interdependent and influence one another from outside but are personally interior to one another. . . . Every divine person is and acts as itself and yet the two other persons are present and act in that person."[16]

In trinitarian theology we see the nature of God as primarily egalitarian instead of hierarchical, relational instead of authoritarian. This emphasis on the relational language of God leads to understanding of relational care through the *imago Dei.* James Torrance writes,

> What we need today is a better understanding of the person not just as an individual but as someone who finds his or her true being-in-communion with God, and with others, the counterpart of a Trinitarian doctrine of God. The God of the New Testament is the God who has his true being as the Father of the Son and as the Son of the Father in the Spirit. God is love, and has his true being in communion, in the mutual indwelling of Father, Son and Holy Spirit—perichoresis, to use a patristic word. This is the God who has created us male and female to find our true humanity in "perichoretic unity" with him and with another, and who renews us in his image in Christ."[17]

Perichoresis may be a term unfamiliar to non-theologians. The Greek phrase was used by many early church fathers to describe the symbiosis of God. John describes a dance of God with God in his Gospel story. "If God is glorified in him, God will glorify the Son in himself, and will glorify him at once" (Jn 13:32). And in chapter 14 we read, "And I will ask the Father, and he will give you another advocate to help you and be with you forever" (Jn 14:16). Father, Son, and Spirit move together and separately. The dance is in how God loves and is

---

[16]Miroslav Volf, "'The Trinity Is Our Social Program': The Doctrine of the Trinity and the Shape of Social Engagement," *Modern Theology* 14, no. 3 (1998): 409.

[17]James B. Torrance, "The Doctrine of the Trinity in Our Contemporary Situation," in *The Forgotten Trinity: A Selection of Papers Presented to the BCC Study Commission on Trinitarian Doctrine Today*, ed. Alasdair I. C. Heron (London: British Council of Churches, 1991), 3-17.

loved by God. Alister McGrath writes that it "allows the individuality of the persons to be maintained, while insisting that each person shares in the life of the other two. An image often used to express this idea is that of a 'community of being,' in which each person, while maintaining a distinctive identity, penetrates the others and is penetrated by them."[18] We see the importance of the trinitarian dance for our own lives in John's words, "A new command I give you: Love one another. As I have loved you, so you must love one another" (Jn 13:34). The dance of God is a model we are to follow as we dance with one another. Therefore, we must learn and teach the dance.

Anthropology. Theological anthropology addresses our understanding of humanity. We read in Genesis about the creation of humans, starting with Adam: "Then the LORD God . . . breathed into his nostrils the breath of life, and the man became a living being" (Gen 2:7). Anthropology is launched from theology. Karl Barth's theological anthropology begins with the Trinity—God is engaged in "self-relationship" and extends himself into human relationship. We see this in John's words at the beginning of his Gospel: "And the Word was God . . . and the Word became flesh and made his dwelling among us" (Jn 1:1-14). The relationship among the members of the Trinity is characterized by a plurality of qualities such as unity, individuality, equality, love, collaboration, and creativity, and these qualities are to characterize our human relationships as well. To Barth, God is the ultimate demonstration of individuality and community.[19]

Theological anthropology is the fusion of theology, social psychology, and individual psychology. The capacity to act in an individual, equal, loving, collaborative, creative manner implies a constant giving—that is, God giving and receiving from God. As humans we are to model parallel giving and receiving. The giving and receiving

---

[18]Alister McGrath, *Christian Theology: An Introduction*, 3rd ed. (Malden, MA: Blackwell, 2001), 325.

[19]Daniel J. Price, *Karl Barth's Anthropology in Light of Modern Thought* (Grand Rapids, MI: Eerdmans, 2002).

does not diminish these qualities of equality, love, collaboration, and creativity, but rather enhances them. This *intrapersonal* demonstration of grace dictates the *interpersonal* demonstration of grace, seen in the acts of God the Father, Son, and Holy Spirit toward creation and, particularly, toward humanity. The characteristics of this relational God become the DNA that defines how we can receive God's grace and how we are to live with one another in this grace. First John 4:19 reads: "We love each other because he loved us first" (NLT). We do it because God did it. We mimic the dance.

Hamartiology. It requires no special insight to grasp that the human condition carries some form of flaw, limitation, vulnerability, or error. Somewhere, somehow, something went terribly wrong. In *Out of the Silent Planet*, C. S. Lewis's first story in his Space Trilogy, the Malacandrans (those who inhabit Mars) refer to those on Earth as "the bent ones."[20] Every code for existence and religious tradition possesses some explanation for this "bent" condition.

Psychological theories have explanation for the origin of this "bentness." Freudians see it as an arrested development from infancy and childhood that stunts the formation of the ego and prompts a lifelong search for secure attachment and succor from our primary object. Humanists attribute it to the suppression of self-development and the emergence of unmet relational needs, often occurring when we meet the demands and expectations of others rather than addressing essential self-need. To Rogers and others, the presence of unconditional positive regard, empathy, and genuineness are necessary and sufficient to create a corrective experience in therapy.[21] Cognitive-behaviorists might view sin as part of one's conditioning in family and cultural contexts, or the acquisition and adoption of inadequate thought processes. Many theories exist, but the counselor

---

[20]C. S. Lewis, *Out of the Silent Planet* (New York: Macmillan, 1946). DigiCat.
[21]Carl R. Rogers, "The Necessary and Sufficient Conditions of Therapeutic Personality Change," *Journal of Consulting Psychology* 21, no. 2 (1957): 95.

working in a church context must be able to speak the language of sin as a part of their empathy and care. McMinn describes an understanding of the weight of sin to be a core learning experience (along with seeing the dignity of all persons and learning empathy expression skills) provided in Christian mental health training programs.[22]

Soteriology. The traditional American hymn "Nothing but the Blood of Jesus" by Robert Lowry connects our human condition of sin with its solution, salvation.

> What can wash away my sin?
> Nothing but the blood of Jesus.
> What can make me whole again?
> Nothing but the blood of Jesus.[23]

The Christian tradition and the professional disciplines of mental health have solutions to make us whole again. This is where the influence of both of Alicia's "parents" plays out in our work. The seminary-trained pastor has ample preparation in understanding the theological components of salvation, usually defined as the covenantal, volitional decision, and baptismal experience that makes a person a Christ-follower. In addition, pastors are exposed to and informed by rich experiences of disciple-making or spiritual formation, defined as "the lifelong, intentional, communal process of growing more aware of God's presence and becoming more like Christ, through the Spirit, in order to live in restored relationship with God, ourselves, and others, in every dimension of life."[24] The church knows something about how to make people whole. That is the influence of one of Alicia's parents.

However, that parent—the religious one—has far more in common with the psychological science parent than is commonly known. Much

---

[22]Mark R. McMinn, *Sin and Grace in Christian Counseling: An Integrative Paradigm* (Downers Grove, IL: InterVarsity Press, 2010), 35.

[23]Robert Lowry, "Nothing but the Blood of Jesus," 1870.

[24]Holly Catterton Allen, *Forming Resilient Children: The Role of Spiritual Formation for Healthy Development* (Downers Grove, IL: InterVarsity Press, 2021).

of the spiritual formation literature is generated in part by disciplines of learning within the field of psychology. Developmental psychology focuses on the study of all aspects of human development, including spiritual development. Social psychology and community psychology are two additional significant branches of psychological science. Both emphasize the role of shared relationship on individual development and the role of the individual in shaping social and community health.

Ecclesiology. Everyone comes from somewhere, at some time and does something, somehow. The history of the church includes the story of everyone everywhere doing everything, in every way. The church has a story. So does each person. The essential learning task is to acquire basic understanding of faith traditions and histories, to know where people come from and what they are doing. When we don't know histories, we make assumptions, and then we make mistakes based on the errant assumptions, which causes harm. Three words serve as a crucial example. Arians, Arminians, and the Armenians. The words are similar, but the life experience and place within the church are vastly different. In case you don't know the difference, Arians represented a group in the early church who followed a third-century heresy that denied Jesus was God. Arminians, however, are not heretics. They are a prominent theological group whose beliefs were articulated by Jacob Arminius, who died in 1609. His writings were juxtaposed to those of Calvin. The Methodists and Wesleyans of today are followers of this theological tradition. Finally, the Armenians are an ethnic group located west of Turkey who follow the Armenian Orthodox faith tradition. They have survived genocide in the early twentieth century and exist as a small nation with a faith tradition that dates back to the early church.

To know something of the flow of history and theology and culture permits one to enter faith groups as informed and inquisitive visitors and guests. Knowledge accelerates the affirmation of another's faith journey. Understanding of and exposure to the broad themes of world religious traditions—Catholic, Protestant, Orthodox, Muslim, Jewish, Hindu, Buddhist, Sikh, and countless others—enables a regard for the searching nature of humanity.

Of crucial importance is the ability to identify with the "nones," or the "undefined" or the "spiritual." Each person has a unique story of how they have faced the basic themes of existence, borne the weights given them, carried the scars acquired, received the blessings bestowed and the hope they see. These events occur in the context of church. This church context might be the Gothic steepled building on the corner of First and Main Streets. Or it could be the nonformal "church" of common sojourners. The expression "I am not religious but I am spiritual" might be the emerging identity of the twenty-first century. Most written thought for Christian audiences has limited use for postmodern seekers of this century. There remains a deep yearning within the nones to address the existential issues of this day. Bohecker and colleagues have found that there is

> a recognition of longing for a reality beyond the physically finite; the search for a deep and abiding meaning to life that includes hope, integrity, respect, and compassion; the desire to see life as bigger and more important than the individual self; and a recognition that spirituality and religion compose a core developmental dimension of human existence.[25]

To be effective working in the church requires being familiar with faith traditions and how to care for each person as they carry the *imago Dei*.

Integrating Our Identity

In Christian graduate or seminary training, the integration described in chapters three and four can be blended with clinical competence

---

[25]Lynn Bohecker, Rita Schellenberg, and Justin Silvey, "Spirituality and Religion: The Ninth CACREP Core Curriculum Area," *Counseling and Values* 62, no. 2 (2017): 128-43.

and theological fluency. Hathaway and Yarhouse describe this growth process in the form of domains, which we believe are helpful in defining the learning experiences for emerging clinicians. The five domains are worldview integration, theoretical integration, applied integration, role integration, and personal integration.[26]

Worldview integration refers to the attempt to reposition contemporary psychology in a coherent biblical worldview. This typically involves the identification of the alternative worldviews informing and shaping psychology and rethinking how psychology is altered or informed when grounded in a biblical worldview.

Theoretical integration attempts to modify psychological theories, especially personality theories, to fit with a Christian theological understanding, to cultivate psychological theories from the soil of Christian thought in a way that enhances psychological theory building, or to use psychological understandings to inform theology.

Applied integration is the attempt to either culturally adapt or accommodate secular interventions or helping approaches for use with a Christian population or to develop explicitly Christian interventions and helping approaches derived from Christian thought and practice. Tan has noted that clinical integration may occur either explicitly or implicitly. Explicit integration involves a treatment that declares itself to be Christian or that utilizes a recognizable technique shaped by Christian thought or practice. Implicit integration occurs when standard practice approaches are used in a way that is guided by Christian beliefs or values despite there being no explicit Christian identification.[27]

Role integration refers to living out role expectations and patterns arising from a psychological vocation in a particular context in a way that is faithful to one's Christian identity.

---

[26]William Hathaway and Mark A. Yarhouse, *The Integration of Psychology and Christianity: A Domain-Based Approach* (Downers Grove, IL: InterVarsity Press, 2021).

[27]Siang-Yang Tan, "Religion in Clinical Practice: Implicit and Explicit Integration," in *Religion and the Clinical Practice of Psychology*, ed. E. P. Shafranske (Washington, DC: American Psychological Association, 1996).

Personal integration refers to the personal discipleship journey of the Christian who is a psychologist (or, by extension, any similar profession). Personal integration is illustrated by what Farnsworth called "wholehearted integration."[28] While much early integration work was conceptual, focusing on the theoretical integration, for instance, personal integration recognizes the central role of cultivation of Christian passions for the fully developed integration project.

Hathaway and Yarhouse's domains bring the complexity of worldview to the level of graduate education. Among Christians, the idea of a biblical worldview has become a cliché. It has been accepted as a shallow categorical description of those who are on "God's side" as opposed to everyone else. Indeed, a biblical worldview helps us live in a nuanced reality where our identity rests in being the grace-full Christian.[29]

Conclusion

We have argued for the mastery of two realms—the mental health discipline and the biblical and theological discipline. Now we must teach wisdom, the integration of these two academic disciplines into effective ministry and mental health services.

Many mental health scholars have identified wisdom as an essential component of curriculum and training. Counseling scholars Hanna, Bemak, and Chang are among those who recognize that good human care is not merely a matter of learning theories. They draw from the ancient concept of wisdom, which is so very prominent in the Bible as an essential component of professional preparation. They write:

> The concept of wisdom contains the essence of personal growth and development. On reflection, the omission of wisdom in the counseling literature makes it seem conspicuous by its absence. Perhaps, through encouraging metacognitive skills, advanced empathy, dialectical

---

[28]Kirk E. Farnsworth, *Wholehearted Integration: Harmonizing Psychology and Christianity Through Word and Deed* (Grand Rapids, MI: Baker Book House, 1985).

[29]William L. Hathaway and Mark A. Yarhouse, *The Integration of Psychology and Christianity: A Domain-Based Approach* (Downers Grove, IL: InterVarsity Press, 2021).

thinking, perspicacity, and sagacity in practice, training, and research, we can learn to foster and cultivate master counselors with wisdom and reach a new plateau of effectiveness. Paradoxically, as ancient as wisdom itself may be as a concept, it may serve as a new paradigm for research to determine the characteristics, skills, and qualities of the highly effective multicultural counselor.[30]

Their list of skills that cultivate wisdom in counselors (encouraging metacognitive skills, advanced empathy, dialectical thinking, perspicacity, and sagacity in practice, training, and research) is like the description offed by Chatrow and Prior in describing the tasks of Christian discipleship to prepare the faithful to engage the complexities of life.

> Wisdom might seem like the most difficult virtue to attain, but it is helpful to think about the constituent parts of wisdom. *These qualities might include reflectiveness, experience, knowledge, deliberation and temperance. All of these are behaviors that can be practiced and cultivated by each of us and will lead to greater wisdom.*
>
> Even so, while human wisdom can be cultivated through practice, godly wisdom comes from God, and it surpasses all human wisdom. *"But the wisdom that comes from heaven is first of all pure, then peace-loving, considerate, submissive, full of mercy and good fruit, impartial and sincere"* (James 3:17).[31]

Mature integration of biblical truth and psychological knowledge applied in context requires mentoring and demonstrating. That we should teach wisdom is hardly a novel idea within the Christian tradition. Teaching wisdom is at the center of millennia of Christian discipleship. The pursuit of wisdom is central to Christian maturity.

James Sire can bring theological fluency, clinical competence, and identity integration to a conclusion with the idea that such efforts are

---

[30]Fred J. Hanna, Fred Bemak, and Rita Chi-Ying Chung, "Toward a New Paradigm for Multicultural Counseling," *Journal of Counseling & Development* 77, no. 2 (1999): 127.

[31]Joshua D. Chatrow and Karen Swallow Prior, *Cultural Engagement: A Crash Course in Contemporary Issues* (Grand Rapids, MI: Zondervan Academic, 2019), 59.

"a fundamental orientation of the heart, that can be expressed as a story or in a set of presuppositions . . . about the basic constitution of reality, and that provides the foundation on which we live and move and have our being."[32]

Preparing mental health professionals to be Christian thinkers and Christian doers is a crucial educational task. In the emerging zeitgeist where practitioners have an active role in church leadership, they must be prepared to live out their worldview as internalized psychology and theology.

Questions for Reflection

1. Articulate the distinction between pastor and counselor within the church community. What are the combined or overlapping roles, and what are the commonalities?

2. What criteria would you use to define "theological fluency" for Christian counselors working in the church? Should they be held to the same standard as pastors trained with seminary degrees?

3. What does it mean to you to be commissioned and commanded as a Christian mental health professional?

---

[32]James W. Sire, *Naming the Elephant: Worldview as a Concept* (Downers Grove, IL: InterVarsity Press, 2004), 122.

Guided by Grace

SUPERVISION IN CHRISTIAN MENTAL HEALTH PRACTICE

I N 1965 PSYCHOLOGISTS Robert Truax and Charles Carkhuff caused quite a stir. For seventy-five years the prominent therapy model was Freudian psychoanalysis. It declared that there was a special class of caregivers: the analyst, who through years of training could help the "suppressed" population be set free from its internalized anger existing in the form of anxiety. Truax and Carkhuff published a study that challenged that thinking. It followed people with mental health needs who were counseled either by graduate students with about one hundred hours of training or by seasoned professionals. "It was found that the trainees could be brought to function at levels of effective therapy quite commensurate to those of more experienced therapists in less than 100 hours of training."[1]

Later, Carkhuff wrote:

The helping professions have asked critical questions concerning the effectiveness of lay training and treatment programs. A review of these programs indicates (a) that lay persons can be trained to function at minimally facilitative levels of conditions related to constructive client change in relatively short periods of time, and (b) that lay counselors can effect significant constructive change in clients. An inference that

---

[1]Robert R. Carkhuff, and Charles B. Truax, "Training in Counseling and Psychotherapy: An Evaluation of an Integrated Didactic and Experiential Approach," *Journal of Consulting Psychology* 29, no. 4 (1965): 333.

we might draw is that whatever allows one individual to help another is not the sole and exclusive province of professional helpers.[2]

Some have protested Carkhuff's research methods and questioned the findings, but there is widespread agreement on one idea: substantial healing can occur when one person, prepared with basic caregiving skills, remains in the presence of another who is in distress. The application of this idea creates opportunity for churches that want to offer mental health ministry. We know it can work—that is conclusive. There is clear evidence that substantial portions of human care can be conducted by lay counselors, particularly under the supervision of properly trained mental health providers who serve as triage agents, mentors, and resource brokers.

Hold fast to the central theme of this book: the call for the reformation of the mental health "industry" and the empowering of churches to create ministries to address human need in local communities. Cling also to this portion of that theme: that graduate training institutions must prepare professionals for the emerging broader realm of mental health ministry, and the related theme that current professionals who forge links with churches should consider preparing themselves for extra-clinical tasks beyond their graduate training. The focus of this chapter is the importance of supervision serving as the backbone of such ministry.

Creating a care system within church contexts generates major logistic challenges. Foremost among them is ensuring the quality of care provided by churches. Some believe that the use of large numbers of lay counselors will leave scores of individuals vulnerable to inappropriate interventions by unqualified and unregulated "do-gooders." They believe that when intention is high and competence is low, harm will inevitably occur. We agree—and we don't.

---

[2]Robert R. Carkhuff, "Differential Functioning of Lay and Professional Helpers," *Journal of Counseling Psychology* 15, no. 2 (1968): 117.

We agree that irresponsible and misguided advice, direction, and "counsel" can be a danger to people at their most vulnerable moments. One need only to read the book of Job and the "help" he received from well-meaning friends, Eliphas, Bildad, and Zophar, to see that good intentions and earnest belief do not make up for incompetence.

> Stop and think! Do the innocent die?
>> When have the upright been destroyed?
> My experience shows that those who plant trouble
>> and cultivate evil will harvest the same. (Job 4:7-8 NLT)

Their "church counsel" followed bad theology: 1. God punishes evil-doers. 2. You are being punished. 3. You must be evil. 4. Therefore, Job, repent from your evil. Yikes! Job's life might have been different if his three "wise counselors" had a supervisor, and that supervisor, listening to the tape or reading the session notes, said, "Hold it right there, let's go back to some basic counseling skills 101 practice."

The guidance offered by the community of faith can be wrong, inappropriate, or not helpful. And worse, it can be harmful. Sometimes it can naively contribute to emotional injury, potential loss of life, or the destruction of families. It is without debate or contrary argument that every counselor—paid or volunteer, professional or lay, serving in a hospital, an office, a church, or around a kitchen table—should become learned, skilled, and as profoundly good as possible in this sacred activity of human care. God's servant Job deserved better. So also does everyone who seeks counsel from the community of faith.

The mental health profession has used the subdiscipline of supervision to ensure the public's protection from charlatans or well-intentioned caregivers who are mistaken in their actions. A primary purpose for supervision to be included in the academic preparation of all masters and doctoral-level clinicians is to promote their growth as they work with clients and to identify, remediate, or impede caregivers who show problems with professional competence (PPC).[3] "PPC includes difficulty acquiring or maintaining developmentally appropriate levels of skill, functioning, attitudes, and/or ethical, professional or interpersonal behavior in functional or foundational domains."[4]

As many as 40 percent of those seeking mental health treatments turn first to clergy for aid,[5] and because most of that support occurs in minimally trained, regulated, and supervised contexts, and because churches are offering mental health services with increasing frequency, we better have a thorough, comprehensive, and progressive system of supervision. This must include supervisory training for every student in graduate mental health training. We must also implement and evaluate systems and programs for supervision at every level of care—*especially within the church!* We want to make certain that the care delivered in churches is thoughtful, comprehensive, and safe.

The need for supervision in church-based mental health settings is more important when you consider the severity of suffering. Bledsoe and colleagues report that that the "National Institute of Mental Health found that clergy are just as likely as mental health specialists to interact with individuals seeking help for a Diagnostic and Statistical Manual of Mental Disorders (DSM) diagnosis, including individuals with severe mental illnesses such as bipolar disorder or schizophrenia."[6] We want to make certain that the clergy and those involved in mental health ministry do so with proper training,

---

[3]Janine M. Bernard and Rodney K. Goodyear, *Fundamentals of Clinical Supervision*, 6th ed. (Boston: Allyn & Bacon, 2019), 241.

[4]David S. Shen-Miller et al., "Professional Competence Problems in Training: A Qualitative Investigation of Trainee Perspectives," *Training and Education in Professional Psychology* 9, no. 2 (2015): 162.

[5]Andrew J. Weaver, "Has There Been a Failure to Prepare and Support Parish-Based Clergy in Their Role as Frontline Community Mental Health Workers: A Review," *Journal of Pastoral Care* 49, no. 2 (1995): 129-47.

[6]T. Scott Bledsoe et al., "Addressing Pastoral Knowledge and Attitudes About Clergy/Mental Health Practitioner Collaboration," *Social Work & Christianity* 40, no. 1 (2013): 23.

oversight, and boundaries. Mental health care in the church is growing fast, very fast. As it grows it must be within intentional, forward-thinking systems of care and protection for those it serves. Increasing the formal preparation and oversight of church-based ministry through greater collaboration with mental health professionals will improve the overall ministry and human services. To accomplish this task, the church must rely on master's- and doctoral-level clinicians who can oversee the work of pastors and lay counselors offering care. Enter supervision.

Training Every Clinician to Be a Supervisor

Supervision is a unique mental health discipline, focused primarily on developing clinical competence in mental health providers.[7] The quality of the supervision new professionals receive is the highest predictor of clinical competence. Bernard and Goodyear identify it as the "signature pedagogy" for mental health training. "Clinical supervision is the instructional strategy that most characterizes the preparation of mental health professionals."[8]

Currently, supervision as an academic discipline is offered primarily at the doctoral level. At the master's level it is rarely offered as part of an academic curriculum. Supervision in master's-level training usually occurs after graduation as part of one's continuing education. The absence of formal training at the master's level is noted by a team of prolific scholars in supervision theory and practice. They note that "although almost all (clinicians) will eventually supervise (Rønnestad et al., 1997), they are typically thrown into that role with no specific training for it and have to rely on what they learned from observing their own supervisors."[9]

---

[7]Bernard and Goodyear, *Fundamentals of Clinical Supervision.*
[8]Bernard and Goodyear, *Fundamentals of Clinical Supervision*, 2.
[9]Heidi Hutman et al., "Training Public Sector Clinicians in Competency-Based Clinical Supervision: Methods, Curriculum, and Lessons Learned," *Journal of Contemporary Psychotherapy* 51, no. 3, (2021): 236.

We advocate for the inclusion of supervision as the centerpiece of mental health care in churches. It must be foundational in the services rendered. If lay caregivers are to be engaged directly with others around human care at any level, there must be oversight by a trained professional to carry the vision and ensure the services provided are of the highest quality. This is the literal meaning of "super-vision." The friends of Job were not under supervision. No one was overseeing their work, assessing their training, or listening to their counsel to ensure that it was indeed godly, wise, accurate, and sound. Simply put, supervision is an essential skill that needs to be taught to all professional clinicians who aspire to work in mental health ministry.

The two most widely used definitions of supervision come from textbooks frequently used in psychology and counseling graduate training programs, one by Bernard and Goodyear and the other by Falendar and Shafranske. While their definitions are similar, both bring important nuances.

Bernard and Goodyear defined supervision in the first edition of their text in 1992. After the sixth edition of the work the definition has remained essentially the same and has been adopted in both the United States and United Kingdom as a standard of understanding. "Supervision is an intervention provided by a more senior member of a profession to a more junior colleague or colleagues who typically (but not always) are members of that same profession."[10] They enhance this definition with the following criteria: supervision must be evaluative and hierarchical, extend over time, and have the simultaneous purposes of enhancing the professional functioning of the more junior person(s); monitoring the quality of professional services offered to the clients that she, he, or they see; and serving as a gatekeeper for the particular profession the supervisee seeks to enter.

---

[10]Bernard and Goodyear, *Fundamentals of Clinical Supervision*, 9.

Falendar and Shafranske's description is similar, but with some slight differences. They define supervision as

> a distinct professional activity in which education and training aimed at developing science-informed practice are facilitated through a collaborative interpersonal process. It involves observation, evaluation, feedback, the facilitation of supervisee self-assessment, and the acquisition of knowledge and skills by instruction, modeling, and mutual problem solving. In addition, by building on the recognition of the strengths and talents of the supervisee, supervision encourages self-efficacy. Supervision ensures that clinical consultation is conducted in a competent manner in which ethical standards, legal prescriptions, and professional practices are used to promote and protect the welfare of the client, the profession, and society at large.[11]

They elaborate on the details of their broad definition with specifics. That supervision is an *intervention* suggests—similar to other types of interventions such as therapeutic, educational, consultative, or managerial—that supervision is both distinct from and like other activities or interventions. It includes an amalgamation of activities, including teaching, therapy, and evaluation, but is not contained by any one activity.

Bernard and Goodyear's reference to the importance of supervision being within the same profession is an important distinction. Almost all the literature addressing mental health supervision focuses on supervision within the educational process, that is, between professors and graduate students. The focus of this type of supervision is to help students form the knowledge, skills, and dispositions needed to become licensed clinicians like their professor/supervisors. This supervision is primarily educational. The definitions we've discussed here, and indeed most of the research, intervention models, and theory of growth in supervision focus on the *professional development*

---

[11]Carol A. Falender and Edward P. Shafranske, *Clinical Supervision: A Competency-Based Approach* (Washington, DC: American Psychological Association, 2008), 9.

of the emerging licensed caregiver. Almost all our supervision knowledge has to do with moving students from beginning to advanced competencies in the process of graduate, post-graduate, and prelicensure education. While our tools for supervision of the emergent professional are abundant, "the literature on supervision of lay Christian counseling is sparse and limited."[12] Hmmm. Sparse and limited is not what we want. Sparse and limited could become frequent and abundant if supervision training is provided at the master's level in all Christian graduate programs. For public safety, supervision training should be adopted as the standard for all mental health graduate students. The church, and the institutions that prepare people to become professionals in a church context, can become leaders in the thought and practice of triaging mental health care.

Supervision in mental health ministry must include education and training of lay providers, but its primary purpose is protective oversight. If the church embraces a community care system, and if practitioners are providing leadership to that system in the areas of program development, guidance and management, education, consultation, and most prominently, supervision, these areas must be part of their training and expertise. Direct observation of the work of lay counselors by viewing recordings and notes, and strategizing about treatment plans helps to ensure the proper placement of need to skill level and proper outcomes.

In addition to a protective focus, supervision in mental health ministry is educational. In this role, supervisors teach pathways of care that move the intuitive and highly motivated layperson through a guarded process of activities "Clinical supervision serves as the 'signature pedagogy' for developing ethical and effective counselors."[13] It is the process where novices in the mental health services form identity,

---

[12]Siang-Yang Tan and Eric T. Scalise, *Lay Counseling: Equipping Christians for a Helping Ministry*, rev. ed. (Grand Rapids: Zondervan, 2016), 136.

[13]Matt Casada, *Skill Competence and Identity Development in Counselor Trainees* (PhD diss., Regent University, 2022), 61.

internalize ethical practices, develop and implement strategies for care, assess previous experiences and plan for future intervention.

Michael Rønnestad and Thomas Skovholt are counseling scholars whose research provides important content on the creation of a counseling ministry. They have dedicated their careers to studying counselor development over the lifetime. By development, they mean the way counselors change with time to integrate new knowledge, personal maturity, advanced skill, and improved quality of care. "There are certain minimal features to the concept of development regardless of philosophical and theoretical orientation. The elements of change, order/structure and succession are thus basic elements of a concept of development."[14] In analyzing counselor development over the lifespan, they discovered stages associated with growth. They are:

- the lay helper
- the beginning student
- the advanced student
- the novice professional
- the experienced professional
- the senior professional

It is their first stage, the lay helper, which is most relevant to our purposes. Through interviewing hundreds of counselors in this stage, they inform us of the challenges faced and the tasks of supervision needed to address them.

The first challenge is to override their intuitive helping behaviors, which have been effective in nonformal efforts. They write that "the lay helper is guided by a personal epistemology and commonsense conceptions of how to assist others when in distress. He/she typically

---

[14]Michael H. Rønnestad and Thomas M. Skovholt, "The Journey of the Counselor and Therapist: Research Findings and Perspectives on Professional Development," *Journal of Career Development* 30 (2003): 7.

projects one's own solutions for the problems encountered."[15] The lay counselor can readily trust themselves more than they trust theories, interventions, protocols, and supervisors. We naturally trust what we know, not what we don't know. Supervisors of lay helpers build trust and form disciplines of self and systemic restraint so that the new counselor doesn't just "say what is felt or believed" but acts from knowledge grounded in established methods. Creating trust in content beyond and outside intuitive knowledge and experience is the most important indicator of the lay counselor's future success. The solution here is forming a relationship with an advanced clinician for the transmission of knowledge, formation of skills, structured rehearsal of knowledge and skill in applied contexts, and the continual discussion and oversight of the interactions between counselor and participant.

A second challenge in lay counseling supervision is the identification and respect of boundaries. Everyone called to care for people will be challenged to form limits in caring. For many, it is difficult to initially comprehend that caring too much creates harm, both to the recipient and the provider. Counseling is emotionally intense for both parties. "Strong identification with the person being helped and an unexamined quality of how best to assist can contribute to over-involvement, which may impede the reflective and investigative character of an effective helping process."[16] The experience can hit the counselor's affections and anxieties hard. If the caregiver gets pulled into the problem, he or she gets lost. Supervision helps maintain boundaries and objectivity, separating the provider's efforts from the other's pain. In other words, supervision reminds everyone that you can't take other people, or their pain, home with you. Without supervision, every caregiver is vulnerable to becoming part of the problem. The requirement of thousands of supervised hours for emerging

---

[15]Rønnestad and Skovholt, "The Journey of the Counselor and Therapist," 10.
[16]Rønnestad and Skovholt, "The Journey of the Counselor and Therapist," 11.

professionals gives credence to the importance of supervision in preventing over-involvement by helpers in the lives of participants. If the
pathway to formal licensure requires four thousand to eight thousand
hours of supervised work during and after years of academic training,
then how much more should supervision be required for the lay
counselor offering care in ministry contexts?

The final concept emphasized by Rønnestad and Skovholt addresses the relational connection between the helper and the participant. They note that lay helpers are more vulnerable to emotional
activation as they receive the pain-infused circumstances articulated
by those they serve.

> The concepts of sympathy and empathy may differentiate the emotion-
> ality of the lay and the professional helper. . . . Counselors/therapists'
> ability to regulate and control their emotional engagement is inherent
> in the conception of professional empathy. Metaphorically, one may
> say that in empathy, the helper puts on the shoes of the other, but the
> helper knows that the shoes are not his/her own. In the experience of
> sympathy, however, the helper has temporarily lost the ability to reg-
> ulate one's own emotional involvement and has temporarily forgotten
> that the shoes are not his/her own. The emotional activation in sym-
> pathy may be conceptualized as over-identification with the other.
> Over-involvement and strong identification may fuel an inclination to
> give specific and strong advice.[17]

Numerous principles can be gleaned from the research of Rønnestad
and Skovholt. Among the most important is helping lay counselors
separate their "lay-counselor self" from their "personal self." A lay
counselor may have gifts and a calling to minister to the addicted. He
or she might have fought that "addictive demon" for decades, and by
grace, support, and personal decisions was delivered from its grip. Now
their desire is to care for others in the same way that they were offered

---

care at crucial times of need. Their experience in recovery could be so powerful that they see every addict through their single experiential lens. Lay helpers bring themselves into the counseling room as the primary teaching tool. Their experience easily creates assumptions about what another should do to bring about healing. It's what they know. Supervision is where the lay counselor learns to blend themselves with external techniques, ethical limitations, and ideas beyond their experience. An effective lay counselor is one who becomes aware of self and informed by ideas beyond themselves. Supervisors make that possible. They guide, direct, and encourage the use of self to be blended with knowledge that may be beyond their understanding.

Second, supervision can provide reflection, and with reflection comes understanding. There must be an ongoing reflection of learning as it fits within the lay counselor's experience. We offer the experience of the lay counselor who grew up in a home where parental addiction and substance abuse was common. Their knowledge of substance abuse may provide compassion, insight, and empathy for the person affected by addiction. But the experience from childhood could invoke the powerful desire to rescue and might override the constraints that protect everyone from unintentionally perpetuating the problem in the name of trying to reduce it.

Third, supervision of lay counselors permits the formation of more complicated "cognitive maps." While we rely on our experience to interpret the emotional journey of those to whom we listen, sometimes the conceptual path understood by the lay counselor is insufficient. Supervisory learning creates options for the caregiver to pursue outside of experience. The caregiver with life experience is transformed into the caregiver who is informed of ideas beyond their experience and is able to use experience alongside knowledge and skill to encourage growth in others.

Fourth, anxiety is a common trait of beginning counselors. Facing anxiety with a supervisor creates trust. It is expressed in the language

conversation then focuses on creating interventions to begin to immediately address that particular need.

Aten says HDI provides volunteers with evidence-based tools. "The good news is, you don't have to be a professional psychologist to offer support that makes a difference," he said.

Mental Health First Aid offers another model to help volunteers to come alongside those in crisis. It teaches them to recognize signs of mental illness and substance use disorders and respond with initial help and support. An Australian nurse, Betty Kitchener, and Dr. Tony Jorm at Melbourne University started it in 2001. It has since trained a small army of 2.5 million people in the United States.

Omaha, Nebraska–based Fresh Hope has developed another short-term peer model that helps people pivot away from their pain toward hope in several conversations with a trained volunteer.

"It doesn't solve problems. It doesn't deal with their whole life problems," says Fresh Hope trainer Joy Stevens, a longtime master facilitator for the Trauma Healing Institute of the American Bible Society, "but it takes them from hopelessness to hope."

Fresh Hope offers online training for those who want to become "hope coaches." Volunteers learn how to listen, help people process their issue, and speak faith-based hope to them, often out of a small piece of a story from the coach's life.

"You do not give advice," says Stevens, "you learn how to listen and listen very deeply and well. You learn how to ask key questions . . . that get to the bottom of their pain and give away ideas for a way forward."

Supervision Through Christian Virtue

Terri Watson "upped our game" regarding ministry and supervision.[19] She took the discipline of supervision and made it Christian.

[19]Terri S. Watson, *Developing Clinicians of Character: A Christian Integrative Approach to Clinical Supervision* (Downers Grove, IL: InterVarsity Press, 2018).

Or rather, she didn't make it Christian. She demonstrated how the Christian tradition can speak to the process of supervision, making it better. Her book offers a dimension to supervision not found anywhere else in the professional literature. We believe training Christian mental health supervisors to offer oversight to lay and pastoral counselors will create a new discipline in the profession. Supervision training is not new. Its curriculum is basic for every doctoral-level psychology, counseling, social work, and marriage and family program. However, at the master's level, only marriage and family therapy has a robust training history for its clinicians. Even still, most of the education models for supervision training are for graduate mental health students and those seeking licensure. We must take the principles from supervision for professional clinicians and apply them to supervision for lay counselors. Training supervisors for oversight of lay counselors and pastors is a new discipline in which academia must create models, curricula, assessments, and evaluation rubrics. For the emerging academician who wishes to contribute significant research, study how to best create standards of care and supervisory oversight for the emerging applications to counseling ministry.

So, for academicians and students, the formation of ministry-centered care will create a new specialization. The professional counselors of the future must also become supervisors. These supervisors must be able to develop capable lay-level mental health caregivers, oversee their work, and prevent those who are not able to promote healing from functioning in this context.

Watson's framework, through which we can think Christianly about the supervisory process, includes four components: virtue and character, professional ethics, supervisory developmental methods, and spiritual formation. She suggests that clinical supervision is about building personal virtue and character into the lives of those who care for others. She writes,

The supervisor is part of God's overall work in the life of the supervisee, and they are both being formed by the Holy Spirit into Christlikeness. A virtue-informed approach recognizes that personal and professional development are inseparable, and that the most impactful supervision helps supervisees develop the habits and character that will prepare them to face the challenges of long-term mental health practice.[20]

Watson identified three purposes for supervision, all of which are essential to the work of effective human care within the church. They are "development of the supervisee toward competency, monitoring the quality of services provided by the supervisee to protect the welfare of the clients and finally, gatekeeping."[21] Each of these concepts warrants explanation.

Competency. Expertise carries you a long way. Watson's core argument is that virtuous Christian supervision (internal disposition) drives competency (external proficiency). Competency has to do with measurable external skills. We are advocating for the heavy utilization of often minimally trained lay counselors and pastors, therefore the importance of competency development cannot be stressed enough. Pulling from other sources, Bernard and Goodyear creatively describe counselors' three frames of competency. They are "known knowns" (I understand all that I know), "known unknowns" (I understand that I don't know much about . . .), and the always dangerous "unknown unknowns" (I don't understand that I don't know anything about . . .). Supervisors instill competence by creating movement in providers from incompetence to competence, and they do so by identifying and reducing the "unknown unknowns." Bernard and Goodyear refer to this as supervisory "metacompetence."[22] Counselors must teach, inspire, model, and instill competence in the nonprofessional caregiver. In supervision with minimally trained

---

[20]Watson, *Developing Clinicians of Character*, 27.
[21]Watson, *Developing Clinicians of Character*, 5.
[22]Bernard and Goodyear, *Fundamentals of Clinical Supervision*, 6.

caregivers, the greatest priority is on the "unknowns" of human care. Because of the absence of formal training and years of supervised experience, lay counselors do not know what they do not know. This potential danger is addressed through in-service training, open discussion between caregivers and supervisors, direct observation, proper screening, and assignment of cases with a match of need and skill set. Supervision provides that essential over-the-shoulder observation and direction. The trained professional mental health provider—functioning as supervisor—must oversee the competency development of each involved in the caregiving role.

Monitoring quality. Watson's second supervision purpose is the monitoring of services. The mental health professional not only instills competence, they must also have direct eyes on the processes of caregiving. Bernard and Goodyear reveal that this task is most likely avoided because of its potential to be "messy." "Most of the time, supervisors are able to perceive themselves as allies of their supervisees. Yet they also must be prepared, should they see harm being done to clients, to risk bruising egos of their supervisees or in extreme cases, even to steer the supervisee from the profession—an ethical obligation of the profession."[23] There is much to unpack here. Counselors, therapists, social workers, and psychologists must be prepared to be the stalwart defense of proper administration of care occurring in ministry contexts. This is a significant expansion of identity beyond the care provider to the care-provision overseer. This identity should be taught first in our master's and doctoral training programs, modeled in internship and supervised experiences for licensure, and supported by the church or ministry context leadership.

Gatekeeping. The third purpose of supervision identified by Watson is the responsibility of gatekeeping. The task of gatekeeping is to protect the public from harm by identifying those who should not

---

[23]Bernard and Goodyear, *Fundamentals of Clinical Supervision*, 16.

be providing services. Think of the metaphor of the gate as that which keeps the wolves out and the sheep in the fold at night. Ladany acknowledges that at the professional level, the gatekeeping role often fails the public by permitting some who are likely to cause harm in their efforts to continue. He states, "We have not properly considered the gatekeeping role, and as a result, we are graduating many therapists who have no business functioning in the role of therapists."[24]

Watson also speaks to this function:

> As supervisors, we manage these multiple roles by keeping in mind our primary responsibilities to the public, the profession, and the clinical training of the supervisee. We are also mindful of the power differential that our gatekeeping and evaluation roles require and the more vulnerable position this places our supervisees in.[25]

Watson considers the application of Christian virtues, such as faith, hope, love, wisdom, temperance, and courage, among others, to be a parallel process of Christian maturity. Christian virtue can reform and reshape the mental structure of the caregiver and, by extension, the care receiver. Paraphrasing renowned Christian philosopher Arthur Holmes, she asks how interacting with the content of supervision (e.g., Christian virtue) might bring forth change. Rather than ask, "What can I do with it (supervision experiences)? . . ." the right question is "What can it (supervision experiences) do to me?"[26] Her aspiration is that supervision be as transformative to the supervisee as the therapeutic potential is for the client. She concludes, "There is no doubt that we need the formative experience of clinical supervision as much for our own sake as for the sake of our supervisees."[27]

---

[24]Nicholas Ladany, "Does Psychotherapy Training Matter? Maybe Not," *Psychotherapy: Theory, Research, Practice, Training* 44, no. 4 (2007): 395.

[25]Watson, *Developing Clinicians of Character*, 34.

[26]Watson, *Developing Clinicians of Character*, 183.

[27]Watson, *Developing Clinicians of Character*, 191.

Conclusion: Forming Competence with Virtue

The foundation to the supervision described by Watson is virtue formation. Most supervision literature focuses on the external development of competence. Instilling and ensuring competence is the primary obligation of supervisors. Virtue, of course, does not replace competence. She states, "The virtue of practical wisdom in the mental health professions is best exemplified by habits and practices that lead to a lifelong commitment to two key professional virtues: maintaining professional competence and developing effective ethical decision-making skills."[28]

Supervision must confirm and sustain external competence, but it's insufficient if it omits the aspiration to become more like Jesus. To Watson, supervision will look like Christian discipleship but with a twist. Supervising to instill Christian virtue must also address clinical excellence. Our commission and command require a commitment to an ethics of preventing harm and doing good, as defined by the state or provincial government and the expectation of the profession. "Professional ethical principles and codes of conduct provide the standards by which competent professional practices are measured."[29]

There remains one virtue that is to be held in the highest regard as we consider the supervision of lay helpers as part of the solution to the mental health crisis: temperance or self-restraint. Watson suggests that "temperance is proposed as a foundational character virtue that protects clinicians from inflicting harm on others through cultivating the disciplines of self-awareness, humility, and self-control."[30]

Supervision is the primary path toward the ethical position of nonmaleficence, "to do no harm." The prevention of injury is encouraged by humble awareness of competencies and boundary limitations. Oversight of lay helpers by clinically competent professional mental

---

[28]Watson, *Developing Clinicians of Character*, 108.
[29]Watson, *Developing Clinicians of Character*, 27.
[30]Watson, *Developing Clinicians of Character*, 143.

health providers who are trained to offer a supportive presence to those who carry pain is essential. Supervision enlarges the scope of the professionals effectiveness, and it provides security that safeguards the public in the expansion of that scope.

Questions for Reflection

1. The Truax and Carkhuff research set off a storm of debate over who should be allowed to be a counselor. It hasn't stopped. What are the difficult truths on both sides of the argument?

2. How do you see Christian virtues such as faith, hope, love, wisdom, justice, temperance, and courage being applied in supervision?

3. The greatest challenge with the core thesis of this book is ensuring that lay counselors are sufficiently trained to provide care to specific needs. Consider how this can be addressed in supervision.

4. An essential task of supervision, described by Watson as "gate-keeping," is identifying those caregivers who lack the ability to be effective in the task. How does our Christian culture contribute to making this task easy, and what factors impede this essential component?

Bridging Perspectives

CONSULTATION BETWEEN CLINICIANS AND THE CHURCH

ASENIOR PASTOR RECEIVES a call from the middle school youth minister. He is a vibrant young seminarian with a passion for kids and a love for the church. He directs the middle school program that has about fifty sixth, seventh, and eighth graders and he has a problem. "Pastor, I have never seen this before. Yesterday, the parents of five students, both boys and girls called to say that their son or daughter has been 'coining' with other kids in the youth group!"

To which the pastor responds, "Um, what is coining? I've never heard of it. Is it bad?"

The youth pastor confesses that he had never heard of it either until a parent called, then another, and a third. By that time he realized that he better learn. "Coining is when you take an object, like a coin, and rub it on the skin back and forth with mild pressure until the skin bruises. You can make designs. It's been done in Asia for centuries to rid the body of 'negative energy.' The parents said that their kid learned it from another kid in the group. It's understood as 'self-abuse.' It's not as dangerous as cutting or mutilation. But five parents have called in the past twenty-four hours."

The pastor pauses, thinks, then says, "We better call Dr. Sarah for this one. And we should move quickly. I will set up a conference call today with her to get her input. Then we can inform the staff and your adult leaders of how we will address it. By tonight we can let parents know, and you can talk to students on Sunday. Maybe she can come to the fellowship hall after church on Sunday to be a resource to parents. If we are going to be helpful to parents and students, then we need to understand what we are dealing with here. But we should move quickly."

Dr. Sarah is a professional counselor who is often called by pastors of about five churches in her community to address mental health themes in congregations. As a Christian counselor she sees clients from these churches. But the churches themselves are also her clients as she serves them as a mental health consultant. She helps them with their "ifs and thens."

The importance of ifs and thens in church consultations cannot be overstated. *If* Christian clinicians are to actively create, provide, supervise, and guide human care ministries within the church, *then* they must be trained to act as consultants to pastors, elders, and church leaders. Concurrently, *if* churches aim to expand their mental health ministries, *then* utilizing mental health consultants to support pastors, elders, and leaders is a prudent decision. And *if* counselors are to be consultants to pastors regarding mental health practices, *then* they must be trained to be effective consultants in the master's and doctoral experience.

The reliance on a consultant is a strong articulation of leadership humility and wisdom. The use of a consultant demonstrates openness to ideas and expertise held by others with greater or different experience. Given the intricate knowledge base encompassing organizational development and human behavior at individual, couple, family, and group levels, mental health consultation in ministry is indispensable. However, being a consultant entails more than possessing knowledge or knowing where to find answers. The skill set required for consultation is distinct and must be honed through learning the discipline, mastering relevant literature, and contemplating ethical implications and best practices.

Clinicians who are passionate about the church's role in a town or city and share a concern for human welfare can offer consultation to congregational leaders and organizations. Competent consultants are invaluable to Christian leaders, particularly in helping churches address the suffering in their communities. A consultant can assist organizations in navigating unknown areas and create opportunities for quality relationships and appropriate interventions to take place.

Contemporary church leaders often find themselves overwhelmed and underprepared for those suffering from mental illness, trauma, or broken relationships. They already grapple with numerous responsibilities, such as managing business needs, preparing sermons, addressing budgets, and connecting with their communities.[1] Consultation with churches entails a deep appreciation for the demanding work of pastoral leadership. For example, in Exodus 17, Moses, the leader of the Israelites, experienced exhaustion in battle. His trusted partners, Aaron and Hur, provided him with support by holding up his arms until sunset, ensuring victory in battle (Ex 17:8-13). This biblical passage illustrates the importance of support and collaboration in leadership.

In order for a clinician to serve as an Aaron or Hur, they need to be trained in consultant competencies. Consultation is a discipline unto its own. Consultation skills related to mental health ministry draw on the ability to apply varied competencies of the mental health discipline to the context of the church.

The mental health consultant is a collaborator. He or she offers support to church leaders by coming alongside and metaphorically holding up their arms. Consultants are sought out for direction, problem solving, strategic growth planning, training, and other areas as determined by the church consultee. They offer advice

---

[1]A. W. Dominguez and M. R. McMinn, "Collaboration Through Research: The Multimethod Church-Based Assessment Process," in *Psychology and the Church*, ed. M. R. McMinn and A. W. Dominguez (New York: Nova Science Publishers, 2005).

from their area of expertise and use appropriate tools to enhance organizational functioning.

One aspect of collaborative consultation involves leader care. Consultants should check in personally on church leaders in ways that are appropriate and invited. Most pastors have high role demands and few individuals to provide listening support without any expectations in return. By being a trusted, confidential, listening ear, consultants can extend their reach in powerful ways to sustain and multiply supportive communities.[2]

Call Me, I Might Be Able to Help

Christian therapists and pastors can support each other strategically and strengthen the community in the process. Sometimes that looks like a brief consult.

Dr. David H. Rosmarin is a Jewish psychologist who teaches at Harvard Medical School and has networked with rabbis across the country for years. It's led to a variety of informal consults. Sometimes a ten-minute phone call with a rabbi can provide a few tools or the needed direction to help a member of their synagogue.

Rosmarin says it often allows the person who is suffering to work through an issue like anxiety on their own, rather than spending the time and money on a series of appointments with a psychiatrist or counselor.

On the flip side, pastors can support therapists and their work, not only with referrals but by coming alongside members of their congregation in therapy, just as they would if they were undergoing surgery or receiving treatment for cancer.

Jeremy Smith, a clinical mental health counselor in Ohio, encourages pastors to remember appointments with therapists and psychiatrists, offering prayer support and encouragement. They can also talk with the counselor if the client gives permission, and they can follow-up after therapy has ended.

---

[2]Dominguez and McMinn, "Collaboration Through Research."

The Pastor, the Sermon, and the Consultant

Consultation can take the form of being available for situations as they arise. Here's one example: in a local church, a new pastor had a vision for his congregation. With Father's Day approaching, he felt called to preach a sermon that would inspire fathers and men in the community to engage with local youth, regardless of whether they had children of their own. The sermon also encouraged the men to evaluate personal limits to their involvement, based on damaged relationships with their earthly fathers, and tied this to attributes of God and his Fatherhood.

The pastor, aware of potential inadvertent pain-causing blind spots in his writing, decided to seek the help of a trusted mental health consultant. Acknowledging that he had never experienced parental abuse or abandonment, the pastor wanted a review from someone who could identify any content that might be triggering or insensitive to others. The consultant, with expertise in human experience, empathy, family dynamics, relationships, trauma, therapeutic communication, attachment, and related research, reviewed the sermon and offered feedback.

Both the pastor and the consultant appreciated the opportunity to collaborate on a significant sermon. This particular partnership between a pastor and practitioner demonstrates the potential for powerful pulpit ministry supported by mental health consultants. By working together, they can review messaging with sensitivity to individual experiences and grounded in faith, ultimately fostering a more supportive and understanding community.

United in crisis. In times of crisis, a consultant can provide invaluable assistance, especially when decisions must be made quickly. For example, a consultant received a phone call from a pastor who explained a dire situation involving a dying child, a distraught father, and numerous other trauma-related issues within an overwhelmed and under-resourced family visiting from another city.

That evening, the consultant decided to spend time with the family, making members of their clinical team available at the hospital as the critical situation unfolded. Alongside the pastoral team, they continued providing support throughout the family's ordeal, ensuring appropriate stable care was in place and initiated before withdrawing from direct involvement.

Although the specific details must be withheld for confidentiality reasons, the consultant and their team were able to support the pastors during a challenging time. They applied crisis intervention skills by assessing the situation, clearly defining and prioritizing the problems, ensuring safety, offering immediate support, examining alternatives, engaging in collaborative planning, and remaining present until follow-up care was accessible.

It's not clear what the outcome might have been had the consultant not received the pastor's call. However, their participation in the family's care during a life-altering situation undoubtedly provided a sense of care and compassion during an incredibly dark time. The presence of the consultant and their team alongside the pastors contributed to the family's welfare and offered support amid the turmoil.

United in care. Although some pastors receive counseling training, many feel ill-equipped to manage mental health issues due to insufficient education.[3] They often face challenges in areas such as family relationships, substance abuse, lifestyle choices, and adjustment issues.[4] This situation presents a dilemma for pastors: whether to refer all such opportunities to professionals or to assist in mental health situations despite limitations in training or time. Consultants can help bridge this gap, supporting pastors in extending their reach and effectiveness. Instead of solely relying on referrals to outside counselors,

---

[3]Halle E. Ross and Matthew S. Stanford, "Training and Education of North American Masters of Divinity Students in Relation to Serious Mental Illness," *Journal of Research on Christian Education* 23, no. 2 (2014): 176-86.

[4]Harold G. Koenig, "Religion, Spirituality, and Health: The Research and Clinical Implications," *International Scholarly Research Notices Psychiatry* (2012).

the consultant can help churches deliver care within their ministry context, informed by science and grounded in pastoral care traditions.[5] Mental health consultants can assist pastors and church leaders in various ways, such as leader care, ministry development, and parishioner care, while fostering a trusting and confidential relationship.

The church, as a natural context for care, presents an opportunity for new paradigms of care delivery. Christians in the mental health field need to think differently about how services can be delivered through the church, using existing or readily available resources to support a larger number of people than the current system allows. Consider the following example.

In a small local church, a pastor found himself grappling with a challenging situation involving a congregant who had been presenting paranoia, delusions, and hostility. Knowing that he needed guidance, the pastor reached out to a trusted mental health consultant for a brief phone call. The consultant, who had been attending a conference several states away, had only forty-five minutes before their presentation. However, recognizing the urgency of the situation, they made time to discuss it with the pastor and his wife. The couple shared their efforts to support the troubled man, including regular phone calls, home visits, arranging medical care, and even holding onto his firearms for safekeeping.

The consultant listened attentively and asked questions. They offered additional resources for the pastor to explore, such as connecting the parishioner with a local mental health professional, suggesting support groups, encouraging family involvement, developing a crisis intervention plan, offering Mental Health First Aid training to the church staff, promoting mental health awareness within the church community, and ensuring ongoing support for the man in crisis.

---

[5]Jay E. Adams, *Competent to Counsel: Introduction to Nouthetic Counseling* (Grand Rapids, MI: Zondervan, 1986).

By incorporating these resources and action steps, the pastor was able to create a more comprehensive and effective plan to help the individual and protect the congregation as a whole. The consultation, completed in less than forty-five minutes, left the pastor and his wife with a number of practical resources and a palpable sense of appreciation, while the consultant felt grateful for the opportunity to assist in the challenging circumstance.

Equipping Students to Provide Effective Consultation to Faith Communities

Educators who instruct graduate students in providing consultation to faith communities should introduce students to the fundamental concepts of organizational consulting psychology within the context of religious organizations. This includes exploring specific applications to comprehend the dynamics of this field in various settings and identifying appropriate goals and methods for church-related work. Consultation education enables students to merge theoretical knowledge with practical experience. To ensure successful outcomes, students should receive training in specific aspects of consultation, such as measurement, evaluation, effectiveness, values, and ethics as this will equip them to apply scientific principles in consulting with churches. Teaching about individual, group, and organizational/systemic domains is crucial when working within a faith-based environment. Students must grasp the unique factors related to individuals within the church system and learn to intervene effectively on a personal level. Furthermore, a strong understanding of group-level dynamics—such as roles, interpersonal conflict, diversity, and interorganizational behavior—is necessary for implementing interventions with groups within the church organization.[6] In addition, training in organizational/systemic levels should encompass

---

[6]Edgar H. Schein and Peter Schein, *Organizational Culture and Leadership* (San Francisco: Jossey-Bass, 2010).

organizational theory, behavior, structure, ecology, effectiveness, diagnosis, culture, change, and ethics.[7]

Effective organizational intervention relies on a comprehensive understanding of the organization itself, regardless of whether the consultation addresses the entire organization or specific segments.[8] By acquiring knowledge in these areas, graduates will be prepared to assess and guide individuals, enhance team performance, and improve the overall quality of church systems.[9]

Beyond Counseling Referrals

With expertise in consultation, research, and assessment, clinicians can complement traditional counseling services while addressing various needs within the community.[10] Collaborating with church leaders enables these professionals to contribute to broader ministry efforts, creating a nurturing environment that fosters overall well-being.

Mental health professionals can provide vital support through both informal and formal consultations to religious leaders and their congregations. Informal consultation may involve guidance to pastors regarding situational concerns, personal needs, or family matters, while formal consultation may entail working with a church or its leadership to address broader issues or develop new programs, such as mental health outreach initiatives, crisis response teams, or support groups.[11]

Bridging the gap between mental health and spiritual guidance, collaborations between mental health professionals and pastors prove crucial in fostering a holistic approach to well-being. Reciprocal ministry partnerships between mental health professionals and pastors

---

[7]John P. Kotter, *Leading Change* (Cambridge, MA: Harvard Business Press, 2012).

[8]Schein and Schein, *Organizational Culture and Leadership*.

[9]Daniel Goleman, Richard E. Boyatzis, and Annie McKee, *Primal Leadership: Unleashing the Power of Emotional Intelligence* (Cambridge, MA: Harvard Business Press, 2013).

[10]McMinn and Dominguez, *Psychology and the Church*.

[11]McMinn and Dominguez, *Psychology and the Church*.

are essential for building a supportive network that fosters collaboration.[12] These partnerships facilitate knowledge exchange, resource sharing, and the development of joint initiatives and programs that integrate mental health and spiritual well-being, such as support groups for grief, divorce, or addiction recovery.[13] Furthermore, counseling professionals and pastors can engage in joint training and educational opportunities to enhance their skills and knowledge in both mental health and spiritual domains.

Working hand-in-hand, Christian clinicians and churches play a pivotal role in challenging mental health stigmas and championing wellness within congregations. By educating church members about prevalent mental health conditions and fostering spaces for candid conversations, churches can dismantle damaging stereotypes. Forming alliances with mental health entities amplifies this impact, ensuring congregants have easier access to essential resources. Especially during challenging times, cultivating resilience and mental fortitude is paramount. Christian clinicians can introduce and educate on vital tools such as stress management techniques, mindfulness exercises, and self-care routines. Additionally, they can facilitate the creation of supportive networks and peer groups for those navigating tumultuous life events.

Crisis intervention protocols are necessary for churches to address mental health emergencies effectively. Providers can work with churches to establish these standard practices and provide training to church staff and volunteers who will implement them. This collaboration ensures that churches have a plan and are prepared to support individuals in crisis.

Also, clinicians can collaborate with churches to conduct research and assessment. This helps churches ensure that their ministry

---

[12]McMinn and Dominguez, *Psychology and the Church.*
[13]Kenneth I. Pargament, Gina M. Magyar-Russell, and Nichole A. Murray-Swank, "The Sacred and the Search for Significance: Religion as a Unique Process," *Journal of Social Issues* 61, no. 4 (2005): 665-87.

effectively addresses congregants' needs, makes the best use of available resources, and maximizes their impact on the community. Research and assessment can provide valuable data to guide decision-making and program development, and contribute to the broader knowledge base on best practices in church-based mental health initiatives.

Internal Consultation

Mental health consultants who are members of or attend the church they consult for should be aware of potential pitfalls. Internal congregational consultation offers both advantages and disadvantages.[14] While possessing deep knowledge of church programs, staff, and cultural fluency, internal evaluators may also experience challenges such as reduced objectivity, competing priorities, and overestimation of their abilities.[15] Trust and intimate cooperation, key components for successful engagement, are notable advantages of internal consultation. However, consultants must remain cognizant of their influence on church settings and relationships, as well as the dual nature of their role.

Navigating the delicate balance between familiarity with church structure and maintaining objectivity is essential for internal consultants. Awareness of this tension, along with a commitment to the overarching goal of strengthening the community, can help manage this challenge. Open communication is critical for handling expectations and growing stakeholder relationships. By discussing limitations and availability, consultants can ensure alignment on performance and accessibility expectations. Moreover, internal church consultants are often tasked with acting as "translators of information" between various organizational groups and different levels of church leadership. To succeed in this role, they must demonstrate

---

[14]Jay A. Conger and Ronald E. Riggio, *The Practice of Leadership: Developing the Next Generation of Leaders* (San Francisco: John Wiley & Sons, 2012).

[15]J. Bradley Cousins and Elizabeth Whitmore, "Framing Participatory Evaluation," *New Directions for Evaluation* 1998, no. 80 (1998): 5-23.

exceptional communication skills, sensitivity to differing goals, and the ability to maintain authenticity, integrity, and trustworthiness across all parties.[16]

Divergent Roles

The following scenarios provide a limited overview of the wide range of potential practice involvement for the Christian clinician in the church. To better understand the full scope of involvement, it is essential to examine the roles counselors may adopt—such as member, professional, or consultant—and the unique ways they integrate these role variations within their faith community.

Scenario 1. Douglas has numerous pastoral connections in his community and is regarded as a trusted referral resource beyond his own church. He offers reduced-rate services to clients who come from church referrals. His role can be characterized as a member-professional, which is a typical practice for many Christian practitioners. Establishing oneself as an ally in the community is crucial and provides needed and trusted care for individuals.

Scenario 2. Andrea is heavily involved with her church and has collaborated with it in various capacities. She offers informal consultation on parishioner needs and ministry response outside of a designated time or space, often through email, text, or phone calls. In addition, she accepts church referrals for traditional counseling at her private practice and has established a scholarship arrangement with the church to help cover costs for those in need. Andrea's role can be described as member-professional-consultant.

Scenario 3. Anna accepts referrals from her congregation and neighboring churches and has an additional space at her church where she is available once a week. She provides support to church staff, assists walk-in community members with pressing needs, and consults

---

[16]Peter Block, *Flawless Consulting: A Guide to Get Your Expertise Used* (San Francisco: Pfeiffer, 2011).

with the church team on intervention levels, caregiver training, program support, and emotional wellness for leaders. She does not charge for her involvement at the church. Instead, she views this dedicated time as her primary ministry to her faith community. Anna also embodies the member-professional-consultant role, extending her assistance beyond referrals and addressing triaging of those in need, while affirming and enhancing the church's ministry offerings.

Scenario 4. Josh consults with his church in multiple areas and has established deep friendships with local pastors. He considers these relationships to be mutually beneficial for both personal and collaborative care, while remaining ethically aware of dual relationships. In partnership with his pastor friends, he has developed a fee structure for various professional activities. Some services, such as providing input on existing ministry care structure and programs, are offered without charge, while more time-consuming tasks like large-scale program evaluations are invoiced to the church. Josh's role can be seen as a combination of member-professional-consultant, emphasizing mutuality and adaptability to evolving needs and activities.

These scenarios underscore the significance of adaptability, collaboration, and ethical consciousness when offering consultation within faith communities. It is crucial for clinicians to be open to diverse roles and opportunities for engagement, while attending to the unique needs and values of the faith community they serve. This approach not only allows professionals to make a meaningful impact on the individuals they counsel but also fosters a stronger connection between mental health professionals and the broader religious community, ultimately promoting mental and emotional well-being across a wider spectrum of people.

Qualities of an Effective Consultant

Empirical evidence indicates that expertise in subject matter, context-appropriate appearance, advanced interpersonal skills, and exemplary communication abilities are crucial in the consulting process.[17] Dr. Katheryn Benes, a psychologist specializing in parish-based consultation, proposed a memorable acronym to describe these qualities: consultants should have TEA with their consultees. *T* represents trustworthiness, *E* signifies expertise, and *A* denotes attractiveness.

Trustworthiness encompasses character attributes such as honesty, discretion, adaptability to organizational hierarchies, availability, punctuality, engagement, shared vision, task continuity, and productivity.[18] In order to be perceived as trustworthy, consultants must demonstrate integrity and commitment to their clients and the consulting process.

Expertise involves managing the consultation project effectively, comprehending organizational behavior and culture, employing critical questioning, soliciting feedback, delineating (and redefining as needed) collaborative direction, and drawing on academic training and research to execute necessary steps and guarantee informed recommendations or outcomes.[19] This level of expertise requires a commitment to continuous learning and an ability to apply theoretical knowledge to real-life situations.

Attractiveness refers to the way consultants present themselves, including professionalism in appearance and language, verbal and written communication, and the presentation of their work.[20] To maintain professional attractiveness, consultants must assess organizational norms and adapt their personal style accordingly. For instance, while the language of the social sciences can be technical and laden with jargon, it is essential to modify communication whenever possible to ensure clarity and comprehension, demonstrating respect for the client and safeguarding understanding. Likewise, avoiding an

---

[17]Block, *Flawless Consulting.*
[18]Schein and Schein, *Organizational Culture and Leadership.*
[19]Block, *Flawless Consulting.*
[20]Schein and Schein, *Organizational Culture and Leadership.*

overly casual demeanor is equally important. The consultant's objective is to strike a balance that embodies competence, authenticity, and unpretentious sophistication.

Begin with Relationship

For the mental health church consultant, the relationship with the clergy lays the foundation for the work. McMinn and colleagues emphasize the significance of relationship, communication, respect, common values, common goals, trust, complementary expertise, and spiritual and psychological mindedness when collaborating with the church.[21] The authors provide recommendations for mental health professionals to develop both basic and advanced competencies in partnering effectively with clergy to support the well-being of their clients. These qualities cannot be forced or artificial. Cultivating genuine relationships with pastors can take time, and it should. Conversations may get difficult, especially around topics such as faith and healing, or perspectives on lifestyle issues. In these moments, it's paramount to exemplify stellar communication, active listening, and a dialogue rooted in respect. It's through these genuine interactions that trust is nurtured and strengthened over time.

In one such real-life exchange, a lead pastor questioned a consultant while working on church organizational development. The pastor's questions included how one should address a teen who identified as the opposite gender, how to respond to a same-sex couple that wanted to serve in the church and asking about the consultant's personal theological perspectives. The consultant recognized that the pastor wanted to understand his values and how congruent they would be within the church, along with how he communicated, and saw the conversation as a valuable opportunity to consider the goodness of fit in collaborating. Having honest and

---

[21]Mark R. McMinn et al., "Psychologists Collaborating with Clergy," *Professional Psychology: Research and Practice* 29, no. 6 (1998): 564.

respectful communication with a pastor or any other individual around sensitive issues is essential for fostering understanding and maintaining a healthy relationship.

To facilitate such conversations, consultants can rely on some essential elements that contribute to good communication. These include active listening, being fully present and attentive, and avoiding interruptions. This demonstrates respect for the other's perspective and helps create an open dialogue. Trying to empathize by putting oneself in the other person's shoes can lead to a better understanding of their feelings and emotions. This approach helps consultants to communicate more compassionately and respond with sensitivity. Adopting a nonjudgmental attitude, approaching the conversation with an open mind, and avoiding assumptions about the other person's beliefs or intentions fosters an atmosphere of trust and mutual respect.

When expressing thoughts and feelings, using familiar "I" statements, such as "I feel" or "I think," can prevent the conversation from becoming accusatory or confrontational. Staying focused on the specific sensitive topic at hand and avoiding unrelated concerns or past issues is important. If possible, choose the right time and place for the discussion by selecting a quiet, private setting and ensuring that both parties are calm and not rushed. Rescheduling difficult conversations if the setting is not conducive to privacy or time constraints may also be necessary.

Sharing thoughts and opinions honestly but tactfully, being mindful of tone, and avoiding harsh or critical words that could escalate the situation are all crucial. Displaying humility and acknowledging that some questions may have elusive or uncertain answers can foster a more open atmosphere. Encouraging the other person to share their thoughts and feelings by asking open-ended questions that invite more than a yes or no answer can lead to a more in-depth and meaningful conversation.

Seeking common ground by identifying shared values, beliefs, or goals can help bridge differences and establish a foundation for mutual understanding. Finally, being willing to compromise, recognizing that both parties may need to make concessions to resolve sensitive issues, and approaching the conversation with a willingness to find a solution that is acceptable to both parties is key.

By employing these techniques, consultants can engage in respectful communication around sensitive issues, foster mutual understanding, and build stronger relationships with pastors and lay leaders. This is the foundation of the proposed collaborative consultation. And this effort, carried out by Christian mental health professionals around the globe, one church community at a time, can have a profound effect.

A Partnership Approach: Pastors and Consultants

Richard Kidd served as a pastor in Virginia Beach and, in this role, he held a deep working knowledge of the church, understanding its distinct traditions, history, structure, mission, personality, and character. This profound insight uniquely positioned him to recognize the limitations of the traditional "messy outsourcing" model where parishioners requiring counseling were sent to external counselors. Influenced by his mentor, Kidd innovated a new structure for the church's care ministry, one that blended the church's core values with the evolving needs of its parishioners. This revamp manifested in a detailed seven-tiered care offering system, with six of those levels provided directly within the church itself.

Upon seeking assistance, a parishioner would first undergo an intake assessment with a licensed counselor who would then determine the level of care required. Depending on their needs, they might receive targeted support from trained paraprofessional laypeople, counseling interns under supervision, or in-house counseling professionals for more specialized therapeutic interventions. Only in situations demanding expertise beyond the church's capabilities would a parishioner be referred to an external professional, making such referrals infrequent.

In this system, Kidd wore the hat of an in-house consultant, while an external clinical mental health professional acted as an additional consultant, initially not being a part of the church's staff. Their collaborative efforts transformed the church's care ministry, leading to the creation of a caring community rather than just a counseling center.

However, this innovative approach to caregiving had its lifespan. After Kidd's departure, the meticulously constructed in-house care system was dismantled, and the church reverted to the original model of outsourcing counseling needs to a local counseling firm. The success of Kidd's model was evident, as it catered to a pressing need, offering community-centric care that resonated with the church's parishioners. Yet, its dissolution underscores the challenge churches face in maintaining such an intricate system without a dedicated professional guiding, managing, and supporting the efforts continuously. Such a model, despite its potential benefits, requires a consistent commitment and vision, which can be a daunting task for any church in the absence of a persistent champion like Kidd.

Implementing and sustaining innovative care models within church settings often demands a robust infrastructure and unwavering dedication from professionals. The dissolution of Kidd's model post his involvement showcases the vulnerabilities of such initiatives when they are not continuously supported by an advocate deeply attuned to the church's unique identity and values.

Consultation as Prevention

Church-based consultation holds immense potential in curbing the progression of mental health challenges among congregation members. Drawing from community psychology, the emphasis is on initiatives that uplift the well-being of church attendees. Within this framework, it's pivotal to integrate primary, secondary, and tertiary preventive measures tailored for the church environment.

Primary prevention serves as a proactive approach, acting as a protective barrier akin to a fence poised at the edge of a cliff, preventing potential mishaps. Secondary prevention, on the other hand, functions as an early detection and intervention mechanism, much like a safety net positioned just below the cliff's edge, catching those on the verge of falling. Tertiary prevention is directed at offering aid and support to those who have already experienced a fall, providing care and assistance in their recovery journey.

Examples of primary prevention within the church include sermons, premarital counseling, discipleship and mentoring groups, Bible study meetings, Sunday school classes, and youth groups, which strengthen individuals who are not necessarily in crisis.[22] Consultation with a faith-based professional can prove valuable in designing or reviewing curricula for such initiatives. While mental health professionals can also consult on tertiary activities like church-based recovery group program development or setting up counseling services, secondary prevention appears to be an underutilized area for collaboration between clinicians and churches.[23]

Mental health professionals, with their vast expertise spanning counseling skills, group dynamics, child development, family systems, and organizational development, can be instrumental in fortifying church ministries that seek to support and engage their communities. Parents striving to foster deeper connections with their children can find guidance through parenting groups led by these experts, which blend research-backed developmental knowledge with effective interventions. For youth groups experiencing dwindling attendance, consultants can offer program evaluations to

---

[22] J. David Hawkins, Richard F. Catalano, and Michael W. Arthur, "Promoting Science-Based Prevention in Communities," *Addictive Behaviors* 27, no. 6 (2002): 951-76.

[23] Abraham Wandersman and Paul Florin, "Community Interventions and Effective Prevention," *American Psychologist* 58, nos. 6-7 (2003): 441. See also Kathryn M. Benes, Joseph M. Welsh, Mark R. McMinn, Amy W. Dominguez, and Daniel C. Aikins, "Psychology and the Church: An Exemplar of Psychologist-Clergy Collaboration," *Professional Psychology, Research and Practice* 31, no. 5 (2000): 515-20.

unearth the underlying issues and suggest evidence-based strategies for revitalization.

Furthermore, these professionals can collaborate with church leaders to develop secondary prevention efforts aimed at early identification and intervention of potential mental health or behavioral issues within the congregation. This could include hosting workshops on recognizing signs of stress, anxiety, or substance abuse, and providing resources or referral systems for those in need. They can also offer training sessions for church staff and volunteers, equipping them with the skills to support members going through challenging times. Additionally, consultants can organize peer support groups or mentorship programs within the church, creating safe spaces for sharing and growth. By forming a synergistic partnership, consultants and church ministries can proactively address challenges and promote holistic well-being within their communities.

A Shift to Indirect Care

The call for a paradigm shift in the approach to church-based mental health collaborations is both urgent and imperative. While the prevailing focus for most mental health practitioners has been on direct care provision, there's a burgeoning need to explore avenues that fortify the church's mental health backbone.

Transitioning from a traditional direct service model, where congregants are simply referred to Christian clinicians for therapy, to an indirect model which cultivates a symbiotic relationship between clinicians and pastors, we not only respect the church's foundational role in spiritual care but also expand its capacity to support a broader spectrum of its members.

An indirect care approach positions mental health professionals as pivotal contributors to organizational growth and program refinement within church settings. This strategic collaboration enriches mental health support, fostering a spiritually and emotionally thriving congregation.

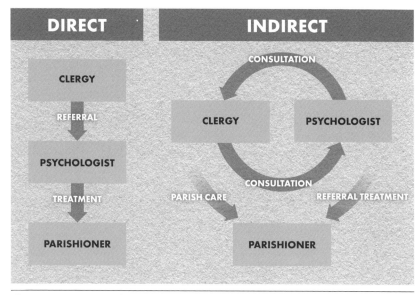

Figure 3. Models of service delivery

Direct consultations with church leaders empower Christian mental health professionals to spearhead the design and enhancement of church-centric mental health initiatives.[24] This synergy encompasses comprehensive program audits, pinpointing growth opportunities, and advising on the alignment of mental health initiatives with pastoral values.[25] Furthermore, these professionals can guide churches in assessing the reach and impact of their mental health endeavors, ensuring they resonate with congregants' needs and nurture overall well-being.

Given the central role churches play in community life, the indirect care model promises a more nuanced mental health framework. This approach invites clinicians to provide a suite of consultative services, from crisis response strategies to group therapy techniques. This shared expertise allows church leaders to seamlessly weave mental

---

[24]Curtis J. VanderWaal, Edwin I. Hernandez, and Alix R. Sandman, "The Gatekeepers: Involvement of Christian Clergy in Referrals and Collaboration with Christian Social Workers and Other Helping Professionals," *Social Work & Christianity* 39, no. 1 (2012).

[25]Schein and Schein, *Organizational Culture and Leadership.*

health insights into their pastoral outreach. Moreover, specialized workshops and training sessions can be introduced, enlightening the congregation about mental health nuances, effective interventions, and self-care strategies vital for those in ministerial roles.

Customized resources, reflective of a congregation's unique requirements, can be crafted. Informative pamphlets, study guides, and support group materials can be curated to address a spectrum of mental health concerns, from mild stressors to complex challenges. This proactive approach not only heightens awareness but also fosters an environment where seeking help is encouraged and destigmatized. Establishing support frameworks, be it through intimate groups, peer mentoring, or digital platforms, further solidifies the church's commitment to mental well-being. The potency and outreach of these initiatives can then be measured through meticulous research and evaluations, ensuring they resonate with and effectively address the needs of the church community.

In sum, the embrace of an indirect care model sets the stage for a more profound and integrated alliance between mental health professionals and churches. By accentuating consultation, program development, and impact assessment, the church amplifies its role as a sanctuary for both spiritual and mental well-being. Such a collaborative paradigm not only enriches the spiritual journey of its members but also fosters a community that's resilient, informed, and empathetic.

Questions for Reflection

1. How do my personal values and beliefs as a Christian mental health provider align with the church's teachings and practices, where do they differ, and how can I ensure that I maintain a balance between maintaining my professional integrity and respecting the church's doctrines?

2. As a Christian clinician, in what ways can I effectively identify and address potential areas of concern within the church community while fostering a trusting and supportive environment that encourages open dialogue and growth?

3. How can I continuously develop my understanding of the unique needs and challenges faced by the church community, in order to provide more tailored and effective consultation services?

Fostering Sanctuary

ADVANCING CHURCH DEVELOPMENT AND EVALUATION

ONCE UPON A TIME, in a quaint little town, a church named Grace Haven was struggling with declining membership and engagement. Pastor John, along with the church leaders, decided to explore organizational development as a means of revitalizing the congregation. They brought in a consultant to assist, understanding that fresh eyes can be an asset. The consultant worked to understand the church's goals, gathered information from stakeholders, and used the data to create a collaborative plan to improve engagement.

The first step helped to create small groups to improve communication and connection among members. These groups led individuals to feel a deeper sense of belonging and fostered a supportive environment. Next, the consultant provided leadership training for church leaders and volunteers. This enhanced decision-making, conflict resolution, and guidance skills, making the church's leadership more effective. To further solidify their direction, the church leaders engaged in strategic planning. This process helped them define a clear mission and vision, ensuring their ministry efforts were more focused. Grace Haven also sought to strengthen its connections with the local community by engaging in outreach programs and partnership-building efforts. This allowed the church to become an integral part of the community, fostering collaboration and service. Last, the consultant recommended sustainable ministry planning, based on assessing needs and resources, improving the church's stewardship. This ensured the long-term sustainability of its ministries and operations.

Over time, Grace Haven experienced a transformation. Membership and engagement grew, the congregation became more connected, and the church enjoyed a renewed sense of unity and purpose. The organizational development initiatives had created a nurturing environment that promoted spiritual growth, well-being, and connection, making Grace Haven a shining example of how this work can revitalize a congregation and its community.

Organizational development, a pivotal aspect of enhancing a church's relational dynamics and operational efficacy, stands as a notable strength that Christian mental health professionals bring to the table. For consultants to be truly transformative, they must delve deeply into the heart of the church's organizational ethos, culture, and objectives. This immersive understanding mirrors the depth counselors seek with their individual clients and underpins impactful church consultation.

To chart a precise roadmap for change, consultants should meticulously explore the church's foundational pillars: its mission, structural design, interpersonal dynamics, incentives, leadership tenets, and other factors shaping its function. By tailoring their interventions to resonate with the church's distinct character and needs, consultants are better positioned to navigate the intricate nuances of ministry and bolster those entrusted with its leadership.

At its core, the aim of organizational development within a church context is to revitalize its operational matrix, enriching both its personnel dynamics and relational ambiance. Church consultants endeavor to foster an invigorating environment characterized by a unified vision, adept leadership, enhanced collaboration, and adept problem resolution. By assisting churches in pinpointing and rectifying their operational gaps, consultants catalyze a culture of enduring self-reliance and continuous improvement.

The action research model, emphasizing problem identification, client collaboration, and actionable solutions, stands as an invaluable tool for church consultants. This framework propels the church into a proactive, introspective learning journey. Consultants, partnering closely with the church, facilitate dialogue around the collated data, assisting in pinpointing core challenges, tracing their origins, and crafting actionable strategies for resolution. Such a cooperative methodology not only equips the church with robust tools for introspection but also ignites a cycle of rejuvenation and self-improvement.[1] Guided by this model, churches embark on an introspective journey, characterized by active learning and self-assessment. Collaboratively examining the collected data with consultants, churches are able to discern and rank pressing issues, trace back to their underlying causes, and formulate actionable strategies for mitigation. Such a partnership not only equips the church with incisive tools for introspection but also sets the stage for a revitalized and self-sustained future.[2]

Examples of organizational development initiatives in churches include:

- *Leadership development:* Providing training and resources to church leaders to improve their decision-making abilities and understanding of the congregation's needs.[3]

- *Team building and collaboration:* Facilitating activities and workshops to strengthen relationships among church staff and volunteers and improve communication.[4]

---

[1]Kurt Lewin, "Action Research and Minority Problems," *Journal of Social Issues* 2, no. 4 (1946): 34-46.

[2]Roger D. Evered and Gerald I. Susman, "An Assessment of the Scientific Merits of Action Research," *Administrative Science Quarterly* 23, no. 4 (1978): 582-603.

[3]Kevin Hall, "Leadership Modeling: Christian Leadership Development Through Mentoring as Informed by Social Learning Theory," *Journal of Applied Christian Leadership* 14, no. 2 (2020): 28.

[4]Katarina Katja Mihelic, Bogdan Lipicnik, and Metka Tekavcic, "Ethical Leadership," *International Journal of Management & Information Systems* 14, no. 5 (2010).

- *Strategic planning:* Assisting churches in creating a clear vision and mission, setting measurable goals, and developing strategies to achieve them.[5]

- *Conflict resolution:* Providing mediation services and training church leaders in effective conflict resolution techniques to address issues that may arise within the congregation or between church staff and volunteers.

- *Staff and volunteer training:* Offering training programs and resources to equip church staff and volunteers with the skills and knowledge needed to effectively serve the congregation and community.

- *Organizational structure and governance:* Assessing and recommending changes to a church's structure and governance systems to improve efficiency, communication, and decision-making.[6]

- *Financial management and stewardship:* Assisting churches in developing sustainable financial practices, improving budgeting, and promoting responsible stewardship of resources.[7]

- *Community outreach and engagement:* Supporting churches in building relationships with their surrounding communities and identifying opportunities for service and collaboration.[8]

Integrating organizational development opportunities within church consultation can be pivotal in shaping an environment that not only addresses mental health issues but also elevates overall well-being and fortifies mental health resources for both the congregation and the broader community. Such initiatives can transform the

---

[5]Thom S. Rainer, *I Am a Church Member: Discovering the Attitude That Makes the Difference* (Nashville: B&H Publishing, 2013).

[6]Gary L. McIntosh and Samuel D. Rima, *Overcoming the Darkside of Leadership* (Grand Rapids, MI: Baker Books, 1997).

[7]George Barna and David Kinnaman, eds., *Churchless: Understanding Today's Unchurched and How to Connect with Them* (Carol Stream, IL: Tyndale House Publishers, 2014).

[8]R. J. Sider, *Churches That Make a Difference: Reaching Your Community with Good News and Good Works* (Grand Rapids, MI: Baker Books, 2005).

church into a beacon of growth, connection, and stability, enhancing its service to its members and the surrounding community.

One evident benefit of these initiatives is the enhancement of communication and teamwork. By embracing team-building activities, everyone from church members to staff and volunteers can forge deeper bonds and more refined communication pathways. This unity fosters a harmonious and collaborative environment. Moreover, targeted training sessions can refine the leadership acumen of church figureheads, empowering them with sharper decision-making, conflict navigation, and a more profound ability to guide their flock.

A strategic planning approach can crystallize the church's vision and mission, endowing it with a renewed clarity and purpose. This clear direction can galvanize more impactful ministerial actions. Furthermore, by reaching out and forging new alliances, churches can bolster their community ties, paving the way for enriched service opportunities and collective endeavors. By also adopting sustainable financial strategies, churches can ensure their operations are both efficient and future-proof, safeguarding the longevity of their missions.

Embedding organizational development strategies within church consultations can profoundly rejuvenate institutional health and vigor. Addressing inherent challenges, amplifying well-being, and enhancing mental health outreach not only cultivates an environment conducive to individual and spiritual wellness but also magnifies the church's positive footprint on its members and the expansive community it serves.

Enhancing Church Programs Through Development and Evaluation

The integration of program development and evaluation into church settings not only contributes to the effectiveness of their activities and use of facilities but also promotes a culture of learning and continuous improvement.[9] This culture fosters collaboration among church staff, volunteers, and congregants, leading to the identification of best practices, the adaptation of new strategies, and the achievement of the church's mission. To promote this kind of environment, consultants can encourage churches to emphasize program evaluation at all levels of the organization. Providing training and resources for church leaders, staff, and volunteers to understand and engage in the evaluation process is essential. This may include workshops, seminars, or online training modules that focus on evaluation techniques, methodologies, and ethical considerations. Consultants can also assist churches in establishing a systematic approach for monitoring and evaluating their programs and activities regularly. This may involve the use of logic models, performance indicators, and data collection systems that facilitate the tracking of program outputs and outcomes. External evaluation can provide valuable insights and an unbiased perspective on the effectiveness of a church's programs and initiatives.

It is crucial for consultants to help create an environment that encourages open communication, feedback, and reflection. By fostering a culture of transparency and accountability, all stakeholders can contribute to the evaluation process, voice their concerns, and share their experiences. This collaborative approach can lead to more accurate assessments of program effectiveness, as well as the identification of areas for improvement and innovation. The integration of program development and evaluation into church settings not only enhances the effectiveness of their activities, programs, and facilities but also promotes a culture of learning, collaboration, and continuous improvement. By providing resources for evaluation, churches can foster this culture, ultimately enabling them to better serve their congregation and fulfill their mission.

---

[9]Michael Quinn Patton, "The Ongoing Evolution of Utilization-Focused Evaluation," in *Evaluation Roots: Theory Influencing Practice*, ed. Marvin C. Alkin and Christina A. Christie (New York: Guilford, 2023), 183.

Nurturing Healthy Church Communities:
The Power of Data-Driven Support Groups

The design, implementation, and continual assessment of any church program lies at the heart of its success. It's not enough to merely start a ministry—the real power lies in continuous reflection, reassessment, and adaptation. From identifying the unique needs of the community to implementing the program and continually monitoring its impact, each stage plays a crucial role in nurturing a supportive and resilient church.

The initial stage involves conducting a thorough needs assessment. This step provides the foundation for the planning process by uncovering the specific issues to be addressed, identifying who or what is affected by these problems, and revealing their scale and impact. For instance, if a church plans to offer a divorce support group, a needs assessment could show critical factors such as the number of divorced people in the area, the level of interest in such a group, and whether the proposed timing and structure of the group are appropriate. The assessment results then help the church to ensure the program meets the true needs of the community.[10]

Identifying the specific target population is the next step. This could range from individuals to groups or even whole communities. It guides the planning process, informs future marketing efforts, and ensures alignment with the church's overarching goals. For instance, if a ministry aims to support marriages within both the church congregation and the larger community, it must identify and understand the needs of those at risk and the demand for the proposed program.

With the needs and target population identified, a "gap analysis" must be performed. This process compares the current situation with the desired one, thereby revealing the gap that the proposed ministry

---

[10]Peter M. Kettner, Robert M. Moroney, and Lawrence L. Martin, *Designing and Managing Programs: An Effectiveness-Based Approach* (Los Angeles: Sage, 2015).

program should address. This information identifies the nature of the problem and develops a targeted approach to address it. After identifying the needs and gaps, it's time to prioritize them and propose potential solutions. The church must evaluate the possible interventions, considering factors like cost-effectiveness, input from church leaders, and the size of the target population. This step also involves assessing the skills and abilities of the ministry leaders and volunteers who will be conducting the interventions.

Once the program has been designed, the next crucial phase is implementation. In this stage the proposed solutions are put into action. This requires careful monitoring to ensure the intended services are being delivered, the target populations are being reached, and the program leaders are adequately qualified. Additionally, this phase requires a keen eye on the ground to spot any issues that surface and make the necessary adjustments.

Despite the importance of the design and implementation stages, the work isn't over once a program is up and running. Establishing a cycle of continual improvement ensures the ministry stays responsive to the community's evolving needs. Regular assessments can reveal new needs or unforeseen challenges and suggest innovative solutions. This iterative process ensures that church programs remain relevant, impactful, and attuned to the community. Another key factor in the successful implementation of church programs is the use of data for informed decision-making. Data provides a comprehensive understanding of the community's needs and helps in measuring the program's effectiveness. Collection methods such as surveys, interviews, or group discussions can uncover not just explicit needs but also latent needs that individuals might not be aware of or willing to express. This evidence-based approach ensures the effectiveness and impact of the church's programs.

How Data Can Bolster Mental Health Ministry

Dr. Lee Underwood has worked for years supervising residential treatment programs for adolescents and adults with severe mental health issues, disruptive behavioral and sexual disorders, and substance abuse.

He knows that churches can help serve these populations and others but also sees trepidation among pastors and staff or outright rejection of any offering that involves clinical counseling.

Underwood suggests support groups for churches that are new to thinking about mental health. "I've never had church leadership say no to a support group, because they don't see it as counseling," he says.

He's also found that data can bolster the pitch to start such groups—and keep them.

For one church he began with a needs assessment in the form of a short survey. It included questions such as: Would you be open to counseling? What issues would you want counseling on? Where do you want it—off-campus or at the church?

Underwood says the feedback made it easy to create a proposal for staff. "The data helped us then go to the leadership of the church and say 'there appears to be a big desire.' Seventy-five percent of your people are saying they're open to counseling. Twenty-five percent of your people are saying they're struggling with lots of grief and loss. Another 15-20 percent are saying they're immobilized with depression, and some are on psychiatric medication."

Underwood advises those leading church support groups to test members at the start, mid-way and at the end to track whether their symptoms and spiritual well-being are improving.

"I find the data to be incredible," he says. What it often shows is not just a reduction in symptoms but an accompanying growth in the person's faith. That's a win for most churches that prioritize individual spiritual growth as well as overall health.

In assessing the effectiveness of a program, churches should take into account several factors. The key question is, Is the program making a positive difference in the lives of the people it was intended to serve? This can be determined through participant feedback, changes in behavior or attitudes, or improvements in well-being. A good program evaluation should be able to discern whether the observed changes can be uniquely attributed to the program or whether other factors may have influenced the results.[11]

Determining which outcomes to assess is important. In the context of our divorce support group example, the goal isn't necessarily to decrease the number of divorces in the community but rather to provide support and maintain meaningful connections for those going through this challenging process. Therefore, the effectiveness of such a program would be more accurately reflected in the well-being of the participants rather than in the divorce rate statistics. Additionally, the metric of cost-effectiveness is paramount. Churches must judiciously balance their financial and resource allocations against the tangible and intangible benefits a program delivers. This doesn't imply that the most economical program automatically tops the list; instead, the value derived—in terms of community enrichment, the support extended, and the bonds fostered—should proportionately reflect the investment made. Essentially, a program that yields higher benefits relative to its costs can be deemed more efficient.

Mental health consultants can offer invaluable guidance throughout this process. By conducting thorough needs assessments, they can uncover the nuanced needs of the community. They can also define the target population, ensuring that those in critical need aren't overlooked. Their expertise can provide guidance on creating a program structure that's responsive to the specific needs and contexts of the

---

[11]Kettner, Moroney, and Martin, *Designing and Managing Programs.*

target audience. During the implementation phase, they can offer on-going support and oversight, helping to troubleshoot challenges, advise on adjustments, and ensure the program remains faithful to its core objectives while adapting to the real-time needs of the partici-pants. They can also contribute significantly to the long-term planning of the ministry, helping to devise strategies for maintaining program efficacy, suggesting measures for scaling the program if necessary, and providing guidance on sustaining the program over time, con-sidering potential shifts in community needs.[12]

In conclusion, the design, implementation, and continual as-sessment of church programs are crucial in creating a nurturing and resilient community of believers. By working with mental health consultants, churches can ensure their programs are not only well-intentioned but also truly effective. The ultimate goal is to provide transformative support to those who need it, and this requires a dedi-cated commitment to understanding and responding to the commu-nity's evolving needs.[13]

Managing the costs of evaluation. It is indeed true that the evalu-ation process can be expensive; however, with careful planning, costs can be minimized. Consider the following strategies for consultants to collaborate with churches while staying within a budget.

- *Simplify the evaluation design:* Streamline the process to reduce complexity and cost by focusing on the most critical aspects of the program.[14]

- *Revise the sample size:* Adjust it to a more manageable and cost-effective number, ensuring that it still provides reliable results.[15]

[12]Kettner, Moroney, and Martin, *Designing and Managing Programs.*
[13]Peter H. Rossi, Mark W. Lipsey, and Gary T. Henry, *Evaluation: A Systematic Approach* (Los Angeles: Sage Publications, 2018).
[14]Patton, "Ongoing Evolution of Utilization-Focused Evaluation."
[15]David Royse, Bruce A. Thyer, and Deborah K. Padgett, *Program Evaluation: An Introduction to an Evidence-Based Approach* (Stamford, CT: Cengage Learning, 2015).

- *Employ economic data collection methods:* Use volunteers for data collection, shorten surveys, or use focus groups and key informants to gather information more cost-effectively.[16]
- *Leverage reliable secondary data:* Search for existing data sources that can be used to supplement primary data collection, saving time and resources.[17]

By addressing time constraints through careful planning, churches can ensure efficient data collection and analysis. Constraints can be tackled by using multiple methods of data collection, such as combining qualitative and quantitative data (e.g., questionnaires with numeric and open-ended questions, focus group data). This mixed-methods approach not only increases validity through triangulation but also saves time and money.

Through diligent planning and collaboration with church leaders and stakeholders, financial and logistic constraints can be managed. A clear understanding of the church's needs prior to evaluation also allows for a streamlined and cost-effective evaluation process while maintaining credibility.[18] The consultant's role is to tailor the evaluation to meet the specific requirements of each church and ministry context, ensuring that the evaluation process is both efficient and valuable.

Using results. A comprehensive final report, including recommendations, is essential for effectively communicating the results of a program evaluation to church leaders. Ensuring that this report is presented in a contextually appropriate manner is crucial for fostering understanding and facilitating the practical application of the findings.[19] One factor that influences the usefulness of the results is their relevance to the evaluation's purpose. It is essential to maintain focus

---

[16]John W. Creswell and Cheryl N. Poth, *Qualitative Inquiry and Research Design: Choosing Among Five Approaches* (Los Angeles: Sage, 2016).

[17]P. Bazeley and K. Jackson, *Qualitative Data Analysis with NVivo* (Los Angeles: Sage, 2013).

[18]Patton, "Ongoing Evolution of Utilization-Focused Evaluation."

[19]Patton, "Ongoing Evolution of Utilization-Focused Evaluation."

when crafting the final report and align it with the evaluation's objectives, even if additional interesting information has been gathered.[20]

Effective communication between evaluators and users of the results, efficient information processing by the users, the credibility of the results, and the degree of user involvement or advocacy all contribute to the practical application of the findings.[21] The final report should be presented in a manner that suits the church leaders' preferences, which could range from a formal presentation at a board meeting to a private review with leaders. The consultant should deliver the report in a language that is easily understood, structured in a way that is meaningful to the recipients, and always open to input and feedback from leaders.[22] By engaging them in the evaluation process and presenting findings in a manner that resonates with their needs and concerns, the results are more likely to be embraced and implemented.

The MCAP: An Assessment and Consultation Model

As a graduate student, I (Amy Trout) found myself driven by a deep passion to combine my love for psychology and my faith in the church. I wanted to use my knowledge and skills to create a meaningful impact on the church community, but I was unsure how to proceed.

During a community psychology class, I was fascinated to learn about the concept of church assessment. This approach involved psychologists working with religious institutions to gather valuable information through surveys, which would provide churches with insights on strengths and areas for improvement. The idea excited me, as it presented a fresh alternative to traditional church-affiliated counseling centers.

---

[20]Royse, Thyer, and Padgett, *Program Evaluation*.
[21]Hallie Preskill and Shanelle Boyle, "A Multidisciplinary Model of Evaluation Capacity Building," *American Journal of Evaluation* 29, no. 4 (2008): 443-59.
[22]Donald B. Yarbrough et al., *The Program Evaluation Standards: A Guide for Evaluators and Evaluation Users* (Los Angeles: Sage, 2010).

However, as I delved deeper, I realized the assessment process was quite standardized and limited in scope, meaning it might not be applicable to all churches or specific situations. Recognizing the untapped potential in this concept, I began to explore ways to refine and expand on the existing model.

This pursuit ultimately led me to develop the "Multimethod Church-based Assessment Process" (MCAP) for my dissertation. The core distinction between MCAP and previously published church-based assessment efforts is the belief that pastors should be able to determine which questions to assess within their congregation. Instead of using standardized questionnaires that are assumed to work equally well for different types of churches, MCAP is a standardized *process* that enables pastors and behavioral scientists to work collaboratively in addressing highly specific church-initiated questions.[23]

During this time, I had the privilege of collaborating with Dr. Mark McMinn, a renowned Christian psychologist who shared my dedication to integrating psychology and faith. Together, we cofounded the Center for Church-Psychology Collaboration at Wheaton College. This center allowed us to use the skills of psychology in service to the church. Working closely together, we applied the MCAP model to various church settings, which allowed us to delve deeper into the dynamics of faith, emotional well-being, and community support. The Center for Church-Psychology Collaboration was ultimately short-lived, but the work we accomplished has had a lasting impact on both the field of psychology and the church community, paving the way for numerous research projects, training programs, and services designed to further integrate psychology tools to accomplish the mission of the church.

---

[23]Amy W. Dominguez and Mark R. McMinn, "Assessment Process," in *Psychology and the Church*, ed. M. R. McMinn and A. W. Dominguez (New York: Nova Science Publishers, 2005), 105.

Now, decades later, I see the impact of the journey that began with my graduate student days and discovery of church assessment. The MCAP model continues to serve as a valuable tool for understanding and addressing the unique challenges faced by churches. It has been used globally and taught at prestigious institutions such as the University of Cambridge in its Church Consultancy Program. I remain committed to exploring new ways to apply psychological principles and research within the context of faith-based organizations, striving to make a difference in the lives of both individuals and communities of faith.

The MCAP provides a collaborative assessment process to create a customized approach for each church, addressing specific needs and developmental areas unique to the organization. Church leadership identifies questions to be the focus of the assessment, and the consultant develops ways, through research, to get answers to those questions. Graduate students in behavioral health are trained in relational skills, interviewing, research methods, systems, group dynamics, consultation, and report writing, all of which are employed in such an assessment.[24] The MCAP model comprises three stages. Stage one, Generating Specific Questions, forms the foundation of the entire project. In this stage, the clinician demonstrates commitment to collaborative involvement through astute observation, insightful feedback, and sensitively building a relational network around a common goal—the church's specific questions that warrant assessment. During stage two, Collecting Information, the consultant generates a written plan outlining appropriate methods to gather relevant data. Multiple methods are used in each assessment area to ensure breadth and depth of data generation. This stage is also executed collaboratively, using planning methods that align with the church's needs.[25]

---

[24]A. W. Dominguez, *Multi-Method Church Assessment Program: An Assessment and Consultation Model* (PsyD diss., Wheaton College, Wheaton, IL, 2001).
[25]Dominguez, *Multi-Method Church Assessment Program.*

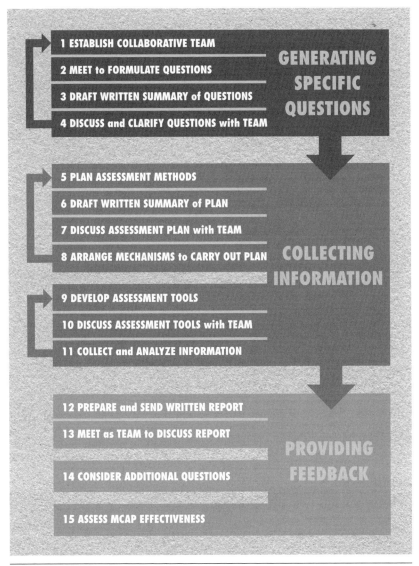

Figure 4. Multimethod Church-Based Assessment Process
Source: Adapted from Amy W. Dominguez and Mark R. McMinn, "Assessment Process," in *Psychology and the Church,* ed. Mark R. McMinn and Amy W. Dominguez (New York: Nova Science, 2005), 108.

For example, some churches may choose to distribute surveys during services, while others may opt for email distribution. The goal is to ensure that the proposed methodology fits the consultee's needs and can be revised as often as necessary to obtain direction and goodness of fit for the church. The consultant implements the agreed-upon methods and analyzes the data. In stage three, Providing Feedback, the consultant prepares a final report with recommendations and discusses it with the church team. Additional assessment questions may also be considered. Afterward, the consultant offers a mechanism for church leaders to provide input on the effectiveness of the assessment process.[26]

By combining multiple methods to address specific questions identified by church leadership, MCAP enables a more comprehensive understanding of complex, interrelated issues that could be misrepresented by relying solely on a single instrument, such as a survey questionnaire.[27] Through a collaborative method that respects the church's authority and prioritizes its unique needs, the MCAP model ensures that the assessment and consultation process yields relevant and useful data for each ministry setting.

Dominguez and McMinn noted that the MCAP consultation model has been successfully applied in a variety of church and parachurch organizations, providing a structured process that retains flexibility to address church-led areas of assessment.[28] Examples of its diverse applications include identifying needs and proposing recommendations for church-based recovery care, understanding community requirements related to church-based homeless outreach, identifying racial tension in a multicultural inner-city church, evaluating motivation for small group participation along with factors limiting engagement, and gauging member satisfaction. This approach ensures that each project is highly individualized, reflecting the unique needs and goals of the congregation under assessment.

---

[26]M. R. McMinn and A. W. Dominguez, "Assessment Process"; Dominguez, *Multi-Method Church Assessment Program*.

[27]McMinn and Dominguez, *Psychology and the Church*.

[28]McMinn and Dominguez, *Psychology and the Church*.

The MCAP consultation model is a valuable tool that allows churches to receive customized guidance and support while addressing the challenges and opportunities in their congregations. The flexibility of the model allows for a wide range of applications and enables church leadership to determine its specific needs and areas of focus. As churches continue to evolve and adapt to the changing needs of their congregations, the model can identify areas for growth and improvement. By working collaboratively with mental health consultants, church leaders can ensure that their ministry programs are effective, efficient, and aligned with their core mission and values. Moreover, the model encourages a spirit of collaboration and partnership between church leaders and consultants, fostering a sense of shared ownership and responsibility for the assessment process. This approach can help build trust, enhance communication, and promote a sense of unity as the church seeks to better understand and address its needs and opportunities. By empowering church leaders to do this, the model has the potential to significantly impact the effectiveness and overall health of church ministries worldwide.

Teaching Organizational Development and Program Evaluation

Organizational development stands as a cornerstone for Christian mental health professionals aspiring to thrive in church settings. For graduate students to flourish in this realm, a robust educational framework is essential, one that melds foundational theory with practical, faith-based application.

Initially, a deep dive into the underpinnings of organizational development is vital. By weaving together systems theory, humanistic psychology, and action research with a faith-centric lens, students can discern the synergy between these paradigms and Christian principles. This synthesis lays a foundational bedrock for effective practice. Equally crucial is cultivating diagnostic acumen. Students must master the art of nuanced evaluations incorporating spiritual insights with empirical data. This entails comprehensive data assimilation through tools like surveys and focus groups, and subsequent discerning analysis to spotlight improvement vectors.

Furthermore, students should be acquainted with faith-sensitive interventions tailored for church settings. These span team building, leadership cultivation, and process consultation. An appreciation for the strengths and nuances of each intervention aids students in making judicious choices in varied church contexts. The psychological and emotional intricacies of change management, especially within religious frameworks, can't be overlooked. Effective, culturally-respectful communication strategies are essential.

Evaluation remains paramount. Students must be trained to craft faith-sensitive metrics, continually monitor intervention efficacy, and effectively communicate findings to church stakeholders. Immersing students in case studies, real-time simulations, and hands-on experiences can fine-tune their proficiency in these facets.

Transitioning to program evaluation, a pivotal component in assessing intervention and program efficacy within church environments, students should be well-versed in its history, current trends, and ethical implications. They should be adept at discerning the unique dynamics of church systems and the tangible role of evaluation in shaping decision-making. Additionally, students need expertise in formulating specialized plans—encompassing question identification, metric selection, data methodology, and evaluation designs apt for religious settings, paired with hands-on data management and analytic techniques.

Navigating ethical waters, like confidentiality and cultural sensitivity, especially in faith-driven program evaluation, is indispensable. Offering students tangible exposure through internships or field assignments can amplify their confidence and adeptness in these realms.

Preparation of future Christian mental health professionals mandates a multifaceted pedagogical approach. By intertwining theoretical rigor with practical skillsets and real-world exposure, educators can forge professionals primed to champion change and refine church programs and interventions.

Questions for Reflection

1. As a Christian clinician, how can you apply your skills, knowledge, and spiritual insights to facilitate organizational development in the church, while respecting the unique culture, values, and beliefs of the congregation?

2. How can you create a collaborative environment with church leaders and members to address organizational challenges, promote open communication, and foster a sense of shared ownership in the development process?

3. As a mental health professional, what are your strengths and areas for growth in conducting program evaluation, and how can you leverage these strengths and address these areas to best serve the church?

4. How can you maintain a balance between providing professional expertise in program evaluation while respecting the autonomy and decision-making authority of church leadership?

Integrity in Christian Mental Health

THE ETHICS AND ECONOMICS OF CARE

HAVING EXPLORED the various practical strategies and best practices that underpin this new model of collaboration between churches and mental health professionals, we now find ourselves at a critical juncture. The mechanics alone are not enough to ensure success. As we move toward the end of this book, we must turn our attention to the deeper philosophical considerations that must guide this collaboration: financial sustainability and ethical responsibility. These are not mere addenda but the very foundation on which our entire approach rests. Without a clear economic model, the stability we seek would crumble, and without unshakable ethics, we risk doing more harm than good. Join us in the concluding section as we delve into these essential elements, ensuring that our vision is not only actionable but also grounded in principles that honor both the human soul and the practical realities of our world.

Operating Within the Arena of Ethics

For mental health professionals. In any professional work, following ethical guidelines is essential to protect all involved parties. For instance, when collaborating with a ministry team in a nonclinical setting, church leaders may question the need for obtaining consent from community members. However, mental health practitioners must practice ethically within their field.[1] To address this issue, Christian practitioners can adopt a different approach and provide clear explanations to help church leaders understand and support the informed consent process.

This explanation should use everyday language, avoid clinical or legal jargon, and be explicit about the services offered, the capacity in which they are provided, and any specific limitations.[2] Consultation models can help create personalized, church-friendly informed consent discussions. Confidentiality is critical and may require explanation and sensitivity in church settings.[3] Christian mental health professionals should protect clients, especially when discussing consultation work in different settings such as the church, guided by their ethical principles.

Dual relationships also need attention. The APA ethics code states that psychologists should avoid multiple relationships that could impair their objectivity, competence, or effectiveness. Similar concepts are expressed in the American Counseling Association and other codes.[4] Mental health professionals must commit to identifying and avoiding situations where their relationships or activities may exploit or cause harm. They should maintain clarity about their role while engaging genuinely with others, particularly in their churches. They must be mindful of conversations and initiate them as necessary, considering the other's well-being. Boundaries can blur when the collaborating mental health professional needs pastoral support from the same person for whom they have provided personal and organizational care.[5]

[1]Celia B. Fisher, *Decoding the Ethics Code: A Practical Guide for Psychologists* (Los Angeles: Sage Publications, 2021).

[2]American Psychological Association, "American Psychological Association Ethics Code," 2017, www.apa.org/ethics/code.

[3]Fisher, *Decoding the Ethics Code.*

[4]American Counseling Association, *American Counseling Association Code of Ethics*, www.counseling .org/knowledge-center/ethics.

[5]Carrie Doehring, *The Practice of Pastoral Care: A Postmodern Approach* (Louisville, KY: Westminster John Knox, 2015).

Practitioners should exercise wisdom and good judgment without being overly guarded. Building trusting, genuine relationships that mutually support and enhance each other is the foundation for effective collaboration. Optimizing role management becomes more streamlined when involvement is envisioned as temporary or non-binding, when ministry support is valued and promoted, and the mental health professional is viewed as a partner with the pastor, like behavioral health consultants and medical staff within integrative care settings.[6]

Stigma can be a significant barrier for people of faith seeking help.[7] When clinicians are integrated into the faith community or have affiliations with one, it can significantly diminish the stigma associated with mental health. The pastoral team plays a pivotal role in this; by valuing and respecting the role of the mental health professional, they further normalize and elevate the importance of mental well-being within the congregation.

Mental health professionals working in a church setting must be aware of the cultural dynamics within the faith community they serve. This includes understanding the specific beliefs, values, and practices, as well as the unique characteristics of the individuals within the congregation. Being culturally competent enables counselors to provide sensitive and appropriate care that respects and acknowledges the faith-based context.[8]

Working in a church setting can be taxing, with consultants often facing high expectations and emotional demands from the congregation and leadership.[9] Therefore, it is crucial for these professionals

[6]M. R. McMinn et al., "Psychology, Theology, and Spirituality in Christian Counseling: An Integrative Approach to Mental Health," in *Christian Counseling Ethics: A Handbook for Psychologists, Therapists, and Pastors,* ed. R. K. Sanders (Downers Grove, IL: InterVarsity Press, 2011), 61-78.
[7]Christopher E. M. Lloyd and Yasuhiro Kotera, "Mental Distress, Stigma and Help-Seeking in the Evangelical Christian Church: Study Protocol," *Journal of Concurrent Disorders* 4, no. 1 (2022): 1-9.
[8]D. W. Sue and D. Sue, *Counseling the Culturally Diverse: Theory and Practice,* 7th ed. (Hoboken, NJ: Wiley, 2017).
[9]Rae Jean Proeschold-Bell et al., "A Theoretical Model of the Holistic Health of United Methodist Clergy," *Journal of Religion and Health* 50 (2011): 700-720.

to prioritize self-care and maintain a healthy work-life balance to prevent burnout and ensure they can continue providing effective care. This includes setting appropriate boundaries, seeking personal support, and engaging regularly in activities such as exercise, relaxation, and leisure pursuits. It is essential for consultants in a church setting to maintain regular supervision and accountability to ensure they practice ethically and effectively.[10] Supervision provides an opportunity for the mental health professional to discuss concerns, receive feedback on their practice, and address potential ethical dilemmas. Ideally, the supervisor should be knowledgeable about the specific context and ethical issues related to consulting in a faith-based setting.

Professionals working in a church setting should maintain accurate and up-to-date records of their work with clients to maintain continuity of care and to meet legal and ethical requirements.[11] This includes keeping records of assessments, treatment plans, progress notes, and consultations. Record-keeping should be done in a manner that protects the confidentiality of the clients and adheres to applicable laws and regulations.

While working in a church setting, one may encounter conflicts between their professional obligations and the expectations or values of the religious community.[12] In such situations, it is important for the counselor to remain aware of their ethical responsibilities and seek guidance and support from colleagues, supervisors, and professional organizations to resolve conflicts ethically.

Church-consulting counselors should continually engage in professional development, attend workshops, or seek additional training

---

[10]Janine M. Bernard and Rodney K. Goodyear, *Fundamentals of Clinical Supervision*, 6th ed. (Boston: Allyn & Bacon, 2019).

[11]American Counseling Association Code of Ethics (2014); American Psychological Association Ethics Code (2017).

[12]Clark D. Campbell and Michelle C. Gordon, "Acknowledging the Inevitable: Understanding Multiple Relationships in Rural Practice," *Professional Psychology: Research and Practice* 34, no. 4 (2003): 430.

related to the unique challenges of working in a faith-based context. This ongoing learning will help counselors stay current with best practices and ethical standards, ensuring they provide the highest level of care to their clients and effectively navigate the complexities of working within a church setting.

It is essential for practitioners to maintain open communication with church leaders and be willing to discuss any ethical concerns that may arise. By fostering a collaborative relationship, mental health professionals can work together with leaders to address potential ethical issues and provide effective, compassionate care.

Professionals working in church settings face unique challenges that require a delicate balance of ethical considerations, cultural competence, and open communication with leaders and the community. By adhering to professional ethical guidelines, being sensitive to the religious context, and engaging in ongoing professional development, mental health providers can successfully navigate the complexities of their role within the faith community. To further enhance their effectiveness, these professionals should develop strong support networks within their profession, including engaging in peer consultation, attending conferences, and participating in professional organizations. These networks can provide additional resources and guidance for tackling the unique challenges of work in a faith-based setting.

Partnering with the Community and Referring Out

Research tells us that churches are frequently the first stop for someone experiencing mental illness, but they're often not equipped to address what may be a myriad of chronic issues, let alone a crisis.

The ability to develop a referral system can make an enormous difference in emergencies where someone is suicidal or when a pastor is in over their head.

It's why Nashville's Mt. Zion Baptist has created a robust referral system under the leadership of pediatrician Dr. Stephanie Walker. "I think it's the pastor's responsibility to be able to say, 'I'm able to do this and I'm not able to do this'—so recognizing their own limitations," said Dr. Walker.

She has led a team to create Mt. Zion's system, available not only to members but to anyone in the community. It connects those in need with Nashville's array of mental health resources, including support groups and medical and counseling practices.

"We're in the health care mecca," she explained. "So as a congregation and as a church we don't have to recreate the wheel. The resources are out there. We have the people. They have the resources. We serve as the connectors."

Mt. Zion has also trained lay leaders and church staff to listen critically when members approach them. "If you were at home and you were having a moment and you decided to call the church and the secretary answers the phone, there are key words that you are listening for," she said. "If the person is saying 'I'm going to hurt myself' you don't say 'well, you know, ma'am, there's no one here today. It's 4:30, everyone has left the office.' You pick up the phone. There's an algorithm sheet. There's a phone number that you call. You say, 'hold on, don't hang up—I will get you help immediately.'"

Mt. Zion leaders have also discussed the long-term nature of caring for people with mental health needs. Their goal is to help people before, during, and after a crisis.

"It's not a sprint, it's a marathon," said Walker. "So we're going to continue to walk you through this. And if at any moment you feel like you need to start over, it's okay. But we're going to surround you with a support system."

For church leaders. As church leaders, the well-being and safety of your congregation is paramount. When considering collaboration with mental health professionals, it is crucial to understand and uphold the ethical aspects involved in providing mental health care services. Ensuring that these standards are maintained within your church community helps to protect everyone involved and fosters a trusting, supportive environment.

Essential ethical practices include informed consent, maintaining confidentiality, cultural and spiritual sensitivity, and ongoing education and training. By understanding and supporting these aspects, church leaders can foster a safe community that promotes the well-being of its members. This commitment to ethical practice is an essential step toward creating more accessible, effective, and compassionate mental health care within faith communities.

Embracing partnerships with Christian counselors offers a unique opportunity to address barriers to access and affordability in mental health care. For instance, your members and attendees may find a counselor-led support group in your church for a nominal fee to be easier to pay for and schedule than a more expensive therapy session in a professional building across town. This type of collaborative approach can significantly benefit individuals, contributing to the overall well-being and resilience of the congregation.

A Valuable Resource for Collaboration and Support

Ministries play a crucial role in addressing the critical issues that arise when partnering with Christian mental health professionals. Having a space where individuals can share their stories, insights, and even offer caution when necessary is essential for those looking to engage in this work respectfully and effectively.

To address this need, we have developed an online platform at www.churchconsultation.net. This resource aims to facilitate collaboration and communication among various stakeholders, including practitioners, church leaders, and others who are interested. The website features several sections focused on church-based consultation, allowing users to discuss relevant situations, resources, models, successes, challenges, and opportunities for growth toward a new model of care.

As the site continues to evolve, its development will be guided by user feedback, ensuring it remains a dynamic and adaptable resource for the community. We are excited to connect with others who share a passion for fostering collaboration between ministries and mental health professionals and look forward to welcoming new users to the platform.

The Question of Money

Some years ago when Jim had a sabbatical from Northern Illinois University, we (Jim and Heather) moved our family to Honduras to study mental health practices in a culture that had only minimal infrastructure to deliver care to its population. In short, Honduras had no mental health "industry." While we don't readily think of mental health as an industry, it is. Consider the businesses constructed around services in clinical care, medicine, inpatient hospitals, community centers, books, magazines, websites, and more. All told, this sector amounts to $24 billion annually in the United States.[13]

Mental health is a vital part of overall health care, focused on preventing, diagnosing, and treating mental, emotional, and behavioral disorders. As mental health issues have gained recognition and awareness, the demand for therapy and other interventions has shot up. However, the current service models can't fully meet this demand, as the industry faces unique challenges such as accessibility, affordability, and stigma. The following are some key economic challenges and a look at potential solutions, emphasizing the role of partnerships with the church.

Like general health care, mental health care operates based on supply and demand. Demand for services is influenced by factors like

---

[13]IBISWorld, "Mental Health and Substance Abuse Centers in the US—Market Size 2003–2029," January 23, 2023, www.ibisworld.com/industry-statistics/market-size/mental-health-substance -abuse-centers-united-states/#:~:text=The%20market%20size%2C%20measured%20 by,industry%20increased%205.4%25%20in%202022.

increased awareness of mental health issues, growing prevalence of disorders, and reduced stigma. On the supply side, providers include psychiatrists, psychologists, counselors, and social workers, many of whom typically have waiting lists.

Another economic challenge is accessibility of services alongside affordability. Sometimes the nearest therapist is located quite a distance away. Some strategies to tackle this challenge include offering incentives for providers to work in underserved areas, using telecare to connect patients with providers remotely, and working with churches to offer prevention-based care.

Government policies and funding play a significant role in shaping the mental health care industry's affordability, or lack thereof. They affect regulations and licensing requirements for providers, public funding for mental health resources, and initiatives aimed at reducing stigma and raising awareness. Addressing the growing demand for mental health care services requires a concerted effort to develop and sustain a skilled workforce. This includes expanding educational opportunities, encouraging interdisciplinary collaboration, and supporting professional development. Church-based care and consultation present an attractive opportunity for mental health professionals wanting to contribute to the emotional well-being of those within the faith community.

The economics of the mental health care industry present unique challenges and opportunities for growth and improvement. Partnering mental health services with the church offers a unique opportunity to address existing barriers to access and affordability, contributing significantly to the well-being of individuals and communities worldwide. Church partnerships can have relevance in offering indirect or direct care at reduced rates, or through ministry assistance. Also, the church can lead anti-stigma initiatives by sharing mental health information and education and offering church-based support networks.

Tackling these challenges requires a comprehensive approach that includes increased public funding and investment in mental health resources, policies that promote an adequate supply of trained professionals, and the integration of innovative technologies to enhance service delivery. Collaborative efforts between governments, health care providers, and community organizations such as the church can play a significant role in overcoming these challenges and fostering a more efficient and equitable mental health care industry.

Moreover, efforts to reduce stigma and raise awareness about mental health issues are crucial in encouraging individuals to seek help and ultimately improving the overall well-being of communities. Collaboration and support from various stakeholders, such as mental health professionals, policymakers, and organizations, contribute to building a more accessible, affordable, and effective mental health care system that addresses the unique challenges faced by this industry. The church, as a key community institution, can play a vital role in fostering emotional well-being by offering valuable resources and working alongside mental health professionals to create supportive environments for those in need.

Financial Models for Offering Consultation Services Within a Church Context

As interest in integrating mental health, organizational consultation, and community outreach services within churches grows, Christian practitioners and faith communities are recognizing the need for a comprehensive approach to well-being, effective administration, and community engagement. Churches can serve as ideal environments for professionals to provide various consultation services, benefiting congregants, the church organization, and the broader community. To achieve a sustainable practice, we must explore different business models and financial considerations. Here are some potential business models and financial strategies that professionals can adopt in such partnerships.

Fee-for-service model. The fee-for-service model can be applied to mental health counseling, organizational consultation efforts, and supportive church and community outreach. In this model, clinicians charge clients directly for their services. This approach allows professionals to set fees based on the type of activity, time required, length of sessions, or specific services provided. Some advantages of this model include flexibility, easy revenue tracking, and the ability to adjust fees to cater to various needs. However, professionals should be aware of the potential financial strain and consider offering sliding scale fees, payment plans, or church-sponsored scholarships to improve accessibility.

Church sponsorship model. In this model, the church sponsors the professional's services, either by providing a salary or covering a percentage of their fees. This allows congregants to access reduced cost or free mental health services. It can also enable the church to receive organizational consultation services to improve its management and operations, and support ministry development and community outreach. It is essential to establish a clear agreement between the church and the professional to ensure transparency and sustainability in using this model.

Grant-funded model. Professionals can secure funding for their services through grants provided by government agencies, foundations, or other organizations. This model offers an opportunity for counseling professionals to offer free or reduced cost mental health services, provide organizational consultation services to the church at little to no cost, and support ministry and community outreach programs and initiatives. Grant-funded models require robust planning, grant writing skills, and continuous reporting to sustain funding. Collaborating with the church to identify grant opportunities and leveraging the church's network and resources can improve the chances of securing funding.

Partnership model. Forming partnerships with local mental health agencies, community organizations, and other professionals can greatly enhance the reach and impact of church ministries and Christian clinicians. Such collaboration constructs a strong referral network that comes into play when a congregant requires services beyond the expertise of the church or the individual consulting professional. Each partner organization contributes unique resources and expertise, leading to a collective pool that ensures better service delivery. Furthermore, the collaboration introduces each entity to the others' client base, thus expanding their reach significantly. The principle of economies of scale applies too; shared operational costs among the partners often result in affordable yet high-quality services that could have been beyond individual budgets. Moreover, these partnerships invariably foster robust community engagement and outreach, creating a holistic and supportive environment that caters to varied community needs. Continuous learning and the sharing of best practices among the partners can lead to innovative solutions for community service, constantly enhancing the quality of services provided. Overall, these partnerships form a symbiotic network where resources are optimized to their fullest, creating a beneficial scenario for all involved parties.

Subscription model. In the subscription model, mental health professionals offer various mental health, organizational consultation, ministry, and community outreach services to congregants, the church, and the community for a fixed monthly or yearly fee. This can include individual or group consultations, workshops, educational resources, and community engagement initiatives. By providing a bundle of services, professionals can generate a stable revenue stream and encourage long-term commitment from clients, the church, and the community.

Additional considerations. Regardless of the chosen business model, practitioners should be mindful of practical considerations. Setting up a consultation practice with a church may require initial investments in office equipment, furniture, marketing materials, and other resources. Professionals should assess their financial capacity and seek ways to minimize costs, such as using shared spaces or collaborating with the church for necessary resources. Additionally, professionals should account for ongoing expenses like rent, utilities, insurance, and licensing fees. Budgeting and tracking these expenses can help ensure financial stability. Developing a pricing strategy that balances accessibility for congregants, the church, and the community with financial viability for the professional is crucial. Offering discounted rates, sliding scale fees, or group sessions can make services more affordable. Still, consultants should periodically review their pricing structure and adjust as needed to account for changes in the market or their expenses.

To maintain financial stability, consulting professionals may need to diversify their income streams. This can include offering workshops, online courses, or writing and selling books or resources related to mental health, faith, organizational development, and community outreach. Diversification can also involve separate private practice and providing consultation services to other organizations, such as schools or community centers, in addition to the church. Investing in marketing and outreach efforts is important for attracting and retaining clients. This can include creating a website, using social media, networking within both the church and the broader community, and collaborating with other professionals or organizations. Word-of-mouth referrals from satisfied clients and church clients can also be a powerful marketing tool. Furthermore, professionals should implement a robust system to monitor income, expenses, and other financial indicators, ensuring the sustainability of their practice. Professionals can ensure that their practice remains financially viable by establishing a system for tracking income, expenses, and other financial metrics. This may involve using accounting software, hiring a bookkeeper, or collaborating with the church's financial management team. By collaborating with the financial management team of the church, professionals can ensure that the services are appropriately compensated while also contributing to the church's mission, giving back to the community, and strengthening the relationship between mental health services and faith-based organizations. This arrangement not only supports the church's mission and contributes to the community but also strengthens the bond between mental health services and faith-based organizations.

Pro bono collaboration. As a Christian, engaging in pro bono work with churches can be a meaningful way to serve your community, share your expertise, and live out your faith through the giving of your professional expertise. In *The Good and Beautiful Community*, James Bryan Smith focuses on the importance of building Christian communities based on the teachings and character of Christ, emphasizing the importance of balancing our own needs with those of others, practicing good stewardship, and being generous in our actions and relationships. Smith encourages individuals to manage their resources responsibly so they are free to effectively support and serve others.[14] This approach aligns with the Christian principles of stewardship and generosity, which encourage believers to use their time, talents, and resources wisely for the benefit of others and the glory of God. That is sage advice for collaborative consultation, in both assessing the church's need and soberly assessing personal resources to determine how to wisely structure partnered engagement.

I (Amy) have always been deeply rooted in my church and its community. This spiritual haven has been a source of unwavering support, a beacon during challenging times, and a guidepost when I sought direction. Drawn to the idea of reciprocating this love, I pondered how I might intertwine my professional acumen with my spiritual journey. While roles like serving refreshments after services or aiding in the nursery are undeniably valuable, my heart felt a pull toward a

---

[14]James Bryan Smith, *The Good and Beautiful Community* (Downers Grove, IL: InterVarsity Press, 2010).

more specialized form of service. Balancing one's personal commitments, I've found, is key to offering genuine assistance without overextending oneself.

My background as a mental health professional offered a distinct avenue of support: providing the church community with consultation services tailored to both emotional and organizational needs. While my initial efforts were centered around my own church community, word spread, and soon, neighboring churches sought similar support. Depending on the need and context, I sometimes offered structured professional models, while at other times, it was a more informal assistance.

The spectrum of my engagements varied: from curating care ministry training sessions, sculpting a support system, mapping community resources, to executing research methods that helped in ministry development. Breakfast workshops emerged as a fruitful endeavor, where I addressed pressing topics like leadership dynamics, emotional well-being, stress alleviation, and personal growth. For those requiring more personalized engagement, individual consultations were also available. While certain specialized services did come with a fee, my primary goal was to offer assistance, especially to churches with financial constraints, often extending pro bono support.

Over the years, the ripple effect of my contributions has been palpable. Pastors and community members alike have voiced their appreciation, viewing my services as a keystone in bolstering their congregational well-being. The opportunity to harness my professional skills in such a spiritual context has been both a privilege and a revelation. As I reflect on my journey, the realization that I've been able to bridge my vocation with my faith to foster more robust, resilient church communities fills me with profound gratitude. Through this blend of professional expertise and spiritual commitment, I've been fortunate to pave paths of healing, growth, and unity.

By offering your professional skills to churches pro bono, you can make a positive impact on your community, help churches accomplish their mission, and deepen your own spiritual journey. Christian mental health professionals can make meaningful contributions to the church in various ways. To begin such an endeavor, take an inventory of your professional skills, experiences, and areas of expertise that could be helpful to a church. Reach out to local churches, develop genuine relationships with these contacts, and inquire about their needs. Offer your services based on your skills and be open to learning about their specific needs.

Additionally, network with other professionals by joining Christian professional counselor groups or online forums where you can connect with others who may be interested in offering their skills to churches pro bono or who already are doing so. Consider how to best partner to support church initiatives by offering skills as a clinician to ongoing projects, ministries, or outreach programs. Maintain a servant's heart as you engage in pro bono work with churches, using care to approach it with humility and a genuine desire to serve. If you have a private practice, you will likely gain referrals from churches you serve as you will become a trusted ally in care. But offering services in this manner is not a marketing tool, rather it is using your talents to contribute to the well-being of others and the kingdom of God.

Pro bono opportunities for mental health professionals in church communities are diverse and valuable contributions to support individuals in need. Providing mental health workshops, seminars, and screenings to church staff and congregants on topics like stress management, anxiety, depression, or self-care can help destigmatize mental health issues and promote well-being within the community. Additionally, establishing support groups for those dealing with issues like grief, addiction, or anxiety can offer a safe space for individuals to share their experiences and find encouragement. Training church leaders, volunteers, and staff to better understand mental health issues, recognize warning signs, and provide appropriate support to congregants is also an essential way to support the community.

Pro bono or reduced-rate individual or family counseling sessions can offer strategic help to church members who may not have access to mental health services due to financial constraints or other barriers. Collaborating on mental health programs and initiatives can also be beneficial, which may involve creating resources, organizing events, or developing partnerships with local mental health organizations to address the specific needs of the church community. Offering to help churches develop guidelines related to mental health is an important way to ensure that policies are informed and compassionate.

Serving as a liaison between the church and local mental health professionals or organizations provides an opportunity to help coordinate services and resources for church members in need. Advocating for awareness within the church community and using your knowledge and experience to highlight mental health issues can also help encourage greater understanding, support, and resources. Finally, if you are experienced in working with faith-based communities, mentoring other mental health professionals interested in offering pro bono services to churches can help expand the network and increase access to care.

Being mindful of your time and energy while providing pro bono services is crucial for maintaining your well-being and ensuring the quality of your work. Balance commitments and avoid burnout when offering pro bono services by careful consideration of personal and professional responsibilities and prioritize accordingly. Thoughtfully determine which pro bono opportunities align best with your values, interests, and available resources. Establish a clear limit for the number of hours you can commit to per week or month to assist in workload management and to prevent overcommitment. Communicate expectations with transparency to the church regarding availability and the scope of services you can provide to prevent misunderstandings. Also, learn to say no. While it can be difficult to turn down requests for help, it's essential to recognize when you're unable to take on additional pro bono work. Politely decline opportunities that would overextend your capacity or create undue stress. Remain committed to scheduling downtime to ensure that you have regular periods of rest and relaxation to recharge and maintain your well-being. While this can be challenging, it is vital to make time for hobbies, exercise, and spending time with loved ones in order to achieve a healthy work-life balance.

Regularly monitor your well-being, assessing your mental, emotional, and physical health. If you notice signs of burnout or excessive stress, consider revising your commitments and seeking support if needed. Invite other professionals or volunteers to share responsibilities and lighten your workload. Collaboration can help distribute tasks more evenly and prevent burnout. Seek support from friends, family, or colleagues for encouragement and guidance when navigating the challenges of balancing pro bono work with other responsibilities. Sharing your experiences and seeking advice can help you manage stress and maintain perspective. Periodically review your pro bono commitments and adjust as needed. Your availability and priorities may change over time, so it's essential to reassess your workload and make changes accordingly. By being conscious of your personal resources, establishing boundaries, and taking measures to maintain a healthy work-life balance, you can minimize potential negative impacts that pro bono services may have on both you and the communities you serve.

"I've Got These People in the Room with Me"

Churches in Colorado have been thinking through mental health issues for years and are helping to lead the national conversation on faith and mental health. Many point to the 1999 Columbine High

School massacre as a turning point. Two shooters killed twelve students and a teacher and left a grief-stricken community battling PTSD, anxiety, and depression. In 2012, a gunman killed twelve people at a movie theater in Aurora, Colorado, and brought more trauma.

In this context, Denver-based Brandon Appelhans cofounded My Quiet Cave to provide small group mental health curriculum for churches wanting to meet the needs of their communities.

"Churches are on the frontline—there's no getting around it," says Appelhans. "This is something that requires a response and an immediate response from churches."

He started the nonprofit with a fellow Denver Seminary student. Together they developed a nine-week curriculum that integrates faith and mental health.

His focus: how people understand their spiritual identity when they hit a crisis. Appelhans says he checked out from regular life at age fourteen after receiving a bipolar diagnosis. During that time, his medical team struggled to find the right mix of medications that could give him some stability. "You hit this crisis and everything disintegrates," he says. "People can say 'God loves me' and believe, but we believe things will go well."

My Quiet Cave, now known as Anchor International, offers short-term Overcome groups that work in that space, connecting teens and adults coming into or coming out of deep turmoil with a deeper understanding of their faith and how it speaks to what they're experiencing. It also oversees Anchor groups, which function as ongoing drop-in places for community.

Group facilitators receive online training and resources. Executive director Kimberly Britt says pastors and other ministry leaders are also requesting the training. "The best thing I think that's come out of the pandemic is putting a spotlight on issues that were already there," she said. "It exaggerated a lot of symptoms, brought a lot of things to the surface, and we were forced to address it—it's right here in the church."

The testimonials from these groups speak to profound need. Forty-year-old Audrey battled depression starting at age thirty-five but went off the deep end when her daughter died in a car accident. She cycled back into an eating disorder and became reclusive. She was seeing a therapist twice a week with no improvement when she discovered the group at her church.

She remembers her first meeting. "I spent quite a while looking at the floor," she recalls.

But as she listened to the stories of other group members she found herself emboldened. "I thought, 'Well, I could probably talk because if you're not safe in your church, where are you safe?'" she said.

Audrey started speaking and her life started changing. She began to cut back on her therapy appointments as she became more secure, content, and at peace.

"I think it was really for me finding out that I was not alone. That God was with me. That I've got these people in the room with me," she said.

Personal Pathways: Bridging Gaps Through Strategy and Finance

As clinicians aim to bridge the gap between mental health care needs and their expertise, it is crucial to consider the most effective financial structures for offering services within a church setting. This may involve adopting a business model with fees or providing pro bono services.[15] Creating a personal strategic plan is essential for a successful collaboration with churches. Drawing inspiration from early Christian communities and their "rules," Christian professionals can develop a plan outlining their direction, values, and goals within the church community. Embracing a growth mindset is vital for continuous improvement and a deeper understanding of one's professional identity and purpose.

Practitioners should actively seek opportunities to apply their skills and training within the church community. Initiating conversations

---

[15]J. E. Barnett, "Psychotherapist Self-Care: Practicing What We Preach," *Psychotherapy* 48, no. 1 (2011): 88-93. doi:10.1037/a0022186.

with church leaders and members to assess needs, generate ideas, and explore possibilities will help bridge the gap between mental health care needs and available expertise. Establishing trust and clear communication is crucial for genuine collaborative engagement[16] and maintaining ethical integrity in collaborative practice.[17] By thoughtfully developing a personal strategic plan and financial structure that aligns with the church community's needs, mental health professionals can foster successful collaboration and provide valuable mental health care services.

Partnerships between mental health services and the church have the potential to greatly impact the accessibility and affordability of mental health care, resulting in substantial benefits for individuals and communities around the globe.[18] By fostering cooperation between health care providers and faith-based organizations, these collaborative efforts can help create a more efficient, equitable, and effective mental health care industry, addressing the unique challenges that it faces. The combined approach not only benefits those in need of mental health services, but also contributes to the overall well-being and resilience of communities at large.

The integration of mental health services and consultation within faith-based settings offers numerous advantages for individuals, church organizations, and the wider community. By examining various business models and financial strategies, mental health professionals can establish a sustainable practice that tackles the distinct obstacles confronted by the mental health care industry, while simultaneously promoting the welfare of faith communities. Open communication and collaboration between mental health professionals,

[16]D. W. Sue and D. Sue, *Counseling the Culturally Diverse: Theory and Practice,* 7th ed. (Hoboken, NJ: Wiley, 2016).

[17]G. Corey, M. S. Corey, C. Corey, and P. Callanan, *Issues and Ethics in the Helping Professions* (Belmont, CA: Brooks, 2010).

[18]Tyler J. VanderWeele, "Religion and Health: A Synthesis," in *Spirituality and Religion Within the Culture of Medicine: From Evidence to Practice,* ed. J. R. Peteet and M. J. Balboni (New York: Oxford University Press, 2017), 357-401.

faith-based organizations, and other relevant stakeholders is crucial for the creation of a comprehensive and accessible mental health support system that accommodates the diverse needs of individuals and communities.

Through such partnerships, mental health services can become more approachable and less stigmatized, as they are offered within a familiar and supportive environment. This can encourage individuals who may have been hesitant to seek help to take the first step toward better mental health. Furthermore, faith-based organizations can provide valuable resources, such as pastoral counseling and spiritual guidance, which can complement and enhance traditional mental health services.

By working together, mental health professionals and church organizations can bridge gaps in access and affordability, creating a more inclusive and effective mental health care system. This collaborative approach not only addresses the pressing challenges faced by the industry but also contributes to the overall well-being and resilience of communities worldwide.

Questions for Reflection

1. How do you ensure that your professional ethical standards align with the values and beliefs of the church community you are working with? Likewise, how can church leaders ensure values alignment with mental health practitioners?

2. How do you envision managing boundaries as mental health providers and church leaders engage in collaborative care?

3. How do counselor and church leaders navigate potential conflicts of interest or power dynamics that may arise when working together?

4. How can you balance your financial needs as a professional with the desire to offer pro bono services to those in need within the church community?

5. What funding models or partnerships can you explore to sustain church-focused consultation work?

6. In what ways can professionals and the church collaborate to create or access funding opportunities for specific services, such as grants, sponsorships, or community-based fundraising initiatives?

The Last Word

UNITING CHURCHES AND
CHRISTIAN MENTAL HEALTH PROFESSIONALS

DURING THE 2020 WORLD ECONOMIC FORUM, experts convened to address the global mental health crisis, advocating for $1 billion in funding for mental health programs. At this event, Don Mordecai, the national leader for mental health and wellness at Kaiser Permanente, introduced the concept of relational health, igniting a spark of hope and inspiration. The term encompasses the quality and strength of connections between individuals and their social networks and communities, emphasizing the importance of fostering supportive and meaningful relationships. Relational health contributes to an individual's overall well-being and emotional resilience, and ultimately reduces the demand on health care systems.

The concept resonates deeply with the central message of this book: addressing the mental health crisis more effectively through collaboration between churches and Christian mental health professionals, rather than relying solely on substantial financial investment or mass media campaigns. When we think of relational health, we are reminded of the Trinity. The Trinity represents the divine dance of interconnectedness, harmony, and love, the ultimate symbol of what it means to be relationally healthy.

In this spirit, we see the church as a catalyst for teaching, modeling, and nurturing people into relationship with themselves, their social networks, the broader culture, and ultimately, with God. We encourage you, the clinician, graduate student, pastor, or lay leader, to embrace your calling and enlist your church in this urgently needed work, fostering relational health and connectedness within your community.

As you reflect on what you may have left undone, consider how your unique training and skills can be used to serve others more effectively. By actively contributing to the emotional and spiritual growth of those around you, you can forge stronger relationships and promote overall well-being. Dedicate yourself to personal growth and explore untapped collaborative opportunities to address the needs at your doorstep.

The power of relational health, exemplified by a simple act like listening to a discouraged friend or delivering a meal to a neighbor in need, should not be underestimated. The constructive collaboration between mental health science and compassionate believers in the church has the potential to harness such acts and build a movement that will significantly impact the growing mental health crisis. As an emerging professional integrating your faith, you possess the ability to forge powerful and transformative collaborations in your community. The time for action is now. Let's get to work.

Dear brothers and sisters, never get tired of doing good.

2 Thessalonians 3:13 NLT

Index

CAPS
INTERNATIONAL

An Association for Christian Psychologists,
Therapists, Counselors and Academicians

CAPS is a vibrant Christian organization with a rich tradition. Founded in 1956 by a small group of Christian mental health professionals, chaplains and pastors, CAPS has grown to more than 2,100 members in the U.S., Canada and more than 25 other countries.

CAPS encourages in-depth consideration of therapeutic, research, theoretical and theological issues. The association is a forum for creative new ideas. In fact, their publications and conferences are the birthplace for many of the formative concepts in our field today.

CAPS members represent a variety of denominations, professional groups and theoretical orientations; yet all are united in their commitment to Christ and to professional excellence.

CAPS is a non-profit, member-supported organization. It is led by a fully functioning board of directors, and the membership has a voice in the direction of CAPS.

CAPS is more than a professional association. It is a fellowship, and in addition to national and international activities, the organization strongly encourages regional, local and area activities which provide networking and fellowship opportunities as well as professional enrichment.

To learn more about CAPS, visit www.caps.net.

The joint publishing venture between IVP Academic and CAPS aims to promote the understanding of the relationship between Christianity and the behavioral sciences at both the clinical/counseling and the theoretical/research levels. These books will be of particular value for students and practitioners, teachers and researchers.

For more information about CAPS Books, visit InterVarsity Press's website at www.ivpress.com/christian-association-for-psychological-studies-books-set.